English Language Arts

Lesson Guide 1

Book Staff and Contributors

Kristen Kinney-Haines *Director, English Language Arts*
Amy Rauen *Director, Instructional Design*
Susan Raley *Text Editor*
Tricia Battipede *Senior Creative Manager*
Julie Jankowski *Senior Visual Designer*
Caitlin Gildrien *Visual Designer*
Sheila Smith *Visual & Cover Designer*
Alane Gernon-Paulsen, Amy Losi *Writers*
Amy Eward *Content Specialist; Senior Manager, Writing and Editing*
Dan Smith *Senior Project Manager*

Doug McCollum *Senior Vice President, Product Development*
Kristin Morrison *Vice President, Design and Product Management*
Kelly Engel *Senior Director, Curriculum*
Christopher Frescholtz *Senior Director, Program Management*
Erica Castle *Senior Director, Creative Design*
Lisa Dimaio Iekel *Senior Production Manager*

Image Credits

All illustrations © Stride, Inc., unless otherwise noted.

Characters
Tommy DiGiovanni, Matt Fedor, Ben Gamache, Shannon Palmer

Cover Illustration
Helen Musselwhite

Interior Pattern
Spiral. © Silmen/iStock.

Interior Images
Book 1 **1** Expressions. © Tetra Images, LLC /Alamy Stock Photo. **53** Giant panda eating. © Mitsuaki Iwago/Minden Pictures. **135** Triceratops. © Jeff Morgan 05/Alamy Stock Photo. **189** Butterfly and bee on a coneflower. © db_beyer/iStock. **261** American scientist George Washington Carver. © Bettmann/Getty Images. **333** Fox. Scott Wakefield.

Book 2 **387** Readers. © FatCamera/iStock. **441** *Sadiq and the Desert Star* cover image by Anjan Sarkar. © Picture Window Books. **477** Foolish Goose. Donald Wu. **547** Arctic fox in the snow. © jimkruger/iStock. **611** Roman toy horse with wheels. © Araldo de Luca/Getty Images. **703** Man who is visually impaired walking with his dog. © Roman/Adobe Stock.

At Stride, Inc. (NYSE: LRN)—formerly K12 Inc.—we are reimagining lifelong learning as a rich, deeply personal experience that prepares learners for tomorrow. Since its inception, Stride has been committed to removing barriers that impact academic equity and to providing high-quality education for anyone—particularly those in underserved communities. The company has transformed the teaching-and-learning experience for millions of people by providing innovative, high-quality, tech-enabled education solutions, curriculum, and programs directly to students, schools, the military, and enterprises in primary, secondary, and post-secondary settings. Stride is a premier provider of K–12 education for students, schools, and districts, including career-learning services through middle and high school curriculum. Providing a solution to the widening skills gap in the workplace and student loan crisis, Stride equips students with real-world skills for in-demand jobs with career learning. For adult learners, Stride delivers professional skills training in healthcare and technology, as well as staffing and talent development for Fortune 500 companies. Stride has delivered millions of courses over the past decade and serves learners in all 50 states and more than 100 countries. The company is a proud sponsor of Future of School, a nonprofit organization dedicated to closing the gap between the pace of technology and the pace of change in education. More information can be found at stridelearning.com, K12.com, destinationsacademy.com, galvanize.com, techelevator.com, and medcerts.com.

ISBN: 978-1-60153-609-9

Printed by Sheridan Kentucky, Versailles, KY, USA, May 2021.

Table of Contents

Interesting People

Fables

English Language Arts 2 Program Overview

Welcome to English Language Arts 2. We are grateful for this opportunity to play a role in the English language arts education of your students. We offer this overview of the content and structure of the course as part of our effort to help you best support them. At any time, if you have questions or would like further clarification, please reach out to us. Let's begin.

English Language Arts 2 encourages students to learn independently. As a Learning Coach, your role is to support and enhance the learning experience. Each lesson includes rich interactivity to ensure that students build depth of understanding. Online interactions provide a wealth of data, so teachers know where students are struggling. Offline practice, during which students write directly in an activity book, offers variety. With rich content that engages and motivates students, and enough practice to reinforce concepts, this course includes the tools and technology that students need to succeed.

Course Components

Online Lessons

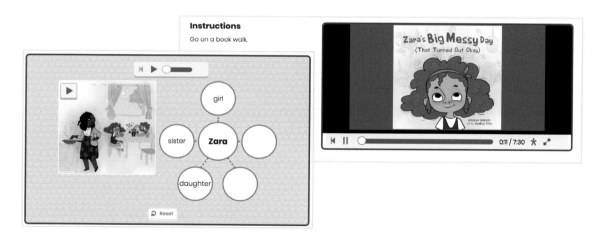

The online lessons provide the core instruction and multiple opportunities for practice in ELA 2. These lessons include:

- Instruction in reading, writing, word study, spelling, and handwriting integrated within a single course

- Practice with speaking and listening skills through opportunities for students to respond to discussion prompts, present work they've done, and reflect on and respond to information presented verbally

- A carefully thought-out progression from guided to independent practice

- Learning experiences that support struggling students

- Computer-scored practice with instant and meaningful feedback
- Independent practice using Stride Skills Arcade, an adaptive tool that offers individualized practice based on specific need
- Student-friendly learning goals
- Engaging games to review and practice skills
- Access to Big Universe, a digital library of thousands of fiction and nonfiction texts

Rich offline print materials support learning with ample opportunity for students to demonstrate mastery of concepts taught online. Contemporary literature, timely and engaging nonfiction, and a digital library give readers a variety of reading experiences.

Lesson Guide

The course is accompanied by a lesson guide that makes it quick and easy for Learning Coaches to understand each lesson at a glance—without logging in. The lesson guide provides an overview of a lesson's content, activities, and materials; answer keys for activity book pages; alerts when special Learning Coach attention is needed; and other features to aid Learning Coaches in supporting students.

Activity Book

ELA 2 includes an activity book where students can put pencil to paper on a daily basis. Key activity book features include:

- Activities that require students to make text-to-self connections, write explanations, analyze and reflect on readings through writing and drawing, and work through the writing process, from brainstorming to publishing
- Custom drafting paper with built-in space for revision marks
- Annotated models of writing assignments
- Revising and proofreading checklists
- Reusable spelling word sorts and choice spelling practice activities
- Reference boxes that state grammar and punctuation rules with clear examples
- Prompts to encourage student reflection and goal setting
- A reading log and badge book to track and celebrate achievements
- Full-color pages with adequate space for answers

Reading Materials

ELA 2 provides students with a rich selection of reading materials, offering diverse perspectives through both classic and contemporary readings in fiction and nonfiction. A variety of print and digital formats are offered.

- *Fables and Folktales:* In this collection of classic and refreshed tales, selections are brought to life through full-color illustrations. Select words and phrases are defined to support comprehension.

- **Trade books:** The course includes contemporary, high-quality trade books that span genres, including nonfiction and chapter books.

- **Nonfiction magazines:** Three full-color magazines are included and focus on high-interest topics related to animals, insects, and ancient Rome. Select words and phrases are defined to support comprehension.

- **Big Universe:** Access to Big Universe, a leveled e-book library, is built into the course. In Big Universe, students have over 14,000 fiction and nonfiction texts from more than 40 publishers on countless topics at their fingertips.

Course Structure

ELA 2 uses a well-balanced approach to literacy that connects reading, writing, grammar, vocabulary, spelling, handwriting, and speaking and listening into one integrated course. The course is designed to lead students through concepts based on current state and national standards. The material is structured to fit a typical 180-day school year, but it can also be adapted to fit individual needs.

The course comprises 12 **units**. Units are divided into a series of **workshops**, which are in turn divided into **daily lessons**. In each workshop, the reading, writing, and word study content is anchored by a focus text or texts. Workshops also include dedicated time for spelling, handwriting, oral fluency practice, independent reading, and independent, personalized practice for remediation and acceleration.

Research shows that literacy blocks lasting from 90 to 120 minutes each day improve literacy outcomes. (See M. Susan Burns, Peg Griffin, and Catherine E. Snow [Eds.], *Starting Out Right: A Guide to Promoting Children's Reading Success* [Washington, D.C.: National Academy Press, 1999] and Catherine E. Snow, M. Susan Burns, and Peg Griffin [Eds.], *Preventing Reading Difficulties in Young Children* [Washington, D.C.: National Academy Press, 1998].) As such, students spend about 2 hours a day working with ELA 2.

Each unit ends with two wrap-up days dedicated to review, assessment, reflection, celebration, goal setting, and discussion.

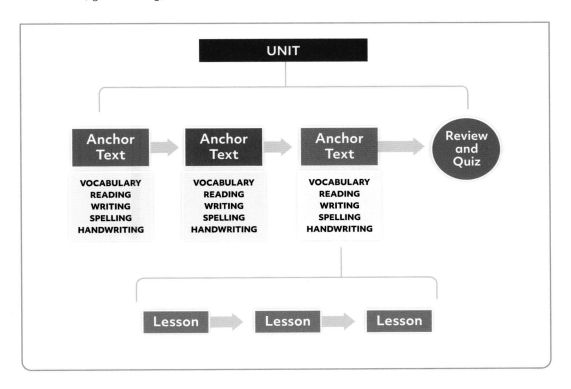

Lesson Model Overview

Workshops in ELA 2 follow a multiday learning cycle. Lessons contain instruction and practice in reading foundations, spelling, vocabulary, comprehension, grammar, composition, and handwriting. The amount of time dedicated to each fluctuates depending on the lesson, the unit, and the semester. For example, the first semester places more emphasis on reading foundations, while the second semester focuses on word analysis. Earlier units emphasize the basics of phonics, story grammar, and writing complete sentences, while later lessons emphasize word relationships, analysis of character traits, and researching a topic to write about. Time on task differs by lesson, with introductions of skills garnering more time, and review and practice requiring slightly less time.

Regardless, the instructional formula across lessons is expressed as three main sections: Get Ready, Learn and Try It, and Wrap-Up.

Lessons also typically contain a Read section, in which students may complete a prereading activity, read from the anchor text, and answer comprehension questions.

GET READY

Get Ready activities introduce and orient students to the lesson content. They may include building background knowledge; introducing important vocabulary words; foundational reading instruction in decoding, concepts of print, and active reading; and any other important prereading activities.

LEARN AND TRY IT

Learn and Try It activities include one or more cycles of bite-size instruction and guided practice, followed by opportunities to apply new skills.

WRAP-UP

Wrap-Up activities include one to three ungraded questions that serve to gauge students' understanding as they exit the lesson. These activities may also include oral fluency practice, independent practice using Stride Skills Arcade, independent reading, and handwriting.

Here is a *sample* workshop flow (as mentioned previously, the precise combination and sequence of activities fluctuates workshop to workshop):

	INITIAL DAY	MIDDLE DAYS	FINAL DAY
GET READY	Lesson Introduction	Lesson Introduction	Lesson Introduction
	Reading Foundations or Word Work	Reading Foundations or Word Work	Vocabulary
	Book Walk		
	Vocabulary	Vocabulary	
	Before You Read		
READ	Think About Reading	Read	Read
	Read	Reflect	
	Check-In	*Brain Break*	
	Reflect		
LEARN AND TRY IT	*Brain Break*	**LEARN AND TRY IT** Reading	**LEARN AND TRY IT** Reading
	LEARN AND TRY IT Writing		*Brain Break*
	Brain Break	*Brain Break*	**LEARN AND TRY IT** Writing
	LEARN Spelling	**TRY IT** Spelling	
WRAP-UP	Formative Assessment	Formative Assessment	Formative Assessment
	Handwriting	Handwriting	*Brain Break*
	Go Read!	Go Read!	Spelling Quiz
			Read and Record
			Stride Skills Arcade
			Handwriting

Activity Descriptions

This table describes each activity type in ELA 2.

*Note: *Brain Break* is not described in the table. *Brain Break* screens are not instructional activities; rather, they are reminders to students to take breaks at natural stopping points throughout each lesson. Simple ways to spend a few minutes taking a break are suggested.

GET READY	Description
Lesson Introduction	The Lesson Introduction introduces the content of each lesson within an engaging context. It also presents the key learning objectives as student-friendly goals and lists the state standards covered in the lesson.
Reading Foundations	Reading Foundations activities serve to remind students of basic reading skills and behaviors mastered in earlier grades. The activities cover topics related to phonics, word parts, and strategies for decoding text.
Book Walk	In Book Walk activities, students preview the major features of a new reading selection, including the title, author, illustrator, pictures, and any key features. These activities, often provided as videos, are designed to help students anticipate reading selection content and connect to the selection.
Vocabulary	Vocabulary activities introduce students to words they'll need to know to understand assigned readings. Scaffolded instruction helps students move from rote knowledge of definitions to deeper understanding of a word and the nuances of its use.
Word Work	Explicit instruction in word relationships and strategies for uncovering word meaning (from dictionaries to roots and affixes) provide students deeper understanding of words, their meanings, and their usage.
Before You Read	Before You Read activities provide background information to set context for the upcoming reading and ask guiding questions to help students set a purpose for reading.

READ	Description
Think About Reading	Students prepare to read by completing activity book pages on which they may make a prediction about the text, respond to a prompt to make a personal connection to the text, or activate prior knowledge by thinking about what they already know about the topic of the upcoming reading.
Read	Read activities direct students to complete an independent reading assignment. These activities may include a read-aloud video for students to follow along with.

READ	Description
Check-In	Check-In activities evaluate students' basic comprehension of what they just read. These activities are not graded, but results are visible to the teacher.
Reflect	Students add to the activity book page they started in the Think About Reading activity by confirming predictions or answering reflection questions.

LEARN & TRY IT	Description
Learn	Learn activities provide direct instruction on reading and writing topics. These activities are always online and provide interactive guided instruction.
Try It	Try It activities provide opportunities for students to practice the reading and writing concepts they've learned. Students may complete online practice or work in their activity book, including work on writing assignments. In some lessons, Try It practice is embedded in the online Learn activity. When Try It practice is online, students receive support via contextual feedback based on their answers.
Spelling	Spelling activities include spelling pattern instruction, online and offline practice sorting words, offline practice in the activity book, timed speed sorts, review games, and graded quizzes.

WRAP-UP	Description
Formative Assessment	Instructional lessons end with a short formative assessment (those activities with "Questions About" in the activity title). They include one to three ungraded questions that gauge students' understanding of reading, writing, and/or spelling skills at the end of the lesson. Although the questions are ungraded, the results are available to teachers.
Quizzes and Graded Assignments	There are two types of quizzes. • **Spelling** Each spelling list cycle ends with a graded online quiz. • **Unit** The last day of most units includes a graded online quiz covering reading, writing, and word study concepts from the unit. Note that the majority of writing content is assessed through the graded writing assignments. In addition to graded online quizzes, there are four graded writing assignments that students must submit to their teacher. These assignments are submitted in the Wrap-Up (A) lesson for the unit.
Read and Record	Read and Record activities allow students to practice reading fluently. Students record themselves reading text aloud, listen to their recording, and evaluate their reading against specific criteria.
Stride Skills Arcade	Throughout each unit, additional independent practice with ELA concepts is provided via Stride Skills Arcade (activities with the title "More Language Arts Practice").

WRAP-UP	Description
Handwriting	Students work at their own pace for 10 minutes in a handwriting workbook to learn and practice handwriting.
Go Read!	Go Read! activities provide dedicated time for independent reading. Students may select a book or magazine of their choice, or they may read something from the Big Universe digital library.
Review	In the Wrap-Up (A) day at the end of each unit, students review unit content in preparation for the next day's unit quiz.
Theme Time	In the Wrap-Up (A) lesson at the end of each unit, students complete work in their activity book that asks them to make connections across the readings from the unit. They may also complete an optional ungraded project.
Your Choice Time	In the Wrap-Up lessons at the end of each unit, time is set aside for students to choose between independent reading or writing, completing the optional Theme Time project, or completing the unit writing assignment.
Reflection	In the Wrap-Up (B) lesson at the end of each unit, students respond to a writing prompt or write about a topic of their choice. This freewriting activity is designed to build writing fluency. Students also set a personal reading or writing goal for the next unit.
Celebrate	In the Wrap-Up (B) lesson at the end of each unit, a Celebrate activity allows students to celebrate accomplishments. They record what they read in the unit in their reading log. They also color the badge for the unit in their badge book, as well as color any relevant badges to celebrate reading accomplishments.
Discussion	In the Wrap-Up (B) lesson at the end of each unit, students respond to a discussion prompt. These prompts often incorporate sharing students' work from the unit. Students should discuss the prompt shown on-screen with an adult. In some cases, teachers may facilitate a group discussion that includes explicit instruction of conversation skills.

A Balance of Online and Offline Time

To enable actionable data and to provide instant feedback to students throughout their learning, ELA 2 online activities make up about 60 percent of core lesson time. However, equally critical to learning is that students put pencil to paper. As such, ELA 2 incorporates daily offline activities in which students complete work in their activity book.

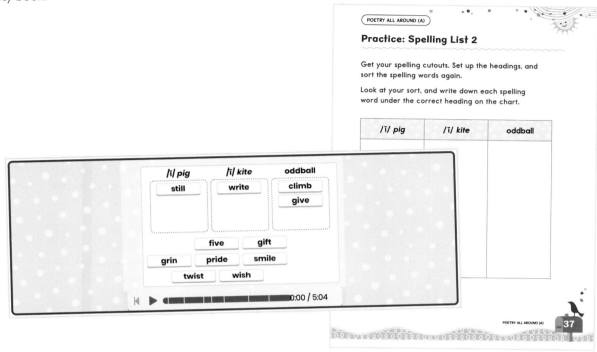

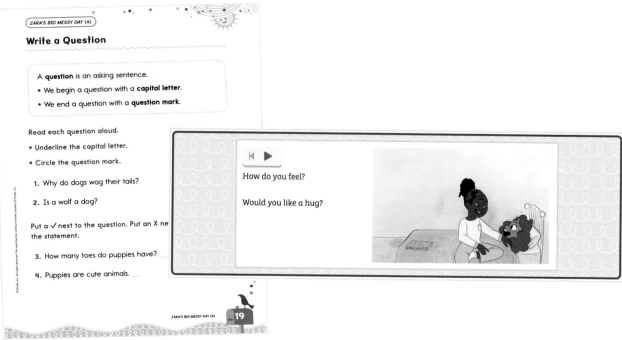

Assessments Overview

To ensure students can show what they have learned and to support high academic outcomes, students need instruction that prepares them for the right cognitive level of tasks they are asked to complete on graded quizzes.

Online Interactive Questions

Online interactive questions provide powerful opportunities for students to demonstrate deep understanding. For this reason, a variety of online question types, including drag-and-drop and fill-in-the-blank, are used throughout the course.

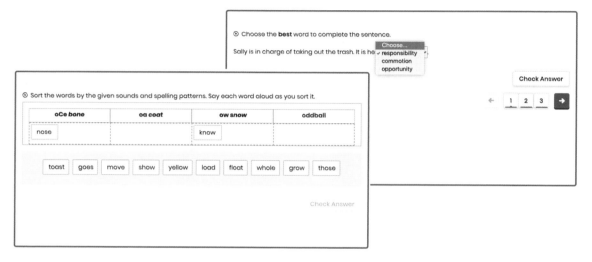

Graded Assessments

ELA 2 includes both online computer-scored quizzes and teacher-graded assignments.

GRADED		
Assessment	**Scoring**	**Location**
Unit Quizzes	computer-scored	Wrap-Up (A) lessons
Spelling Quizzes	computer-scored	throughout units (every 4 or 5 lessons)
Writing Assignments – Published	teacher-graded	Units 2, 5, 9, 11

Instructional Approach: Reading

Close Reading and Textual Analysis

ELA 2 uses a close-reading approach to instruction. Students read first for comprehension and then reread to support further study of texts. Research shows that students who participate in repeated readings of instructional-level text demonstrate better outcomes.

Students are first introduced to a reading selection through prereading activities. These activities might include a Book Walk video and/or activity book pages in which they make a prediction or connection to the text.

Students then spend dedicated time reading independently. Independent reading may begin with a read-aloud video.

In the Learn activity, students engage in guided analysis of the text.

A Mix of Contemporary and Classic Literature and Engaging Informational Texts

The reading activities engage students in works of literature from various genres. Works are grouped thematically to help students make connections among texts or genres. The course requires students to read often, think critically about what they have read, evaluate the ideas, and apply the skills they have learned. All this is done using works of literature and engaging informational texts.

In grade 2, students engage with an even balance of fiction and nonfiction authentic texts. Contemporary reading selections by a diverse group of authors and illustrators allow for an exciting comparison of genres. Classic stories, rich illustrations, and engrossing story lines provide opportunities for students to make meaningful connections with the readings. Nonfiction materials—from books to magazines—cover a variety of topics, including insects, animals, biographies, and the history of ancient Rome. In all, students learn about narrative nonfiction, fairy tales, folktales, fables, scientific and historical texts, poetry, drama, novels, opinion pieces, and biographies in their journey through the grade 2 program.

Grade 2 Reading List

TITLE	AUTHOR	DELIVERY	GENRE
What Do You Do With a Problem?	Kobi Yamada	trade book	fiction
Zara's Big Messy Day (That Turned Out Okay)	Rebekah Borucki	trade book	fiction
Finding the Rhyme in a Poem	Valerie Bodden	Big Universe	poetry
Pizza and Other Stinky Poems	Harriet Ziefert	Big Universe	poetry
Arnold and Louise: Lost and Found	Erica S. Perl	trade book	fiction
"Bears in Danger"	Stride	*K12 World: Astounding Animals*	nonfiction
Choice of: *Bears* *Black Bears* *Brown Bears* *Chipmunks* *Eastern Chipmunks*	Backyard Wildlife series My First Animal Library series In My Backyard series North American Animals series	Big Universe	nonfiction
Goldilocks and the Three Bears	Jan Brett	trade book	fiction
Goatilocks and the Three Bears	Erica S. Perl	trade book	fiction
Brownilocks and the Three Bowls of Cornflakes	Enid Richemont	Big Universe	fiction
Brontorina	James Howe	trade book	fiction
If the Dinosaurs Came Back	Bernard Most	trade book	fiction
Truth or Lie: Dinosaurs!	Erica S. Perl	trade book	nonfiction
Choice from Digging for Dinosaurs series	Amicus Publishing	Big Universe	nonfiction
"The Life of a Butterfly"	Stride	*K12 World: Invaluable Insects*	nonfiction
Praying Mantis	Tamara B. Orr	Big Universe	nonfiction
"Honey from the Hive"	Stride	*K12 World: Invaluable Insects*	nonfiction
"I See a Honeybee"	Stride	*K12 World: Invaluable Insects*	nonfiction
"The Bee's Knees: Insects Are Awesome!"	Stride	*K12 World: Invaluable Insects*	nonfiction
"Insect"	Stride	activity book	poetry
"How Many?"	Stride	activity book	poetry
"Housefly"	Stride	activity book	poetry

Grade 2 Reading List

TITLE	AUTHOR	DELIVERY	GENRE
"A Caterpillar's Job"	Stride	activity book	poetry
"Pesky Pests"	Stride	activity book	poetry
A Weed is a Flower	Aliki	trade book	nonfiction – biography
The Girl Who Thought in Pictures	Julie Finley Mosca	trade book	nonfiction – biography
The Fabled Life of Aesop	Ian Lendler	trade book	fable
"The Ant and the Dove"	retold from Aesop by Stride	*Fables and Folktales*	fable
"The Tortoise and the Hare"	retold from Aesop by Ian Lendler in *The Fabled Life of Aesop*	trade book	fable
"The Boy Who Cried Wolf"	retold from Aesop by Ian Lendler in *The Fabled Life of Aesop*	trade book	fable
"The Fox and the Grapes"	retold from Aesop by Ian Lendler in *The Fabled Life of Aesop*	trade book	fable
"The Goose and the Golden Egg"	retold from Aesop by Ian Lendler in *The Fabled Life of Aesop*	trade book	fable
The Grasshopper and the Ant	retold from Aesop by Stride	*Fables and Folktales*	fable – drama
"The Lion and the Fox"	retold from Aesop by Stride	*Fables and Folktales*	fable
"The Hound and the Hare"	retold from Aesop by Stride	*Fables and Folktales*	fable
Choice of: "The North Wind and the Sun" "The Donkey and the Lapdog" "The Fox and the Crow" "The Town Mouse and the Country Mouse" "The Ant and the Grasshopper" "The Lion and the Statue"	retold from Aesop by Ian Lendler in *The Fabled Life of Aesop*	trade book	fable
Where Are You From?	Yamile Saied Méndez	trade book	fiction
I Am Enough	Grace Byers	trade book	fiction
Just Ask!	Sonia Sotomayor	trade book	fiction
Sadiq and the Desert Star	Siman Nuurali	trade book	fiction – novel
"The Three Wishes"	rewritten by Stride	*Fables and Folktales*	folktale

Grade 2 Reading List

TITLE	AUTHOR	DELIVERY	GENRE
"The Fisherman and His Wife"	rewritten by Stride	*Fables and Folktales*	folktale
The Foolish Goose	Leora Robinson	*Fables and Folktales*	folktale – drama
Astrid & Apollo and the Starry Campout	V.T. Bidania	trade book	fiction – novel
"Each Animal in Its Place"	Stride	*K12 World: Astounding Animals*	nonfiction
"Bring On the Bats!"	Stride	*K12 World: Astounding Animals*	nonfiction – opinion
Felina's New Home	Loran Wlodarski	Big Universe	nonfiction
"Animals in Winter"	Stride	*K12 World: Astounding Animals*	nonfiction
"A Day in Ancient Rome"	Stride	*K12 World: Journey Through Rome*	nonfiction
"Gods and Spirits of Ancient Rome"	Stride	*K12 World: Journey Through Rome*	nonfiction
Choice of: *Italy* *Colosseum*	Sarah Tieck Kristine Spanier	Big Universe	nonfiction
"Living with Latin"	Stride	*K12 World: Journey Through Rome*	nonfiction
Volcanoes! Mountains of Fire	Eric Arnold	trade book	nonfiction
"Pliny Saw It All"	Stride	*K12 World: Journey Through Rome*	nonfiction
"Animal Helpers"	Stride	*K12 World: Astounding Animals*	nonfiction
Choice from Animals with Jobs series	Amicus Publishing	Big Universe	nonfiction
Buddy: The First Seeing Eye Dog	Eva Moore	trade book	nonfiction
Zoey and Sassafras: Dragons and Marshmallows	Asia Citro	trade book	fiction – novel

Instructional Approach: Writing

A Balance of Explicit Instruction and Authentic Writing Experiences

Learning to express one's ideas in writing is a fundamental requirement of an educated person. ELA 2 prepares students to express themselves as educated people in the twenty-first century.

Grammar, usage, and mechanics activities are an integral part of writing instruction. These activities involve close examination of sentences from the reading selections in which students explore the effect of a writer's choices on a sentence's meaning. After examining and answering guided questions about the choices of expert writers, students apply grammar, usage, and mechanics skills to their own writing to communicate effectively in standard English. These skills are also reinforced in revising and proofreading of students' graded writing assignments. Grammar, usage, and mechanics activities focus on grammatical terms, sentence construction and manipulation, recognizing how grammar and punctuation affect the meaning of a sentence, and fixing errors.

Through authentic writing experiences, students analyze writing models and then work through the writing process to develop original compositions of their own. An emphasis on thoughtful planning takes the fear out of writing as students learn tangible strategies to make the process manageable. Throughout ELA 2, students complete 10 major writing assignments. For the four teacher-graded assignments, they follow the complete writing process: prewriting, drafting, revising, proofreading, and publishing. Students are not required to formally revise, proofread, and publish all the ungraded writing assignments.

The assignments include:

- four sentences
- informational paragraph (graded)
- short research task
- how-to
- book review (graded)

- descriptive paragraph
- friendly letter
- personal story (graded)
- persuasive essay
- research report (graded)

Students also complete structured speaking assignments. These assignments include reading a poem aloud, telling a personal story, and giving a persuasive speech.

Research skills are an integral part of the writing work. In ELA 2, students learn and apply research skills, including determining whether a source is appropriate, identifying a question or purpose for research, and taking notes from research sources to answer a question. Students conduct and incorporate research into two of their writing assignments.

Instructional Approach: Word Study

Reading Foundations, Vocabulary, and Spelling

In ELA 2, word study includes instruction on foundational reading skills, vocabulary, and spelling, providing a thorough word study experience that helps grow students' decoding, comprehension, writing, spelling, and speaking and listening skills.

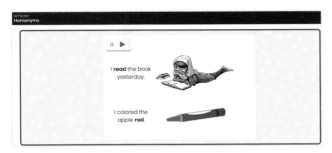

Reading Foundations

Foundational activities focus on concepts related to phonological awareness, phonics, word parts, word relationships, and strategies for decoding text.

Vocabulary

Vocabulary includes explicit instruction on words students need to know to comprehend the reading selections, as well as instruction on word relationships and strategies for uncovering word meaning.

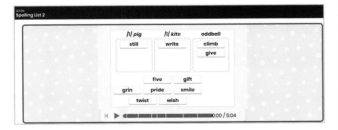

Spelling

Spelling instruction focuses on learning to recognize, understand, and apply patterns rather than memorizing rules. Research shows that good readers and spellers do not decode (read) and encode (spell) rules but rather letter patterns that help them identify words and differentiate one word from another. Students can learn to spell words quickly by studying these spelling patterns that are common to many words. Word sorts are a key instructional strategy used in ELA 2 spelling.

Individualized Learning

ELA 2 is designed to help all students succeed.

Stride Skills Arcade An engaging teaching tool that motivates students toward mastery and rewards learning with games. At least twice a unit, students practice related concepts based on their specific needs. Time to use Stride Skills Arcade is integrated right into the course to ensure sufficient independent practice time.

Stride Skills Arcade's adaptive technology guides each student to practice where most needed. It then serves up a variety of lively and engaging content. Stride Skills Arcade's vast database of questions, video lessons, and printable resources delivers grade-level appropriate content aligned to the rigor of the Common Core and individual state standards. Stride Skills Arcade's benchmark and formative assessments identify where students are performing on specific grade-level standards throughout the year and help identify critical foundational gaps missed in prior grade levels.

Test prep capabilities pinpoint student strengths and weaknesses for improved student outcomes on end-of-year assessments.

The Help Me Button Located on the lesson menu, this is an additional personalization feature that lets students opt into activities that are dynamically chosen based on the concept they are studying. Recommendations are powered by a sophisticated engine designed to serve up the activities most likely to be effective for the individual student.

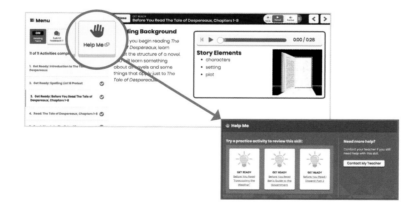

How to Use This Guide

This lesson guide contains information that will be helpful to you as you begin English Language Arts 2 and daily as you work through the program. Here is what the lesson guide contains and how to use it.

Lesson Title
The lesson title indicates the lesson topic and matches the title you will see in the online course.

Learning Coach Check-In
This label indicates that your participation is particularly important for the activity it appears in. A description of how to support students is included with the specific activity in the Activities section of the lesson guide.

Synopsis
This section gives a brief summary of the reading selection.

Lesson Goals
The goals indicate what students will do in the lesson.

Activities
Each lesson is broken down into three or more main sections Get Ready, Read, Learn and Try It, Quiz, and Wrap-Up. Each section is broken down into individual activities.

Lesson Overview Table
This table shows an overview of the lesson's activities, their approximate times, and whether students complete them offline or online.

Content Background
This information will help you better understand the content students will be learning.

Materials
This box lists all materials needed for the lesson and indicates whether each material is Supplied or Also Needed.

Keywords
The definitions of key terminology specific to lesson concepts are given here.

Answer Key
The lesson guide includes answer keys for activity book pages.

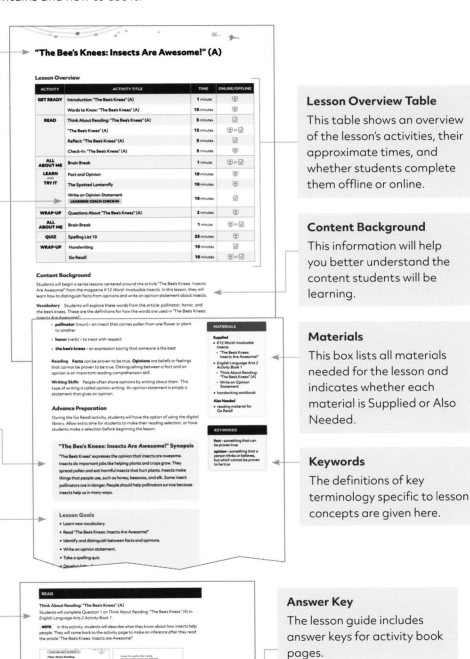

Lessons with Graded Assessments

Check in with students when a lesson has a graded assessment.

- The final lesson of most units has a computer-scored quiz. Check to make sure students have completed and submitted this quiz.

- Four teacher-graded assignments appear throughout the course. You may need to help students submit these assignments to their teacher. Discuss with the teacher the best method of turning in students' work.

Remember

Academic support at home is critical to student success. While ELA 2 empowers students to work independently, this guide is designed to help you support your students each day to help them maximize their learning.

English Language Arts 2 Keywords

adjective – a word that describes a noun or a pronoun
Examples: *purple, prickly, difficult*

adverb – a word that describes a verb, an adjective, or another adverb
Examples: *slowly, sweetly, very*

alliteration – the use of words with the same or close to the same beginning sounds
Example: **B**onnie **b**aked **b**ananas.

antonym – a word that means the opposite of another word

audience – a writer's readers or a speaker's listeners

author's point – a writer's claim or belief about a topic

author's purpose – the reason the author wrote a text: to entertain, to inform, to express an opinion, or to persuade

base word – a word that can have a prefix or suffix added to it
Example: *happy* is the base word of *unhappy*

biography – the story of a person's life written by another person

body (of a friendly letter) – the main text of a friendly letter

body (of an essay) – the main text of a piece of writing

bold type – type that is darker than the surrounding text that draws attention to a word or phrase

book review – a piece of writing that gives an opinion about a book and tells about it

brainstorming – before writing, a way for the writer to come up with ideas

caption – writing under a picture that describes the picture

cause – the reason something happens

character – a person or animal in a story

closing – the part of a friendly letter that follows the body
Examples: *From, Yours truly*

command – a sentence that gives an order or makes a request
Example: Speak a little louder.

compare – to explain how two or more things are alike

compound word – a word made from two smaller words

comprehension – understanding

concluding sentence – the last sentence of a paragraph; often summarizes the paragraph

conclusion (in writing) – the final paragraph of a written work

concrete poem – a poem whose words are written in a shape that relates to what the poem is about; also called a "shape poem"

conjunction – a word that joins parts of a sentence
Examples: *and, but, or, although, because*

connection – a link readers make between themselves, information in text, and the world around them

consonant-le syllable – a syllable that comes at the end of a word that is made up of a consonant followed by *–le*

content word – vocabulary related to a specific subject
Examples: *cell, mitosis*

context – the parts of a sentence or passage surrounding a word

context clue – a word or phrase in a text that helps you figure out the meaning of an unknown word

contraction – a shortened word where an apostrophe replaces missing letters
Examples: *don't, you're*

contrast – to explain how two or more things are different

description – words that show how something looks, sounds, feels, tastes, or smells
Example: The sky is a soft, powdery blue, and the golden sun feels warm on my face.

detail – a fact or description that tells more about a topic

dialogue – the words that characters say in a written work

dictionary – a reference work made up of words with their definitions, in alphabetical order

drafting – the step in which a writer first writes a piece

drama – another word for *play*

effect – the result of a cause

exclamation – a sentence that shows strong feeling
Example: I can't believe it!

fable – a story that teaches a lesson and may contain animal characters

fact – something that can be proven true

fantasy – a story with characters, settings, or other elements that could not really exist

fiction – make-believe stories

figurative language – words that describe something by comparing it to something completely different; figure of speech
Example: Rain fell in buckets and the streets looked like rivers.

first-person point of view – the telling of a story by a character in that story, using pronouns such as *I*, *me*, and *we*

folktale – a story, which usually teaches a lesson important to a culture, that is passed down through many generations

formal language – the choice of words, phrases, and sentences that adhere to the conventional standards of grammar, usage, and mechanics

friendly letter – a letter used to share thoughts, feelings, and news

glossary – a list of important terms and their meanings that is usually found in the back of a book

graphic – a picture, photograph, map, diagram, or other image

greeting – the part of a letter that begins with the word *Dear* followed by a person's name; also called the "salutation"

heading (of a friendly letter) – the first part of a letter that has the writer's address and the date

heading (within a text) – a title within the body of a text that tells the reader something important about a section of the text

hook – a surprising idea or group of words used to grab the reader's attention, usually at the beginning of a work

how-to paper – a paragraph or essay that explains how to do or make something

illustration – a drawing

imagery – language that helps readers imagine how something looks, sounds, smells, feels, or tastes

index – an alphabetical list at the end of a book or magazine that tells the pages where a subject or name can be found

infer – to use clues and what you already know to make a guess

inference – a guess you make using the clues in a text and what you already know

introduction – the first paragraph of an essay, identifying the topic and stating the main idea

irregular verb – a verb that does not add *–d* or *–ed* to form the past or past participle
Examples: *ran*, *wore*, *knew*

literal recall – the ability to describe information stated directly in a text

logical order – a way to organize that groups details in a way that makes sense

main idea – the most important idea in a paragraph or text

moral – the lesson of a story, particularly a fable

narrator – the teller of a story

nonfiction – writings about true things

noun – a word that names a person, place, thing, or idea
Examples: *nurses*, *Pennsylvania*, *phone*, *happiness*

onomatopoeia – the use of words that show sounds
Examples: *boom*, *quack*, *grrrrr*

open syllable – a syllable that ends with a vowel, making the vowel sound long

opinion – something that a person thinks or believes, but which cannot be proven to be true

order words – words that connect ideas, a series of steps, or create a sequence
Examples: *first*, *next*, *later*, *finally*

outline – an organized list of topics in an essay

paragraph – a group of sentences about one topic

past tense – the verb form that tells what already has happened
Examples: *walked*, *knew*

personal story – an essay about a personal experience of the writer

personification – giving human qualities to something that is not human
Example: The thunder shouted from the clouds.

perspective – what a character thinks or believes

persuasive essay – an essay in which the writer tries to convince readers to agree with a stand on an issue

plot – what happens in a story; the sequence of events

plural noun – a word that names more than one person, place, thing, or idea
Examples: *men*, *mountains*, *books*, *freedoms*

possessive noun – a noun that shows ownership
Examples: *Amara's*, *children's*

predicate – the verb or verb phrase in a sentence
Example: Mateo reads every evening. (The predicate is "reads every evening.")

prediction – a guess about what might happen that is based on information in a story and what you already know

prefix – a word part with its own meaning that can be added to the beginning of a base word or root to make a new word
Example: *un–* is a prefix in the word *unhappy*

prewriting – the step in which a writer chooses a topic, gathers ideas, and plans what to write

problem – an issue a character must solve in a story

proofreading – the step in which a writer checks for errors in grammar, punctuation, capitalization, and spelling

publishing – the step in which a writer makes a clean copy of the piece and shares it

purpose – the reason for writing

question – a sentence that asks something
Example: What time is it?

reason – a statement that explains why something is or why it should be

reference – a work that contains useful information for a writer, such as an encyclopedia, a dictionary, or a website

reflexive pronoun – a pronoun that refers back to another noun or pronoun in a sentence
Examples: *myself*, *yourselves*

repetition – the use of a word or phrase more than once

research – to find information through study rather than through personal experience

research report – a type of essay based mainly on the author's research

retelling – using your own words to tell a story that you have listened to or read

revising – the step in which a writer reviews and fixes ideas and organization

rhyme – the use of words that end with the same sounds
Example: *Cat* and *hat* rhyme.

rhyme scheme – the pattern of rhymes made by the last sounds in the lines of a poem, shown by a different letter of the alphabet to represent each rhyme
Example: In a poem with the rhyme scheme AABB, lines 1 and 2 rhyme, and lines 3 and 4 rhyme.

rhythm – a distinctive beat

root – a word part that gives a word meaning and must have other word parts added to it
Example: *vis* is the root of *visit* and *revise*

scene – a part of an act of a play that happens at a fixed time and place

sensory language – language that appeals to the five senses

sentence – a group of words that tells a complete thought
Example: David wrote a story.

sequence – the order in which things happen

setting – when and where a story takes place

sidebar – a short text within a larger text that tells something related but not necessary to the main story

signature – the writer's name at the end of a letter, usually written in cursive

simile – a comparison between two things using the word *like* or *as*
Example: He was as quiet as a mouse.

solution – how a character solves a problem in a story

source – a provider of information; a book, a historical document, online materials, and an interviewee are all sources

spelling pattern – a sequence of letters that works together to represent a sound, such as *ay* in *day* and *pay*, or a sequence of vowels and consonants, such as the vowel-consonant-e (VCe) pattern like in *cake* or the consonant-vowel-consonant (CVC) pattern like in *hat*

stage directions – instructions in a play that tell the actors what to do

statement – a sentence that tells something
Example: The fox ran into the woods.

story structure elements – components of a story; they include character, setting, plot, problem, and solution

subject – a word or words that tell whom or what the sentence is about
Example: Mateo reads every evening. (The subject is "Mateo.")

subject-verb agreement – the way a subject and verb match when both are singular or both are plural
Examples: The hawk glides, and the eagles soar.

suffix – a word part attached to the end of a root or base word to create a new word
Example: *–er* is a suffix in the word *reader*

summary – a short retelling that includes only the most important ideas or events of a text

supporting detail – a detail that gives more information about a main idea

syllable – a word part that contains a vowel or vowel sound
Examples: *pa - per, a - lone*

synonym – a word that means the same, or almost the same, as another word

table of contents – a list at the start of a book that gives the titles of the book's stories, poems, articles, chapters, or nonfiction pieces and the pages where they can be found

text feature – part of a text that helps a reader locate information and determine what is most important; some examples are the title, table of contents, headings, pictures, and glossary

text structure – the organizational pattern of a text, such as cause and effect, compare and contrast, and chronological order

theme – the author's message or big idea

time line – a line showing dates and events in the order that they happened

time order – the arrangement of ideas according to when they happened

topic – the subject of a text

topic sentence – the sentence that expresses the main idea of the paragraph

trait – a quality of a person or other object; what something is like

transition – a word or phrase that connects ideas
Examples: *also, first, for example*

verb – a word that shows action or links ideas
Examples: *jump* (action), *is* (linking)

visual – a graphic, picture, or photograph

visualize – to picture things in your mind as you read

voice – the way a piece of writing sounds

vowel team syllable – a syllable that contains a vowel sound spelled with two or more letters

Problems and Solutions

What Do You Do With a Problem? (A)

Lesson Overview

ACTIVITY	ACTIVITY TITLE	TIME	ONLINE/OFFLINE
GET READY	Introduction: *What Do You Do With a Problem?* (A)	**1** minute	🖥
	Book Walk: *What Do You Do With a Problem?* (A)	**10** minutes	🖥
	Words to Know: *What Do You Do With a Problem?* (A)	**10** minutes	🖥
READ	Think About Reading: *What Do You Do With a Problem?* (A) LEARNING COACH CHECK-IN	**10** minutes	📄
	What Do You Do With a Problem? (A)	**10** minutes	🖥 and 📄
LEARN AND **TRY IT**	How a Character Feels	**15** minutes	🖥
	How Do You Feel? LEARNING COACH CHECK-IN	**15** minutes	📄
ALL ABOUT ME	Brain Break	**1** minute	🖥 or 📄
LEARN AND **TRY IT**	Sentences	**10** minutes	🖥
	Begin and End a Sentence LEARNING COACH CHECK-IN	**15** minutes	📄
WRAP-UP	Questions About *What Do You Do With a Problem?* (A)	**2** minutes	🖥
ALL ABOUT ME	Brain Break	**1** minute	🖥 or 📄
WRAP-UP	Handwriting	**10** minutes	📄
	Go Read!	**10** minutes	🖥 or 📄

Content Background

Students will begin a series of lessons centered around the book *What Do You Do With a Problem?* by Kobi Yamada. In this lesson, they will learn about describing a character and explore how a sentence begins and ends.

Vocabulary   Students will explore these words from the story: *avoid*, *disguise*, and *opportunity*. These are the definitions for how the words are used in *What Do You Do With a Problem?*

- **avoid** (verb) – to stay away from

- **disguise** (verb) – to change how something looks or sounds so that people will not recognize it

- **opportunity** (noun) – a chance

Reading Students will use text and illustrations to describe a character's feelings. For example, the character in *What Do You Do With a Problem?* has a problem and says, "I didn't want it. I didn't ask for it. I really didn't like having a problem." From this, we can determine that the character does not like what is happening and feels upset.

Writing Skills A **sentence** is a complete thought. Every sentence begins with a capital letter and ends with a punctuation mark. That punctuation mark is usually a period.

> **Example: W**e jumped in the puddles**.**

Note that students will explore the idea of a "complete thought" more thoroughly in a later lesson. This lesson focuses on sentence beginnings and endings.

Advance Preparation

During the Go Read! activity, students will have the option of using the digital library. Allow extra time for them to make their reading selection, or have students make a selection before beginning the lesson.

What Do You Do With a Problem? Synopsis

One day a child suddenly has a problem. The child is worried about the problem and attempts to avoid and to hide from it. Eventually, the child decides to face the problem and discovers something important—the problem is no longer something to be scared of. Instead, it is a chance to grow and learn.

MATERIALS

Supplied
- *What Do You Do With a Problem?* by Kobi Yamada
- *English Language Arts 2 Activity Book 1*
  - Think About Reading: *What Do You Do With a Problem?* (A)
  - How Do You Feel?
  - Begin and End a Sentence
- handwriting workbook

Also Needed
- crayons or markers (optional)
- reading material for Go Read!

KEYWORDS

character – a person or animal in a story

sentence – a group of words that tells a complete thought
Example: David wrote a story.

Lesson Goals

- Learn new vocabulary.
- Read *What Do You Do With a Problem?*
- Determine how a character feels.
- Compare one's own feelings and experiences to those of a character.
- Begin a sentence with a capital letter, and end it with a period.
- Develop letter formation fluency.
- Read independently to develop fluency.

GET READY

Introduction: *What Do You Do With a Problem?* (A)

Students will get a glimpse of what they will learn about in the lesson.

Book Walk: *What Do You Do With a Problem?* (A)

Students will preview the major features of the new reading selection, including the title, author, illustrator, and pictures. This activity is designed to help students anticipate story content and connect to the selection.

TIP Have students follow along with the book walk using their own copy of the book.

Words to Know: *What Do You Do With a Problem?* (A)

Students will preview and answer questions about three vocabulary words from the reading selection.

READ

Think About Reading: *What Do You Do With a Problem?* (A)

Students will complete Think About Reading: *What Do You Do With a Problem?* (A) in *English Language Arts 2 Activity Book 1.*

NOTE Students may wish to use crayons or markers to draw their picture.

LEARNING COACH CHECK-IN As needed, help students read the activity page.

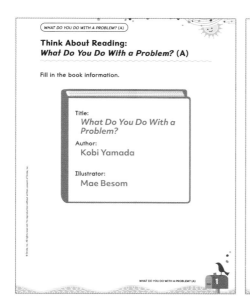

WHAT DO YOU DO WITH A PROBLEM? (A)

Think About Reading:
What Do You Do With a Problem? (A)

Fill in the book information.

Title:
*What Do You Do With a
Problem?*

Author:
Kobi Yamada

Illustrator:
Mae Besom

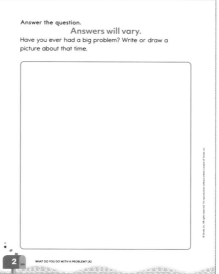

Answer the question.
Answers will vary.
Have you ever had a big problem? Write or draw a
picture about that time.

What Do You Do With a Problem? (A)

Students will listen to *What Do You Do With a Problem?* by Kobi Yamada. Students may choose to read the story on their own. Encourage them to reread their favorite passages.

LEARN AND TRY IT

LEARN   How a Character Feels

Students will learn that one way to describe a character is to talk about the character's feelings. Using text and illustrations from *What Do You Do With a Problem?*, students will identify how the main character feels.

NOTE   The gender of the child in the story is unclear. We can infer that this choice was intentional to help **all** children relate to the child's feelings and experiences.

TRY IT   How Do You Feel?

Students will complete How Do You Feel? in *English Language Arts 2 Activity Book 1*. After identifying how the main character feels at the beginning of the story, students will compare their own feelings and experiences to those of the main character.

LEARNING COACH CHECK-IN   As needed, help students read the activity page.

LEARN Sentences

Through guided exploration of sentences from *What Do You Do With a Problem?*, students will learn that a sentence begins with a capital letter and ends with a punctuation mark. They will learn that most sentences end with a period.

TIP Have students identify capital letters and ending punctuation marks in the book *What Do You Do With a Problem?* or in one of their favorite books.

TRY IT Begin and End a Sentence

Students will complete Begin and End a Sentence in *English Language Arts 2 Activity Book 1*.

LEARNING COACH CHECK-IN As needed, help students read the activity page. It may be helpful for students to answer Questions 8 and 9 aloud before writing their responses.

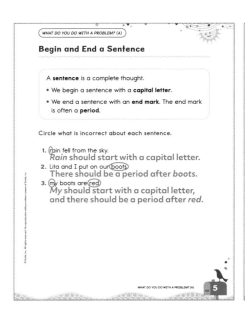

Questions About *What Do You Do With a Problem?* (A)

Students will answer questions to show that they understand the reading and writing skills they learned in this lesson.

Handwriting

Students should gather their handwriting workbook and a sharpened pencil. Begin by reviewing the table of contents with students, and explain that they will work for 10 minutes to complete workbook pages on their own. Students should not race to complete lots of pages. Instead, they should take their time to form letters carefully and correctly. Students should work at their own pace, completing pages until 10 minutes have passed.

TIP Set a timer to help students stay focused during handwriting practice.

Go Read!

Students will read for pleasure. They should choose a book or a magazine that interests them, or they may choose a selection from the digital library, linked in the online lesson.

- Have students read aloud a few paragraphs of their selection.

- Then have students read silently for the rest of the time.

SUPPORT Students should make no more than five errors in decoding when they read aloud a few paragraphs of their Go Read! selection. If students struggle or make more than five errors, they need to select a different (and easier) text for the Go Read! activity.

TIP Have students select something to read ahead of time to help them stay focused.

What Do You Do With a Problem? (B)

Lesson Overview

ACTIVITY	ACTIVITY TITLE	TIME	ONLINE/OFFLINE
GET READY	Introduction: *What Do You Do With a Problem?* (B)	**1** minute	🖥️
	Words to Know: *What Do You Do With a Problem?* (B)	**15** minutes	🖥️
LEARN	Who Is Telling the Story?	**20** minutes	🖥️
ALL ABOUT ME	Brain Break	**1** minute	🖥️ or 📄
LEARN AND TRY IT	Complete Sentences	**15** minutes	🖥️
	Identify a Complete Sentence **LEARNING COACH CHECK-IN**	**20** minutes	📄
ALL ABOUT ME	Brain Break	**1** minute	🖥️ or 📄
LEARN	Spelling List 1 **LEARNING COACH CHECK-IN**	**25** minutes	🖥️ and 📄
WRAP-UP	Questions About *What Do You Do With a Problem?* (B)	**2** minutes	🖥️
	Handwriting	**10** minutes	📄
	Go Read!	**10** minutes	🖥️ or 📄

Content Background

Students will continue a series of lessons centered around the book *What Do You Do With a Problem?* by Kobi Yamada. In this lesson, they will learn to identify the narrator of a story and learn the two parts of a complete sentence.

Vocabulary   Students will explore these words from the story: *shooed*, *scowled*, and *declared*. These are the definitions of the words as used in *What Do You Do With a Problem?*

- **shoo** (verb) – to try to make something go away by waving your hands at it

- **scowl** (verb) – to make an angry face

- **declare** (verb) – to say strongly

Reading   The **narrator** is who is telling a story. Students will learn about two types of narrators. The terms *first-person point of view* and *third-person point of view* will not be introduced. Instead, students will learn that a narrator can be inside of a story or outside of a story. A narrator inside of a story is a character in the story who is taking part in the action. When a narrator is outside of a story, it's as if somebody is watching and describing what is happening in the story but is not taking part in it.

Writing Skills   A complete sentence has two parts, a *subject* and a *predicate*. The **subject** is the naming part of the sentence—it's who or what the sentence is about. The **predicate** is the action part of the sentence. Often, the predicate is simply called the *verb* or *verb phrase*.

In these examples and throughout the course, the subject is underlined once, and the predicate is underlined twice.

Examples:

Amar claps.

We jumped in the puddles.

Shirene and Jo ran.

The white bookshelf is full of books.

Note that students will explore only *simple sentences* in this lesson. A simple sentence has one subject and one predicate. Students are not expected to know this term *simple sentence*.

Spelling   Throughout the course, the goal of spelling instruction is for students to develop knowledge of spelling patterns that represent sounds or units of meaning in written words. Instruction is designed for students to analyze and understand the English spelling system, not for students to memorize the spelling of words.

A **spelling pattern** is a sequence of letters that represent a sound—for example, the letters *ay* in *day* represent the sound of long a. A spelling pattern can also be a predictable pattern of vowels and consonants that enable students to know what sound to say when they read words. For example, the letter sequence *ake* in the word *cake* is a vowel-consonant-e (VCe) pattern. Students can predict that this pattern will lead to a long vowel sound when pronouncing the word.

In this lesson, students will learn the following symbols and spelling patterns:

- /ă/ is the symbol for the sound of short a. It is the sound of the letter *a* in the word *hat*.

- /ā/ is the symbol for the sound of long a. It is the sound of the letter *a* in the word *cake*.

- The consonant-vowel-consonant (CVC) pattern leads to a short vowel sound. It is the pattern in the word *hat*. Students will not be taught the terminology of CVC pattern. Instead, they will be taught the more student-friendly idea that a single vowel surrounded by consonants has a short

MATERIALS

Supplied
- *What Do You Do With a Problem?* by Kobi Yamada
- *English Language Arts 2 Activity Book 1*
  - Identify a Complete Sentence
  - Spelling List 1
- handwriting workbook

Also Needed
- crayons or markers
- scissors
- envelope or baggie to store spelling cutouts
- reading material for Go Read!

KEYWORDS

narrator–the teller of a story

predicate–the verb or verb phrase in a sentence Example: Mateo reads every evening. (The predicate is "reads every evening.")

spelling pattern–a sequence of letters that works together to represent a sound, such as *ay* in *day* and *pay*, or a sequence of vowels and consonants, such as the vowel-consonant-e (VCe) pattern like in *cake* or the consonant-vowel-consonant (CVC) pattern like in *hat*

subject–a word or words that tell whom or what the sentence is about Example: Mateo reads every evening. (The subject is "Mateo.")

vowel sound. Even though a word such as *fast* has two consonants following the letter *a*, it still has a short vowel sound. It has a short vowel sound because the word has a single vowel with consonants before and after it.

- The vowel-consonant-e (VCe) pattern leads to a long vowel sound. It is the pattern in the word *cake*. Students will learn that the silent e in the VCe pattern is a signal that the letter *a* has the long vowel sound /ā/.

Students will sort words into groups. For a word to fit into a group, it must match *both* the target sound and the spelling pattern.

- The word *man* fits into the group /ă/ *hat* because *man* has both the sound of short a and the pattern of a single vowel surrounded by consonants (CVC) that results in a short vowel sound.

- The word *have* does *not* fit into the group /ă/ *hat*. While *have* does have the short a sound /ă/, it does not have the CVC pattern that typically results in a short vowel sound.

A word like *have* is called an oddball because it doesn't match the expectation for the sound that the spelling pattern VCe represents. Students will place oddball words into a separate group when they sort their spelling words.

Advance Preparation

During the Go Read! activity, students will have the option of using the digital library. Allow extra time for them to make their reading selection, or have students make a selection before beginning the lesson.

Lesson Goals
- Learn new vocabulary.
- Identify the narrator of a story.
- Determine how a character feels.
- Compare one's own feelings and experiences to those of a character.
- Identify a complete sentence.
- Sort words by sound, spelling pattern, or units of meaning.
- Develop letter formation fluency.
- Read independently to develop fluency.

GET READY

Introduction: *What Do You Do With a Problem?* (B)

Students will get a glimpse of what they will learn about in the lesson.

Words to Know: *What Do You Do With a Problem?* (B)

Students will preview and answer questions about three vocabulary words from the reading selection.

LEARN AND TRY IT

LEARN   Who Is Telling the Story?

Students will explore how to determine if a narrator is inside of a story or outside of a story. They will also continue to identify the feelings of the child in the story.

LEARN   Complete Sentences

Through guided exploration of sentences from *What Do You Do With a Problem?*, students will learn what makes a sentence a "complete thought." They will learn the terms *subject* and *predicate*, identify the subject and the predicate of a sentence, and determine whether a sentence is complete.

NOTE   Remembering the terms *subject* and *predicate* is less important than being able to identify the naming part and the action part of a sentence (and ultimately being able to write complete sentences that have both these parts). Writing complete sentences is the important eventual outcome, and students will have more exposure to the terminology over the years.

TRY IT   Identify a Complete Sentence

Students will complete Identify a Complete Sentence in *English Language Arts 2 Activity Book 1*.

NOTE   Students will need crayons or markers to complete this activity page.

LEARNING COACH CHECK-IN   As needed, help students read the activity page.

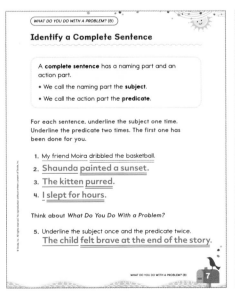

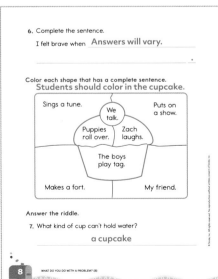

LEARN   Spelling List 1

Students will learn and sort words with sounds and spelling patterns for short a and long a.

- In an online activity, students will learn about the spelling patterns and the sounds they represent. They will learn how to sort words according to those sounds and patterns. They will also complete a word sort.

- In *English Language Arts 2 Activity Book 1*, students will complete Spelling List 1.

NOTE   Students will need scissors to cut out the spelling words on the activity page. Have students store their cutouts in a safe place, such as an envelope.

LEARNING COACH CHECK-IN   As needed, help students read the activity page.

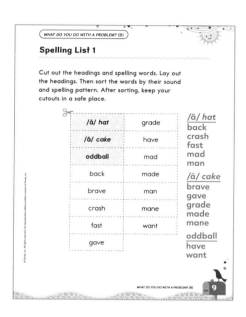

This is the complete list of words students will work with to learn the spelling patterns for the sounds of short a and long a.

short a	long a	oddball
back	brave	have
crash	gave	want
fast	grade	
mad	made	
man	mane	

NOTE   For a word to fit into a category, it must meet two criteria: (1) It must have the target sound. (2) It must have the target spelling pattern. The term "oddball" is used for words that meet only one of the criteria.

Questions About *What Do You Do With a Problem?* (B)

Students will answer questions to show that they understand the reading, writing, and spelling skills they learned in this lesson.

Handwriting

Students should gather their handwriting materials and begin where they left off. Remind students to form letters carefully and correctly.

TIP Set a timer to help students stay focused during handwriting practice.

Go Read!

Students will read for pleasure. They should choose a book or a magazine that interests them, or they may choose a selection from the digital library, linked in the online lesson.

- Have students read aloud a few paragraphs of their selection.

- Then have students read silently for the rest of the time.

SUPPORT Students should make no more than five errors in decoding when they read aloud a few paragraphs of their Go Read! selection. If students struggle or make more than five errors, they need to select a different (and easier) text for the Go Read! activity.

TIP Have students select something to read ahead of time to help them stay focused.

What Do You Do With a Problem? (C)

Lesson Overview

ACTIVITY	ACTIVITY TITLE	TIME	ONLINE/OFFLINE
GET READY	Introduction: *What Do You Do With a Problem?* (C)	**1** minute	🖥
	Blend and Segment Compound Words	**5** minutes	🖥
	Review Words to Know from *What Do You Do With a Problem?*	**10** minutes	🖥
LEARN	How a Story Makes You Feel	**30** minutes	🖥
ALL ABOUT ME	Brain Break	**1** minute	🖥 or 📄
LEARN AND **TRY IT**	Statements	**10** minutes	🖥
	Write a Statement **LEARNING COACH CHECK-IN**	**15** minutes	📄
ALL ABOUT ME	Brain Break	**1** minute	🖥 or 📄
TRY IT	Practice: Spelling List 1 **LEARNING COACH CHECK-IN**	**20** minutes	🖥 and 📄
WRAP-UP	Questions About *What Do You Do With a Problem?* (C)	**2** minutes	🖥
	Read and Record	**15** minutes	🖥
	Handwriting	**10** minutes	📄

Content Background

Students will conclude a series of lessons centered around the book *What Do You Do With a Problem?* by Kobi Yamada. In this lesson, they will learn how an author uses words and pictures to convey feelings and learn how to identify and write a statement.

Reading Foundations   **Phonemic awareness** is the ability to hear, identify, and manipulate sounds in spoken words. Since phonemic awareness is related to the sounds students hear in words, students will not see words in print during phonemic awareness activities.

In this lesson, students will **blend**, or put together, the smaller words that make up a compound word. This activity is an oral activity. So, students will hear two words, such as *some* and *thing*. They will then be asked to say aloud the word the two smaller words make when they are put together, *something*.

Students will then be asked to **segment**, or take apart, a compound word. They will hear a compound word, such as *bedroom*. Then they will be asked to say aloud the two smaller words that make up the compound word, *bed* and *room*.

Reading   Authors use words and pictures to let readers know what a character is like and how the character feels. The authors' goal is also to make readers feel a certain way. Usually authors want readers to feel the same things as characters in a story. For example, in *What Do You Do With a Problem?*, the text states, "What if my problem sneaks up and gets me?" The author likely wants to show that the character feels scared and wants readers to feel the same way. Many authors write stories for children in this way to help them develop **empathy**, the ability to share and understand another person's feelings, which promotes a child's social and emotional growth.

Writing Skills   There are four types of sentences. Grammarians refer to these sentences as *declarative*, *interrogative*, *exclamatory*, and *imperative*.

- **declarative** – a telling sentence, or *statement*

- **interrogative** – an asking sentence, or *question*

- **exclamatory** – a sentence that shows a strong feeling, or *exclamation*

- **imperative** – a sentence that gives an order or request, or *command*

In this course, students will learn and use only the friendly terms *statement*, *question*, *exclamation*, and *command*.

In this lesson, students learn about *statements*. A **statement** is a telling sentence. It begins with a capital letter and ends with a period. It is the most common type of sentence used in English.

> **Examples:**
>
> Sean likes to cook.
>
> A leap year has 366 days.
>
> There are several pine trees in the park.

Advance Preparation

Gather students' cutouts from the Spelling List 1 activity page from *What Do You Do with a Problem?* (B). They will use the cutouts during Try It: Practice: Spelling List 1.

MATERIALS

Supplied
- *What Do You Do With a Problem?* by Kobi Yamada
- *English Language Arts 2 Activity Book 1*
  - Write a Statement
  - Practice: Spelling List 1
- handwriting workbook

Also Needed
- crayons or markers (optional)
- Spelling List 1 activity page cutouts from *What Do You Do With a Problem?* (B)

KEYWORDS

compound word – a word made from two smaller words

statement – a sentence that tells something
Example: The fox ran into the woods.

Lesson Goals

- Review new vocabulary.
- Orally blend and segment compound words.
- Determine a character's feelings.
- Determine how an author wants readers to feel.
- Explain how a character changes from the beginning of the story to the end.
- Write a statement.
- Identify and write spelling patterns that stand for sounds within words.
- Read aloud to practice fluency.
- Develop letter formation fluency.

GET READY

Introduction: *What Do You Do With a Problem?* (C)

Students will get a glimpse of what they will learn about in the lesson.

Blend and Segment Compound Words

In this oral activity, students will manipulate sounds in spoken words. They will practice blending small words to form a compound word. Then they will practice segmenting, or breaking apart, a compound word into its two smaller words.

Review Words to Know from *What Do You Do With a Problem?*

Students will review and answer questions about the vocabulary words from the reading selection.

LEARN AND TRY IT

LEARN   How a Story Makes You Feel

This activity reinforces that authors use words and pictures to convey how a character feels. Students will learn that authors use words and pictures to make readers feel the same as a character, which helps readers better understand the character and the story.

NOTE   The concept of empathy could be discussed at this point if time allows and students seem interested.

LEARN Statements

Through guided exploration of sentences from *What Do You Do With a Problem?*, students will how to identify and write a statement.

TIP Have students practice identifying both spoken and written statements using materials that interest them. Statements are in songs, on posters, and so on.

TRY IT Write a Statement

Students will complete Write a Statement in *English Language Arts 2 Activity Book 1*.

NOTE Students may wish to use crayons or markers to draw their picture.

LEARNING COACH CHECK-IN As needed, help students read the activity page. It may be helpful for students to answer Questions 6 and 7 aloud before writing their responses. Similarly, it may be helpful for students to say their statement aloud before writing it.

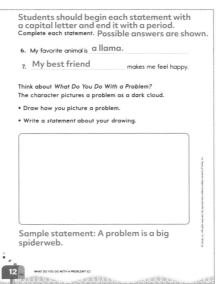

TRY IT Practice: Spelling List 1

Students will practice with the words from Spelling List 1.

- In *English Language Arts 2 Activity Book 1*, students will complete Practice: Spelling List 1.

- Online, students will answer questions that require them to reflect on the spelling patterns.

NOTE Students will need their cutouts from the Spelling List 1 activity page to complete Practice: Spelling List 1.

LEARNING COACH CHECK-IN As needed, help students read the activity page.

WHAT DO YOU DO WITH A PROBLEM? (C)

Practice: Spelling List 1

Get your spelling cutouts. Set up the headings, and sort the spelling words again.

Look at your sort, and write down each spelling word under the correct heading on the chart.

/ă/ hat	/ā/ cake	oddball
back	brave	have
crash	gave	want
fast	grade	
mad	made	
man	mane	

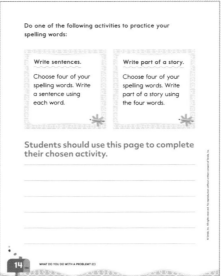

Do one of the following activities to practice your spelling words:

Write sentences.

Choose four of your spelling words. Write a sentence using each word.

Write part of a story.

Choose four of your spelling words. Write part of a story using the four words.

Students should use this page to complete their chosen activity.

WRAP-UP

Questions About *What Do You Do With a Problem?* (C)

Students will answer questions to show that they understand the reading, writing, and spelling skills they learned in this lesson.

Read and Record

Good readers read quickly, smoothly, and with expression. This is called *fluency*. Students will record themselves reading aloud. They will listen to their recording and think about how quick, smooth, and expressive they sound.

TIP   Encourage students to rerecord as needed.

Handwriting

Students should gather their handwriting materials and begin where they left off. Remind students to form letters carefully and correctly.

TIP   Set a timer to help students stay focused during handwriting practice.

Zara's Big Messy Day (A)

Lesson Overview

ACTIVITY	ACTIVITY TITLE	TIME	ONLINE/OFFLINE
GET READY	Introduction: *Zara's Big Messy Day* (A)	**1** minute	🖥️
	Count and Blend Syllables	**5** minutes	🖥️
	Book Walk: *Zara's Big Messy Day* (A)	**5** minutes	🖥️
	Words to Know: *Zara's Big Messy Day* (A)	**5** minutes	🖥️
READ	Think About Reading: *Zara's Big Messy Day* (A) LEARNING COACH CHECK-IN	**5** minutes	📄
	Zara's Big Messy Day (A)	**8** minutes	🖥️ and 📄
	Check-In: *Zara's Big Messy Day* (A)	**5** minutes	🖥️
LEARN AND **TRY IT**	Zara's Character and Identity	**8** minutes	🖥️
	Who Am I? LEARNING COACH CHECK-IN	**9** minutes	📄
ALL ABOUT ME	Brain Break	**1** minute	🖥️ or 📄
LEARN AND **TRY IT**	Questions	**10** minutes	🖥️
	Write a Question LEARNING COACH CHECK-IN	**15** minutes	📄
ALL ABOUT ME	Brain Break	**1** minute	🖥️ or 📄
TRY IT	Apply: Spelling List 1 LEARNING COACH CHECK-IN	**20** minutes	🖥️ and 📄
WRAP-UP	Questions About *Zara's Big Messy Day* (A)	**2** minutes	🖥️
	Handwriting	**10** minutes	📄
	Go Read!	**10** minutes	🖥️ or 📄

Content Background

Students will begin a series of lessons centered around the book *Zara's Big Messy Day* by Rebekah Borucki. In this lesson, they will learn about social identity and how to identify and write a question.

Vocabulary   Students will explore these words from the story: *responsibility*, *commotion*, and *relieved*. These are the definitions of the words as used in *Zara's Big Messy Day*:

- **responsibility** (noun) – something you are in charge of or expected to do

- **commotion** (noun) – a lot of noise and confusion

- **relieved** (adjective) – feeling glad or relaxed because something unpleasant has not happened or has stopped happening

Reading Foundations   Students will continue to develop their **phonemic awareness**, the ability to hear, identify, and manipulate sounds in spoken words. They will count the syllables in a word that they say aloud. They will then hear the syllables of a word and **blend**, or put together, the syllables to say the complete word.

A **syllable** is a unit of spoken language. These units make up words. A syllable is built around a vowel sound. Every syllable must have a vowel sound. The number of vowel sounds you hear in a word is the same as the number of syllables—for example, the word *cat* has one vowel sound, /ă/. The word *cat* has one syllable. The word *funny* has two vowel sounds, /ŭ/ and /ē/. The word *funny* has two syllables.

Reading   Students will learn about **social identity**, people's sense of who they are based on how they view themselves and how others view them. Aspects of people's social identity are often derived from groups to which they belong such as social class, family, racial groups, and even sports teams. These group memberships can be sources of pride. For example, a child who lives in Texas may strongly identify with being from Texas. Being a Texan is a source of pride and an aspect of the child's social identity.

Students will learn about aspects of the character Zara's social identity. For example, Zara's mother is Black and her father is white. So, Zara is biracial. Being biracial is part of Zara's social identity.

Writing Skills   Students will continue to learn about the four types of sentences. In this lesson, students will learn about *questions*. A **question** is an asking sentence. It begins with a capital letter and ends with a question mark. Some common words that begin questions are *who*, *what*, *where*, *when*, *why*, *how*, *will*, *can*, *do*, *is*, and *are*.

Examples: Who wrote that book?

How will we celebrate the holiday?

Are you going outside now?

MATERIALS

Supplied
- *Zara's Big Messy Day* by Rebekah Borucki
- *English Language Arts 2 Activity Book 1*
  - Think About Reading: *Zara's Big Messy Day* (A)
  - Who Am I?
  - Write a Question
  - Apply: Spelling List 1
- handwriting workbook

Also Needed
- reading material for Go Read!

KEYWORDS

prediction – a guess about what might happen that is based on information in a story and what you already know

question – a sentence that asks something
Example: What time is it?

syllable – a word part that contains a vowel or vowel sound
Examples: *pa - per*, *a - lone*

While students will explore complete and incomplete questions, they will not be expected to identify the subject and the predicate of a question in this course.

Advance Preparation

During the Go Read! activity, students will have the option of using the digital library. Allow extra time for them to make their reading selection, or have students make a selection before beginning the lesson.

Zara's Big Messy Day Synopsis

Seven-year-old Zara is a responsible girl who becomes upset and frustrated with all the commotion her brother Sam creates. Zara's mother teaches her a technique to deal with emotions that feel too big to handle. Zara learns to breathe in deeply as if she's smelling flowers, and then breathe out, as if she's blowing out candles. Zara uses this technique to calm herself down throughout a difficult day. By the end of the day, Zara has learned that she can make herself feel better when she does not like how she is feeling.

Lesson Goals

- Learn new vocabulary.
- Read *Zara's Big Messy Day*.
- Orally blend syllables of multisyllabic words.
- Predict what will happen in a story.
- Identify parts of a character's social identity.
- Determine parts of one's own social identity.
- Write a question.
- Identify reasons for when and how to use certain spelling patterns.
- Develop letter formation fluency.
- Read independently to develop fluency.

GET READY

Introduction: *Zara's Big Messy Day* (A)

Students will get a glimpse of what they will learn about in the lesson.

Count and Blend Syllables

In this oral activity, students count the number of syllables in multisyllabic words. Then they will hear the syllables of a word and blend the syllables together to say the complete word.

Book Walk: *Zara's Big Messy Day* (A)

Students will preview the major features of the new reading selection, including the title, author, illustrator, and pictures. This activity is designed to help students anticipate story content and connect to the selection. In this book walk, making predictions will be reinforced.

TIP   Have students follow along with the book walk using their own copy of the book.

Words to Know: *Zara's Big Messy Day* (A)

Students will preview and answer questions about three vocabulary words from the reading selection.

READ

Think About Reading: *Zara's Big Messy Day* (A)

Students will complete Think About Reading: *Zara's Big Messy Day* (A) in *English Language Arts 2 Activity Book 1*. They will make a prediction about what will happen in the story.

LEARNING COACH CHECK-IN   As needed, help students read the activity page.

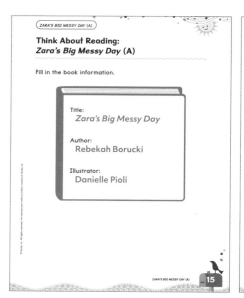

Zara's Big Messy Day (A)

Students will listen to *Zara's Big Messy Day* by Rebekah Borucki. They may choose to read the story on their own. Encourage them to reread their favorite passages.

Check-In: *Zara's Big Messy Day* (A)

Students will answer several questions to demonstrate their comprehension of *Zara's Big Messy Day*.

LEARN AND TRY IT

LEARN   Zara's Character and Identity

Students will study illustrations of the story's main character, Zara, to determine parts of Zara's social identity.

TRY IT   Who Am I?

Students will complete Who Am I? in *English Language Arts 2 Activity Book 1*.

LEARNING COACH CHECK-IN   As needed, help students read the activity page and determine parts of their social identity. Refer to and discuss the example chart for the character of Zara. Use the information about Zara as a springboard for guiding questions, such as the following:

- Are you a brother/sister?

- How do your parents/guardians think of you? Are you their son/daughter?

- Are there things you do that you're proud of, like playing soccer? Do you think of yourself as a soccer player?

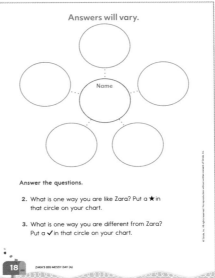

LEARN   Questions

Through guided exploration of sentences from *Zara's Big Messy Day*, students will learn how to identify and write a question.

TIP   Have students practice rephrasing a question as a statement and vice versa.

- Say, "I am wide awake. Am I wide awake?" Discuss how the order of the words changed to make the question.

- Say, "You have pigtails today. Do you have pigtails today?" Discuss how the word *Do* was added to make the question.

TRY IT   Write a Question

Students will complete Write a Question in *English Language Arts 2 Activity Book 1*.

SUPPORT   If students write incomplete questions, try having them read the question aloud, or try reading it aloud to them. Discuss whether that is how they would say the question. Often reading our own writing aloud (versus reading it silently) is enough to help us recognize incomplete sentences.

LEARNING COACH CHECK-IN   As needed, help students read the activity page. It may be helpful for students to answer Questions 5–7 aloud before writing their responses. Similarly, for Question 8, it may be helpful for students to say their question to a character aloud before writing it.

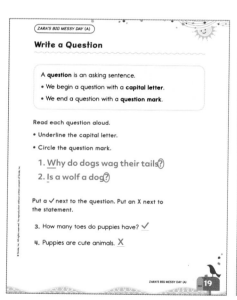

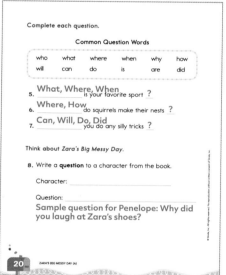

TRY IT   Apply: Spelling List 1

Students will apply what they have learned about the spelling patterns of the words in Spelling List 1.

- In an online activity, students will play a game to review spelling words and answer reflection questions about the spelling patterns learned.

- In *English Language Arts 2 Activity Book 1*, students will complete Apply: Spelling List 1.

LEARNING COACH CHECK-IN   As needed, help students read the activity page.

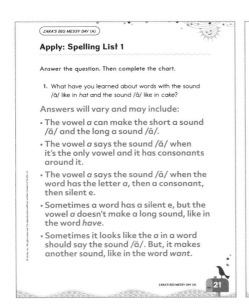
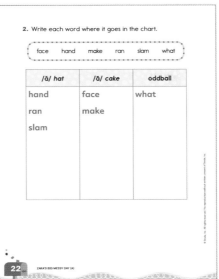

The two worksheet images show:

Page 21 (ZARA'S BIG MESSY DAY (A))

Apply: Spelling List 1

Answer the question. Then complete the chart.

1. What have you learned about words with the sound /ă/ like in *hat* and the sound /ā/ like in *cake*?

Answers will vary and may include:

- The vowel *a* can make the short a sound /ă/ and the long a sound /ā/.
- The vowel *a* says the sound /ă/ when it's the only vowel and it has consonants around it.
- The vowel *a* says the sound /ā/ when the word has the letter *a*, then a consonant, then silent e.
- Sometimes a word has a silent e, but the vowel *a* doesn't make a long sound, like in the word *have*.
- Sometimes it looks like the *a* in a word should say the sound /ā/. But, it makes another sound, like in the word *want*.

Page 22 (ZARA'S BIG MESSY DAY (A))

2. Write each word where it goes in the chart.

face   hand   make   ran   slam   what

/ă/ hat	/ā/ cake	oddball
hand	face	what
ran	make	
slam		

WRAP-UP

Questions About *Zara's Big Messy Day* (A)

Students will answer questions to show that they understand the reading, writing, and spelling skills they learned in this lesson.

Handwriting

Students should gather their handwriting materials and begin where they left off. Remind students to form letters carefully and correctly.

TIP   Set a timer to help students stay focused during handwriting practice.

Go Read!

Students will read for pleasure. They should choose a book or a magazine that interests them, or they may choose a selection from the digital library, linked in the online lesson.

- Have students read aloud a few paragraphs of their selection.

- Then have students read silently for the rest of the time.

SUPPORT   Students should make no more than five errors in decoding when they read aloud a few paragraphs of their Go Read! selection. If students struggle or make more than five errors, they need to select a different (and easier) text for the Go Read! activity.

TIP   Have students select something to read ahead of time to help them stay focused.

Zara's Big Messy Day (B)

Lesson Overview

ACTIVITY	ACTIVITY TITLE	TIME	ONLINE/OFFLINE
GET READY	Introduction: *Zara's Big Messy Day* (B)	**1** minute	🖥️
	Count and Segment Syllables	**3** minutes	🖥️
	Review Words to Know from *Zara's Big Messy Day*	**5** minutes	🖥️
READ	*Zara's Big Messy Day* (B)	**12** minutes	🖥️ and 📄
LEARN AND **TRY IT**	Beginning, Middle, and End	**14** minutes	🖥️
	What Happens When? **LEARNING COACH CHECK-IN**	**13** minutes	📄
ALL ABOUT ME	Brain Break	**1** minute	🖥️ or 📄
LEARN AND **TRY IT**	Exclamations	**10** minutes	🖥️
	Write an Exclamation **LEARNING COACH CHECK-IN**	**13** minutes	📄
WRAP-UP	Questions About *Zara's Big Messy Day* (B)	**2** minutes	🖥️
ALL ABOUT ME	Brain Break	**1** minute	🖥️ or 📄
QUIZ	Spelling List 1	**25** minutes	🖥️
WRAP-UP	Handwriting	**10** minutes	📄
	Go Read!	**10** minutes	🖥️ or 📄

Content Background

Students will continue a series of lessons centered around the book *Zara's Big Messy Day* by Rebekah Borucki. In this lesson, they will learn the basic structure of a story: beginning, middle, and end. They will also learn how to identify and write an exclamation.

Reading Foundations   Students will continue to develop their **phonemic awareness**, the ability to hear, identify, and manipulate sounds in spoken words. They will count the syllables in a word that is spoken aloud. They will then hear a spoken word and orally **segment**, or break apart, the syllables in the word.

Reading   Students will learn the basic structure of a story: beginning, middle, and end. They will learn that in the beginning of a story the characters, setting, and problem are introduced. The bulk of the story is the middle, which is when most of the story's events happen as characters try to solve the problem. The story comes to a close in the end, and we learn how the problem is solved.

Writing Skills   Students will continue to learn about the four types of sentences. In this lesson, students will learn about *exclamations*. An **exclamation** is a sentence that shows excitement or another strong feeling. It begins with a capital letter and ends with an exclamation mark.

> **Examples:**   That is my brother on TV!
>
> The baby took his first steps!

Advance Preparation

During the Go Read! activity, students will have the option of using the digital library. Allow extra time for them to make their reading selection, or have students make a selection before beginning the lesson.

Lesson Goals

- Reread and reflect on *Zara's Big Messy Day*.
- Review new vocabulary.
- Describe what happens at the beginning, middle, and end of a story.
- Explain how the parts of a story work together to tell the story.
- Write an exclamation.
- Take a spelling quiz.
- Develop letter formation fluency.
- Read independently to develop fluency.

MATERIALS

Supplied
- *Zara's Big Messy Day* by Rebekah Borucki
- *English Language Arts 2 Activity Book 1*
  - What Happens When?
  - Write an Exclamation
- handwriting workbook

Also Needed
- scissors
- glue stick
- reading material for Go Read!

KEYWORDS

exclamation – a sentence that shows strong feeling Example: I can't believe it!

GET READY

Introduction: *Zara's Big Messy Day* (B)

Students will get a glimpse of what they will learn about in the lesson.

Count and Segment Syllables

In this oral activity, students will count the number of syllables in multisyllabic words. Then they will hear a multisyllabic word and segment the word into its syllables.

Review Words to Know from *Zara's Big Messy Day*

Students will review and answer questions about the vocabulary words from the reading selection.

READ

Zara's Big Messy Day (B)

Students will have another opportunity to listen to *Zara's Big Messy Day* by Rebekah Borucki. They may choose to read the story on their own.

LEARN AND TRY IT

LEARN   Beginning, Middle, and End

Students will learn about the structure of a story: beginning, middle, and end. They will also learn how the parts of a story build on each other to tell the complete story.

TRY IT   What Happens When?

Students will complete What Happens When? in *English Language Arts 2 Activity Book 1*.

NOTE   Students will need scissors and a glue stick to complete this activity page.

LEARNING COACH CHECK-IN   As needed, help students read the activity page.

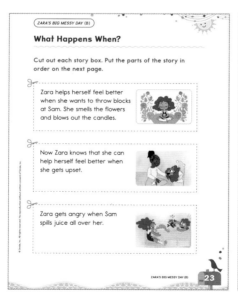
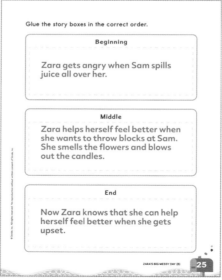

LEARN Exclamations

Through guided exploration of sentences from *Zara's Big Messy Day*, students will learn how to identify and write an exclamation.

TIP Emphasize the oral–written connection by saying statements and exclamations aloud and having students state which punctuation they would use if they were to write each sentence.

NOTE There are often multiple correct ways to write a sentence. What is "correct" depends on what the author is trying to convey. For example, "I was thrilled." and "I was thrilled!" are both correct but have different meanings. When students ask, "Is this right?" try responding with, "Tell me what you're trying to say."

TRY IT Write an Exclamation

Students will complete Write an Exclamation in *English Language Arts 2 Activity Book 1*.

LEARNING COACH CHECK-IN As needed, help students read the activity page. It may be helpful for students to answer Questions 9 and 10 aloud before writing their responses. Similarly, for Question 11, it may be helpful for students to say their exclamation to Penelope aloud before writing it.

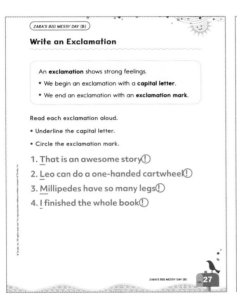

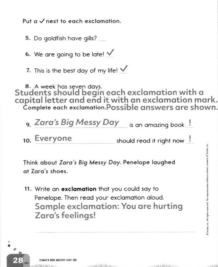

WRAP-UP

Questions About *Zara's Big Messy Day* (B)

Students will answer questions to show that they understand the reading and writing skills they learned in this lesson.

Spelling List 1

Students will take the Spelling List 1 quiz.

Handwriting

Students should gather their handwriting materials and begin where they left off. Remind students to form letters carefully and correctly.

TIP Set a timer to help students stay focused during handwriting practice.

Go Read!

Students will read for pleasure. They should choose a book or a magazine that interests them, or they may choose a selection from the digital library, linked in the online lesson.

- Have students read aloud a few paragraphs of their selection.

- Then have students read silently for the rest of the time.

SUPPORT Students should make no more than five errors in decoding when they read aloud a few paragraphs of their Go Read! selection. If students struggle or make more than five errors, they need to select a different (and easier) text for the Go Read! activity.

TIP Have students select something to read ahead of time to help them stay focused.

Zara's Big Messy Day (C)

Lesson Overview

ACTIVITY	ACTIVITY TITLE	TIME	ONLINE/OFFLINE
GET READY	Introduction: *Zara's Big Messy Day* (C)	**1** minute	🖥
	Author's Purpose	**10** minutes	🖥
READ	*Zara's Big Messy Day* (C)	**15** minutes	🖥 and 📄
LEARN	Retell a Story	**10** minutes	🖥
ALL ABOUT ME	Brain Break	**1** minute	🖥 or 📄
LEARN AND TRY IT	Commands	**10** minutes	🖥
	Write a Command **LEARNING COACH CHECK-IN**	**15** minutes	📄
ALL ABOUT ME	Brain Break	**1** minute	🖥 or 📄
LEARN	Spelling List 2 **LEARNING COACH CHECK-IN**	**25** minutes	🖥 and 📄
WRAP-UP	Questions About *Zara's Big Messy Day* (C)	**2** minutes	🖥
	Read and Record	**10** minutes	🖥
	More Language Arts Practice	**10** minutes	🖥
	Handwriting	**10** minutes	📄

Content Background

Students will conclude a series of lessons centered around the book *Zara's Big Messy Day* by Rebekah Borucki. In this lesson, they will learn how to retell a story and how to identify and write a command.

Reading Students will learn that retelling a story is a good way to check that they understand what they have read. A retelling should include a story's most important details in the order they happen. Learning will build on the story structure of beginning, middle, and end that students have previously learned. So, students will be asked to determine important details, such as the characters and the most important events, in the beginning of the story; then, the middle of the story; and finally, the end of the story.

An important detail is one that would change the story if it were left out. For example, in *Zara's Big Messy Day*, Sam spills orange juice on Zara, which makes her feel very upset. The story would be very different if this detail wasn't in the story. So, this detail should be included in a retelling of the story.

Writing Skills   Students will finish learning about the four types of sentences. In this lesson, students will learn about *commands*. A **command** is a sentence that gives an order or makes a request. It begins with a capital letter and usually ends with a period. A strong command may end with an exclamation mark.

> **Examples:**   <u>Pick up that trash.</u>
>
> <u>Watch out for the bike!</u>
>
> Please <u>shut the door.</u>

A command is always spoken to a person or a group of people (or in some cases, an animal or an object!). Therefore, the subject of a command is *you*, either as a singular or plural pronoun. The subject is simply understood; it is not shown as part of the sentence.

Spelling   Students will learn about spelling patterns that represent the short i sound, /ĭ/, and the long i sound, /ī/. Students will sort words under the headings **/ĭ/ *pig***, **/ī/ *kite***, and **oddball**.

The short i sound, /ĭ/, is found in words with a consonant-vowel-consonant (CVC) pattern. Students will learn that when the vowel i is the only vowel in a word and it is surrounded by consonants, the sound of the vowel *i* is usually /ĭ/. When students sort the spelling words, words with the sound /ĭ/ and a CVC spelling pattern go under the heading **/ĭ/ *pig***.

The long i sound, /ī/, is found in words with a vowel-consonant-silent e (VCe) pattern. Students will learn that when the vowel *i* is followed by a consonant and then silent e, the sound of the vowel *i* is usually /ī/. When students sort the spelling words, words with the sound /ī/ and a VCe spelling pattern go under the heading **/ī/ *kite***.

In some words, the vowel *i* does not represent the sound that would be expected based on the spelling pattern—for example, the word *give* has a VCe spelling pattern. Usually, the vowel *i* within a VCe pattern represents the sound /ĭ/. However, the *i* in the word *give* has the short i sound, /ĭ/. So, the word *give* is considered an oddball and would be placed under the **oddball** heading when students sort the spelling words.

Lesson Goals

- Reread *Zara's Big Messy Day*.
- Identify details to include in a retelling of the beginning, middle, and end of a story.
- Write a command.
- Sort words by sound and spelling pattern.
- Read aloud to practice fluency.
- Develop letter formation fluency.

GET READY

Introduction: *Zara's Big Messy Day* (C)

Students will get a glimpse of what they will learn about in the lesson.

Author's Purpose

Students will build background knowledge about an author's purpose, or the reasons an author writes a story.

READ

Zara's Big Messy Day (C)

Students will have another opportunity to listen to *Zara's Big Messy Day* by Rebekah Borucki. They may choose to read the story on their own.

LEARN AND TRY IT

LEARN   Retell a Story

Students will learn about retelling a story's important details from the beginning, middle, and end of a story. They will learn how to determine whether a detail is important enough to include in a retelling.

LEARN   Commands

Through guided exploration of sentences from *Zara's Big Messy Day*, students will learn how to identify and write a command.

SUPPORT   Students may have difficulty differentiating commands from statements and exclamations. Discuss how these sentences are alike and different. Focus not only on punctuation but also on the meaning of each sentence. Use these sentences, or create sentences that relate to students' interests.

- Statement: Marley plays basketball.

- Command: Go play basketball.

- Exclamation: The dog just sat!

- Command: Sit!

NOTE There are often multiple correct ways to write a sentence. What is "correct" depends on what the author is trying to convey. For example, "Stop." and "Stop!" are both correct commands but have different meanings. When students ask, "Is this right?" try responding with, "Tell me what you're trying to say."

TRY IT   Write a Command

Students will complete Write a Command in *English Language Arts 2 Activity Book 1*. This activity page combines what students have learned about commands, other types of sentences, and retelling a story.

LEARNING COACH CHECK-IN   As needed, help students read the activity page. For Question 9, it may be helpful for students to say their command aloud before writing it. Questions 11 and 12 require students to respond orally. Listen and provide feedback.

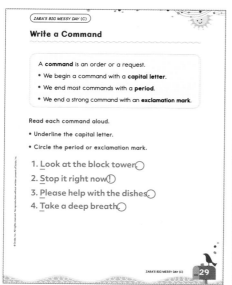

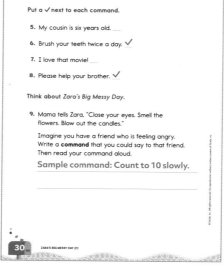

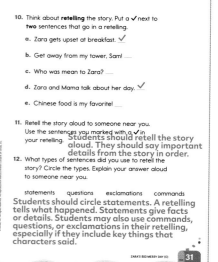

LEARN   Spelling List 2

Students will learn and sort words with sounds and spelling patterns for short i and long i.

- In an online activity, students will learn about the spelling patterns and the sounds they represent. They will learn how to sort words according to those sounds and patterns. They will also complete a word sort.

- In *English Language Arts 2 Activity Book 1*, students will complete Spelling List 2.

NOTE   Students will need scissors to cut out the spelling words on the activity page. Have students store their cutouts in a safe place, such as an envelope.

LEARNING COACH CHECK-IN   As needed, help students read the activity page.

This is the complete list of words students will work with to learn the spelling patterns for the sounds of short i and long i.

short i	long i	oddball
gift	five	climb
grin	pride	give
still	smile	
twist	write	
wish		

NOTE   For a word to fit into a category, it must meet two criteria: (1) It must have the target sound. (2) It must have the target spelling pattern. The term "oddball" is used for words that meet only one of the criteria.

Questions About *Zara's Big Messy Day* (C)

Students will answer questions to show that they understand the reading, writing, and spelling skills they learned in this lesson.

Read and Record

Good readers read quickly, smoothly, and with expression. This is called *fluency*. Students will record themselves reading aloud. They will listen to their recording and think about how quick, smooth, and expressive they sound.

TIP Encourage students to rerecord as needed.

More Language Arts Practice

Students will practice skills according to their individual needs.

Handwriting

Students should gather their handwriting materials and begin where they left off. Remind students to form letters carefully and correctly.

TIP Set a timer to help students stay focused during handwriting practice.

Poetry All Around (A)

Lesson Overview

ACTIVITY	ACTIVITY TITLE	TIME	ONLINE/OFFLINE
GET READY	Introduction: Poetry All Around (A)	**1** minute	🖥️
	Learning About Poetry	**15** minutes	🖥️
LEARN AND **TRY IT**	*Finding the Rhyme in a Poem*	**25** minutes	🖥️
	Rhyme and Beat	**21** minutes	🖥️
ALL ABOUT ME	Brain Break	**1** minute	🖥️ or 📄
TRY IT	Write Four Sentences **LEARNING COACH CHECK-IN**	**15** minutes	📄
ALL ABOUT ME	Brain Break	**1** minute	🖥️ or 📄
TRY IT	Practice Spelling List 2	**20** minutes	🖥️ and 📄
WRAP-UP	Questions About Poetry All Around (A)	**1** minute	🖥️
	Handwriting	**10** minutes	📄
	Go Read!	**10** minutes	🖥️ or 📄

Content Background

Students will begin learning about poetry. In this lesson, students will learn some of the elements of poetry: rhyme, rhythm, and rhyme scheme. They will also practice writing the four types of sentences.

Reading   Students will learn some of the structural elements of poetry. Poems are written in short lines instead of paragraphs. The lines are grouped into stanzas. Poems are meant to be read aloud. Like music, poems have a rhythm that can be heard when readers stress certain words or syllables. The beat of the stressed syllables creates the rhythm.

Poems often have a rhyme scheme, which is a pattern of rhymes made by the last sounds of lines. Rhyme scheme is often shown by a different letter of the alphabet to represent each rhyme. At this grade level, students will be taught to identify rhyme scheme by naming the lines that rhyme with each other—for example, lines 1 and 2 rhyme, and lines 3 and 4 rhyme.

Advance Preparation

Gather students' cutouts from the Spelling List 2 activity page from *Zara's Big Messy Day* (C). They will use the cutouts during Try It: Practice: Spelling List 2.

During the Go Read! activity, students will have the option of using the digital library. Allow extra time for them to make their reading selection, or have students make a selection before beginning the lesson.

Lesson Goals

- Activate and build background knowledge of poetry.
- Identify rhyme, rhythm, and rhyme scheme of a poem.
- Write four types of sentences.
- Identify and write spelling patterns that stand for sounds within words.
- Develop letter formation fluency.
- Read independently to develop fluency.

MATERIALS

Supplied

- *Finding the Rhyme in a Poem* by Valerie Bodden (in digital library; link in online lesson)
- *English Language Arts 2 Activity Book 1*
  - Write Four Sentences
  - Practice: Spelling List 2
- handwriting workbook

Also Needed

- Spelling List 2 activity page cutouts from *Zara's Big Messy Day* (C)
- crayons or markers (optional)
- reading material for Go Read!

KEYWORDS

rhyme – the use of words that end with the same sounds
Example: *Cat* and *hat* rhyme.

rhyme scheme – the pattern of rhymes made by the last sounds in the lines of a poem, shown by a different letter of the alphabet to represent each rhyme
Example: In a poem with the rhyme scheme AABB, lines 1 and 2 rhyme, and lines 3 and 4 rhyme.

rhythm – a distinctive beat

GET READY

Introduction: Poetry All Around (A)
Students will get a glimpse of what they will learn about in the lesson.

Learning About Poetry
Students will learn some important background information about the genre of poetry.

LEARN AND TRY IT

LEARN   *Finding the Rhyme in a Poem*
Students will learn about the elements of poetry: rhyme, rhythm, and rhyme scheme.

NOTE   The reading selection for this activity is located in the digital library, which is linked in the online lesson.

TRY IT   Rhyme and Beat
Students will answer questions to demonstrate their knowledge of the elements of poetry.

TRY IT Write Four Sentences

Students will complete about half of Write Four Sentences in *English Language Arts 2 Activity Book 1*. They will have time to complete this activity page in Poetry All Around (B).

LEARNING COACH CHECK-IN As needed, help students read the activity page and understand the directions.

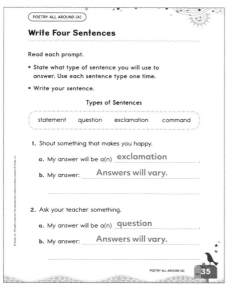

TRY IT Practice: Spelling List 2

Students will practice the spelling patterns for Spelling List 2.

- In *English Language Arts 2 Activity Book 1*, students will complete Practice: Spelling List 2.

- Online, students will answer questions that require them to reflect on the spelling patterns.

NOTE Students will need their cutouts from the Spelling List 2 activity page to complete Practice: Spelling List 2.

NOTE Students may wish to use crayons or markers to draw their pictures or comic strip.

LEARNING COACH CHECK-IN As needed, help students read the activity page.

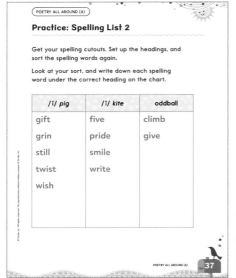

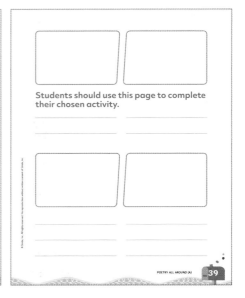

WRAP-UP

Questions About Poetry All Around (A)

Students will answer questions to show that they understand the reading and spelling skills they learned in this lesson.

Handwriting

Students should gather their handwriting materials and begin where they left off. Remind students to form letters carefully and correctly.

TIP Set a timer to help students stay focused during handwriting practice.

Go Read!

Students will read for pleasure. They should choose a book or a magazine that interests them, or they may choose a selection from the digital library, linked in the online lesson.

- Have students read aloud a few paragraphs of their selection.

- Then have students read silently for the rest of the time.

SUPPORT Students should make no more than five errors in decoding when they read aloud a few paragraphs of their Go Read! selection. If students struggle or make more than five errors, they need to select a different (and easier) text for the Go Read! activity.

TIP Have students select something to read ahead of time to help them stay focused.

Poetry All Around (B)

Lesson Overview

ACTIVITY	ACTIVITY TITLE	TIME	ONLINE/OFFLINE
GET READY	Introduction: Poetry All Around (B)	**1** minute	🖥️
	Onset and Rime	**10** minutes	🖥️
LEARN AND **TRY IT**	Elements of Poetry	**20** minutes	🖥️
	All About Alliteration **LEARNING COACH CHECK-IN**	**25** minutes	📄
ALL ABOUT ME	Brain Break	**1** minute	🖥️ or 📄
TRYT IT	Finish Writing Four Sentences **LEARNING COACH CHECK-IN**	**20** minutes	📄
ALL ABOUT ME	Brain Break	**1** minute	🖥️ or 📄
TRY IT	Apply: Spelling List 2 **LEARNING COACH CHECK-IN**	**20** minutes	🖥️ and 📄
WRAP-UP	Questions About Poetry All Around (B)	**2** minutes	🖥️
	Read and Record	**10** minutes	🖥️
	Handwriting	**10** minutes	📄

Content Background

Students will continue learning about poetry. In this lesson, they will review rhyme, rhythm, and rhyme scheme, and learn a new element, alliteration. They will also complete writing their four sentences.

Reading Foundations   Students will continue to develop their **phonemic awareness**, the ability to hear, identify, and manipulate sounds in spoken words. They will hear the onset and rime of a single syllable word. Then they will blend the onset and rime together to say the complete word.

The **onset** is the initial sound unit heard in any word—for example, the *d* in *dog*. The **rime** is the letters that follow the onset, usually a vowel and final consonants—for example, *–og* in *dog*.

Students will hear the onset and rime of a word in the following manner: "What word is /sm/ [pause] ile?" Students should respond by blending the sounds together to say "smile."

Reading   Students will learn that poets often use **alliteration**, the use of words with the same beginning sound. Tongue twisters have alliteration and are used as an example to help students understand alliteration.

The tongue twister "Sally sells seashells by the seashore" is an example of alliteration because of the repeated sound of s.

A poem can have alliteration with as few as two words beginning with the same sound. For example, the line of a poem that says "One day a boy went walking" uses the letter w in the words *went walking* to create alliteration. A poem does not need to have most words beginning with the same sound, like a tongue twister, for the poet to create alliteration.

Advance Preparation

Gather students' in-progress Write Four Sentences activity page from Poetry All Around (A). They will complete this page during Try It: Finish Writing Four Sentences.

Gather students' cutouts from the Spelling List 2 activity page from *Zara's Big Messy Day* (C). They will use the cutouts during Try It: Apply: Spelling List 2.

Lesson Goals

- Orally blend onset and rime of single syllable words.
- Identify rhyme, rhythm, rhyme scheme, and alliteration in poetry.
- Write four types of sentences.
- Identify reasons for when and how to use certain spelling patterns.
- Read aloud to practice fluency.
- Develop letter formation fluency.

GET READY

Introduction: Poetry All Around (B)

Students will get a glimpse of what they will learn about in the lesson.

Onset and Rime

In this oral activity, students will blend together the onset and rime of a word and say the word aloud.

MATERIALS

Supplied
- *Pizza and Other Stinky Poems* by Harriet Ziefert (in digital library; link in online lesson)
- *English Language Arts 2 Activity Book 1*
  - All About Alliteration
  - Apply: Spelling List 2
  - My Speed Sort Times
- handwriting workbook

Also Needed
- crayons or markers (optional)
- in-progress Write Four Sentences activity page from Poetry All Around (A)
- Spelling List 2 activity page cutouts from *Zara's Big Messy Day* (C)

KEYWORDS

alliteration – the use of words with the same or close to the same beginning sound Example: **B**onnie **b**aked **b**ananas.

LEARN AND TRY IT

LEARN   Elements of Poetry

Students will review the elements of poetry, rhyme, rhythm, and rhyme scheme. They will learn about another poetic element, alliteration.

NOTE   The reading selection for this activity is located in the digital library, which is linked in the online lesson.

TRY IT   All About Alliteration

Students will complete All About Alliteration in *English Language Arts 2 Activity Book 1*.

NOTE   Students may wish to use crayons or markers to draw their picture.

LEARNING COACH CHECK-IN   As needed, help students read the activity page and understand the directions. If students struggle to write the tongue twister, help them brainstorm words that begin with the letter *m*. Students have been given the sentence starter "Many monkeys." Guide them to choose from the words they brainstormed to create a structurally correct sentence—for example, a verb is needed after the starter "Many monkeys."

TRY IT   Finish Writing Four Sentences

Students will complete Write Four Sentences in *English Language Arts 2 Activity Book 1*.

LEARNING COACH CHECK-IN   As needed, help students read the activity page and understand the directions.

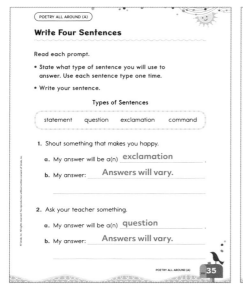

Write Four Sentences

Read each prompt.

- State what type of sentence you will use to answer. Use each sentence type one time.
- Write your sentence.

Types of Sentences

statement   question   exclamation   command

1. Shout something that makes you happy.
   a. My answer will be a(n) _exclamation_
   b. My answer: _Answers will vary._

2. Ask your teacher something.
   a. My answer will be a(n) _question_
   b. My answer: _Answers will vary._

3. Tell what you love to learn about.
   a. My answer will be a(n) _statement_
   b. My answer: _Answers will vary._

4. Give a friend advice on how to have a great day.
   a. My answer will be a(n) _command_
   b. My answer: _Answers will vary._

TRY IT   Apply: Spelling List 2

Students will apply what they have learned about the spelling patterns for Spelling List 2.

- In an online activity, students will complete a word sort and answer reflection questions.

- In *English Language Arts 2 Activity Book 1*, students will complete Apply: Spelling List 2.

   NOTE   Students will need their cutouts from the Spelling List 2 activity page to complete Apply: Spelling List 2.

   TIP   Have students record their speed sort times on the My Speed Sort Times activity page, which is located at the back of the activity book. It can be motivating for students to see their progress as their ability to complete speed sorts should improve over time

   LEARNING COACH CHECK-IN   As needed, help students read the activity page.

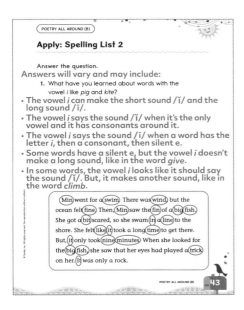

Questions About Poetry All Around (B)

Students will answer questions to show that they understand the reading and spelling skills they learned in this lesson.

Read and Record

Good readers read quickly, smoothly, and with expression. This is called *fluency*. Students will record themselves reading aloud. They will listen to their recording and think about how quick, smooth, and expressive they sound.

TIP Encourage them to rerecord as needed.

Handwriting

Students should gather their handwriting materials and begin where they left off. Remind students to form letters carefully and correctly.

TIP Set a timer to help students stay focused during handwriting practice.

Problems and Solutions Wrap-Up (A)

Lesson Overview

ACTIVITY	ACTIVITY TITLE	TIME	ONLINE/OFFLINE
GET READY	Introduction: Problems and Solutions Wrap-Up (A)	**1** minute	🖥
QUIZ	Spelling List 2	**25** minutes	🖥
ALL ABOUT ME	Brain Break	**1** minute	🖥 or 📄
GET READY	More Onset and Rime	**5** minutes	🖥
REVIEW	Problems and Solutions	**25** minutes	🖥
ALL ABOUT ME	Brain Break	**1** minute	🖥 or 📄
WRAP-UP	Theme Time: Problems and Solutions LEARNING COACH CHECK-IN	**42** minutes	📄
	Your Choice Time	**20** minutes	🖥 or 📄

Advance Preparation

During the Your Choice Time activity, students will be given the option to read something of their choice. If they are using the digital library, allow extra time for them to make their reading selection, or have them make a selection before beginning the lesson.

MATERIALS

Supplied
- *English Language Arts 2 Activity Book 1*
  - Theme Time: Problems and Solutions

Also Needed
- reading material for Your Choice Time (optional)

Lesson Goals

- Take a spelling quiz.
- Orally segment single syllable words into onset and rime.
- Review writing, vocabulary, and reading skills from the unit.
- Make connections among the texts in the unit.

GET READY

Introduction: Problems and Solutions Wrap-Up (A)

Students will get a glimpse of what they will do in the lesson.

QUIZ

Spelling List 2

Students will complete the Spelling List 2 quiz.

GET READY

More Onset and Rime

In this oral activity, students will develop their phonemic awareness by segmenting words into onset and rime.

REVIEW

Problems and Solutions

Students will answer questions to review the vocabulary, writing, and reading skills they learned in the unit.

WRAP-UP

Theme Time: Problems and Solutions

Students will complete Theme Time: Problems and Solutions in *English Language Arts 2 Activity Book 1*.

NOTE   This activity page includes an optional ungraded project. Students may need additional materials to complete the project.

LEARNING COACH CHECK-IN   As needed, help students read the activity page. Discuss students' responses.

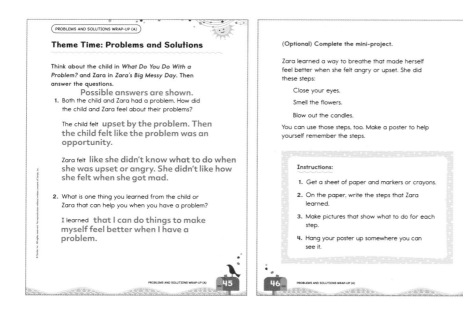

Your Choice Time

Students will choose among the following activities:

- Independent reading

- Independent writing

- Completing the optional project from the Theme Time: Problems and Solutions activity page

Problems and Solutions Wrap-Up (B)

Lesson Overview

ACTIVITY	ACTIVITY TITLE	TIME	ONLINE/OFFLINE
GET READY	Introduction: Problems and Solutions Wrap-Up (B)	**1** minute	🖥️
QUIZ	Problems and Solutions	**33** minutes	🖥️
ALL ABOUT ME	Brain Break	**1** minute	🖥️ or 📄
REFLECTION	Go Write! and Set a Goal **LEARNING COACH CHECK-IN**	**30** minutes	📄
WRAP-UP	Celebrate: Problems and Solutions	**20** minutes	📄
	Discussion: How Do You Learn? **LEARNING COACH CHECK-IN**	**15** minutes	🖥️
	More Language Arts Practice	**10** minutes	🖥️
	Your Choice Time	**10** minutes	🖥️ or 📄

Advance Preparation

During the Your Choice Time activity, students will be given the option to read something of their choice. If they are using the digital library, allow extra time for them to make their reading selection, or have them make a selection before beginning the lesson.

Lesson Goals

- Take a quiz on the writing, vocabulary, and reading skills from the unit.
- Freewrite to develop fluency and reflect on learning.
- Set a goal for future learning.
- Celebrate accomplishments from the unit.
- Participate in a discussion.

MATERIALS

Supplied
- *English Language Arts 2 Activity Book 1*
  - Go Write! and Set a Goal
  - My Reading Log
  - My Badge Book

Also Needed
- crayons or markers
- reading material for Your Choice Time (optional)

Introduction: Problems and Solutions Wrap-Up (B)

Students will get a glimpse of what they will do in the lesson.

QUIZ

Problems and Solutions

Students will complete the Problems and Solutions quiz.

REFLECTION

Go Write! and Set a Goal

Students will complete Go Write! and Set a Goal in *English Language Arts 2 Activity Book 1*.

NOTE   The Go Write! activity is intended to build writing fluency. Students should write for 10 minutes.

LEARNING COACH CHECK-IN   As needed, help students read the activity page. Discuss their goal, including any steps they can take as well as support you can provide in helping them meet it.

A goal is something that you want to do.

You are getting ready to start a new unit. Choose one goal for yourself as a reader or writer. Or, write your own goal.

My GOAL!

☐ Read each book twice.

☐ Read for 10 minutes a day.

☐ Read to someone in my family.

☐ Use complete sentences in my writing.

☐ _____

Write one thing you can do to help reach your goal.

I will _____

WRAP-UP

Celebrate: Problems and Solutions

Students will celebrate accomplishments from the unit.

- They will record what they read this unit in their reading log.

- They will color the badge for this unit in their badge book. They may also color a badge to celebrate reading accomplishments.

NOTE The My Reading Log and My Badge Book activity pages are located at the back of the activity book.

NOTE Students will need crayons or markers to color in their badges.

Discussion: How Do You Learn?

Students will respond to a discussion prompt.

LEARNING COACH CHECK-IN Students should discuss the questions shown on-screen with an adult. In some cases, teachers may facilitate a group discussion.

More Language Arts Practice

Students will practice skills according to their individual needs.

Your Choice Time

Students will choose among the following activities:

- Independent reading

- Independent writing

- Completing the optional project from the Theme Time: Problems and Solutions activity page

Bears

Arnold and Louise: Lost and Found (A)

Lesson Overview

ACTIVITY	ACTIVITY TITLE	TIME	ONLINE/OFFLINE
GET READY	Introduction: *Arnold and Louise: Lost and Found* (A)	**1** minute	🖥
	Book Walk: *Arnold and Louise: Lost and Found* (A)	**10** minutes	🖥
	Words to Know: *Arnold and Louise: Lost and Found* (A)	**10** minutes	🖥
	Before You Read: Does It Make Sense?	**5** minutes	🖥
ALL ABOUT ME	Brain Break	**1** minute	🖥 or 📄
READ	Think About Reading: *Arnold and Louise: Lost and Found* (A) **LEARNING COACH CHECK-IN**	**10** minutes	📄
	Arnold and Louise: Lost and Found (A)	**15** minutes	🖥 and 📄
	Check-In: *Arnold and Louise: Lost and Found* (A)	**5** minutes	🖥
LEARN	Read Between the Lines	**15** minutes	🖥
ALL ABOUT ME	Brain Break	**1** minute	🖥 or 📄
LEARN	Spelling List 3 **LEARNING COACH CHECK-IN**	**25** minutes	🖥 and 📄
WRAP-UP	Questions About *Arnold and Louise: Lost and Found* (A)	**2** minutes	🖥
	Handwriting	**10** minutes	📄
	Go Read!	**10** minutes	🖥 or 📄

Content Background

Students will begin a series of lessons centered around the book *Arnold and Louise: Lost and Found* by Erica S. Perl. In this lesson, they will learn how to make inferences.

Vocabulary   Students will explore these words from the story: *collect*, *treasure*, *consider*, and *trustworthy*. These are the definitions of the words as they are used in *Arnold and Louise: Lost and Found*:

- **collect** (verb) – to gather things together

- **treasure** (noun) – something very special or valuable

- **consider** (verb) – to think about carefully

- **trustworthy** (adjective) – deserving of trust

Reading   An **inference** is a conclusion reached based on facts. Readers **infer** by putting together clues in a text with their background knowledge.

Students at this grade level will be taught the student-friendly phrase "reading between the lines." They will learn that an author doesn't always state things directly in a story. But, students can read between the lines, or make inferences, about the story's characters and events. These inferences are based on what students know from their own experiences, their background knowledge, and clues in the text. For example, it can be inferred that collecting things makes the character of Arnold happy. This inference is based on story details that say Arnold finds things that are special to him and an image that shows Arnold smiling as he put items on his shelves. These details, combined with readers' background knowledge that they know how happy they feel when they find something special, help readers make an inference about Arnold.

Spelling   Students will learn about spelling patterns that represent the sounds of short o, /ŏ/, and long o, /ō/. Students will sort words under these headings: **/ŏ/ box**, **/ō/ bone**, **oddball**.

The short o sound, /ŏ/, is found in words with a consonant-vowel-consonant (CVC) pattern. Students will learn that when the vowel *o* is the only vowel in a word and it is surrounded by consonants, the sound of the vowel *o* is usually /ŏ/. When students sort the spelling words, words with the sound /ŏ/ and a CVC spelling pattern will go under the heading **/ŏ/ box**.

The long o sound, /ō/, is found in words with a vowel-consonant-silent e (VCe) pattern. Students will learn that when the vowel *o* is followed by a consonant, and then silent e, the sound of the vowel *o* is usually /ō/. When students sort the spelling words, words with the sound /ō/ and a VCe spelling pattern will go under the heading **/ō/ bone**.

In some words, the vowel *o* does not represent the sound that would be expected based on the spelling pattern. For example, the word *both* has a CVC spelling pattern. Usually, the vowel *o* within a CVC pattern represents the sound /ŏ/. However, the *o* in the word *both* has the long o sound, /ō/. So, the word *both* is considered an oddball and would be placed under the **oddball** heading when students sort the spelling words.

MATERIALS

Supplied
- *Arnold and Louise: Lost and Found* by Erica S. Perl
- *English Language Arts 2 Activity Book 1*
  - Think About Reading: *Arnold and Louise: Lost and Found* (A)
  - Spelling List 3
- handwriting workbook

Also Needed
- scissors
- envelope or baggie to store spelling cutouts
- reading material for Go Read!

KEYWORDS

infer – to use clues and what you already know to make a guess

inference – a guess you make using the clues in a text and what you already know

Advance Preparation

During the Go Read! activity, students will have the option of using the digital library. Allow extra time for students to make their reading selection, or have students make a selection before beginning the lesson.

Arnold and Louise: Lost and Found, Chapter One Synopsis

Arnold and Louise are best friends. Arnold likes to collect things. Louise often loses things, usually Arnold's things. When Arnold finds the best treasure ever, Louise begs him to let her borrow it. Arnold is reluctant but finally agrees. Louise tells Arnold that he won't be sorry. But, Arnold's not so sure.

Lesson Goals

- Learn new vocabulary.
- Read Chapter One of *Arnold and Louise: Lost and Found*.
- Use background knowledge and text information to make inferences.
- Sort words by sound and spelling pattern.
- Develop letter formation fluency.
- Read independently to develop fluency.

GET READY

Introduction: *Arnold and Louise: Lost and Found* (A)

Students will get a glimpse of what they will learn about in the lesson.

Book Walk: *Arnold and Louise: Lost and Found* (A)

Students will preview the major features of the new reading selection, including the title, author, illustrator, and pictures. This activity is designed to help students anticipate story content and connect to the selection.

TIP   Have students follow along with the book walk using their own copy of the book.

Words to Know: *Arnold and Louise: Lost and Found* (A)

Students will preview and answer a question about four vocabulary words from the reading selection.

Before You Read: Does It Make Sense?

Students will learn about using context clues to help them decode an unknown word.

READ

Think About Reading: *Arnold and Louise: Lost and Found* (A)

Students will complete Think About Reading: *Arnold and Louise: Lost and Found* (A) in *English Language Arts 2 Activity Book 1*.

LEARNING COACH CHECK-IN   As needed, help students read the activity page.

Arnold and Louise: Lost and Found (A)

Students will read Chapter One of *Arnold and Louise: Lost and Found* by Erica S. Perl. Encourage them to reread their favorite passages.

Check-In: *Arnold and Louise: Lost and Found* (A)

Students will answer questions to demonstrate their comprehension of Chapter One of *Arnold and Louise: Lost and Found*.

LEARN

Read Between the Lines

Students will learn how to make inferences. Then they will answer questions that require them to make inferences about the characters in Chapter One of *Arnold and Louise: Lost and Found*.

Spelling List 3

Students will learn and sort words with sounds and spelling patterns for short o and long o.

- In an online activity, students will learn about the spelling patterns and the sounds they represent. They will learn how to sort words according to those sounds and patterns. They will also complete a word sort.

- In *English Language Arts 2 Activity Book 1*, students will complete Spelling List 3.

NOTE Students will need scissors to cut out the spelling words on the activity page. Have students store their cutouts in a safe place, such as an envelope.

LEARNING COACH CHECK-IN As needed, help students read the activity page.

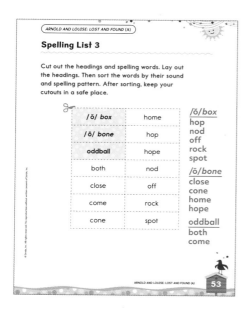

This is the complete list of words students will work with to learn the spelling patterns that represent the sounds of short o and long o.

short o	long o	oddball
hop	close	both
nod	cone	come
off	home	
rock	hope	
spot		

Questions About *Arnold and Louise: Lost and Found* (A)

Students will answer questions to show that they understand the reading and spelling skills they learned in this lesson.

Handwriting

Students should gather their handwriting materials and begin where they left off. Remind students to form letters carefully and correctly.

TIP Set a timer to help students stay focused during handwriting practice.

Go Read!

Students will read for pleasure. They should choose a book or a magazine that interests them, or they may choose a selection from the digital library, linked in the online lesson.

• Have students read aloud a few paragraphs of their selection.

• Then have students read silently for the rest of the time.

SUPPORT Students should make no more than five errors in decoding when they read aloud a few paragraphs of their Go Read! selection. If students struggle or make more than five errors, they need to select a different (and easier) text for the Go Read! activity.

TIP Have students select something to read ahead of time to help them stay focused.

Arnold and Louise: Lost and Found (B)

Lesson Overview

ACTIVITY	ACTIVITY TITLE	TIME	ONLINE/OFFLINE
GET READY	Introduction: *Arnold and Louise: Lost and Found* (B)	**1** minute	🖥
	Blend Phonemes	**5** minutes	🖥
	Words to Know: *Arnold and Louise: Lost and Found* (B)	**5** minutes	🖥
READ	Think About Reading: *Arnold and Louise: Lost and Found* (B) **LEARNING COACH CHECK-IN**	**10** minutes	📄
	Arnold and Louise: Lost and Found (B)	**15** minutes	🖥 and 📄
	Reflect: *Arnold and Louise: Lost and Found* (B) **LEARNING COACH CHECK-IN**	**5** minutes	📄
ALL ABOUT ME	Brain Break	**1** minute	🖥 or 📄
LEARN AND **TRY IT**	Describing Characters	**15** minutes	🖥
	Describe Arnold and Louise **LEARNING COACH CHECK-IN**	**20** minutes	📄
ALL ABOUT ME	Brain Break	**1** minute	🖥 or 📄
TRY IT	Practice: Spelling List 3	**20** minutes	🖥 and 📄
WRAP-UP	Questions About *Arnold and Louise: Lost and Found* (B)	**2** minutes	🖥
	Handwriting	**10** minutes	📄
	Go Read!	**10** minutes	🖥 or 📄

Content Background

Students will continue a series of lessons centered around the book *Arnold and Louise: Lost and Found* by Erica S. Perl. In this lesson, they will learn about describing characters.

Reading Foundations   Students will continue to develop their **phonemic awareness**, the ability to hear, identify, and manipulate sounds in spoken words. They will hear the individual phonemes of a one-syllable word. Then they will blend the phonemes together to say the complete word.

A **phoneme** is the smallest part of spoken language that you hear in words—for example, the word *sun* consists of three phonemes: /s/ /u/ /n/. Sometimes, one phoneme is represented by more than one letter—for example, a digraph, such as *ch*, is written with two letters, but it represents one phoneme or sound.

Students will hear the individual phonemes of a word in the following manner: "What word is /r/ /ŏ/ /k/?" Students should respond by blending the sounds together to say, "rock."

Vocabulary   Students will explore these words from the story: *dart*, *relax*, and *sigh*. These are the definitions of the words as they are used in *Arnold and Louise: Lost and Found*:

- **dart** (verb) – to move or shoot out suddenly and quickly

- **relax** (verb) – to feel calmer and less worried

- **sigh** (verb) – to let out a long loud breath to express feelings such as sadness, relief, or tiredness

Reading   Students will learn about describing **characters** in a story. They will learn that some descriptions are stated directly in the story—for example, the story directly states that Arnold collects things. So, we can describe Arnold as somebody who collects things.

Some descriptions can be inferred from what a character says and does— for example, the story says that Louise darts into the bushes. From our background knowledge, we know that chipmunks tend to move quickly. So, we can infer that Louise moves around quickly.

Advance Preparation

Gather students' cutouts from the Spelling List 3 activity page from *Arnold and Louise: Lost and Found* (A). They will use the cutouts during Try It: Practice: Spelling List 3.

During the Go Read! activity, students will have the option of using the digital library. Allow extra time for students to make their reading selection, or have students make a selection before beginning the lesson.

MATERIALS

Supplied
- *Arnold and Louise: Lost and Found* by Erica S. Perl
- *English Language Arts 2 Activity Book 1*
  - Think About Reading: *Arnold and Louise: Lost and Found* (B)
  - Describe Arnold and Louise
  - Practice: Spelling List 3
- handwriting workbook

Also Needed
- Spelling List 3 activity page cutouts from *Arnold and Louise: Lost and Found* (A)
- reading material for Go Read!

KEYWORDS

character – a person or animal in a story

Arnold and Louise: Lost and Found, Chapters Two and Three Synopsis

Arnold seeks out Louise to collect the treasure she borrowed from him the day before. When Arnold asks for the treasure, Louise tells him that she has hidden it, and he must play a new game that she has invented to find the treasure. After Arnold becomes frustrated with the game, Louise directs him to climb a tree to find his treasure. At the top of the tree, Arnold finds a nest of birds. The baby birds are dancing in front of his treasure, using it as a mirror.

Lesson Goals

- Orally blend the individual phonemes of one-syllable words.
- Learn new vocabulary.
- Read Chapters Two and Three of *Arnold and Louise: Lost and Found*.
- Make and confirm a prediction about reading.
- Describe characters.
- Identify reasons for when and how to use certain spelling patterns.
- Develop letter formation fluency.
- Read independently to develop fluency.

GET READY

Introduction: *Arnold and Louise: Lost and Found* (B)
Students will get a glimpse of what they will learn about in the lesson.

Blend Phonemes
In this oral activity, students will hear and then blend together the phonemes of a word and say the word aloud.

Words to Know: *Arnold and Louise: Lost and Found* (B)
Students will preview and answer questions about three vocabulary words from the reading selection.

Think About Reading: *Arnold and Louise: Lost and Found* (B)

Students will complete Question 1 on Think About Reading: *Arnold and Louise: Lost and Found* (B) in *English Language Arts 2 Activity Book 1*.

NOTE In this activity, students will make a prediction about Chapters Two and Three of *Arnold and Louise: Lost and Found*. Students will come back to the activity page to confirm their prediction after they complete the reading.

LEARNING COACH CHECK-IN As needed, help students read the activity page.

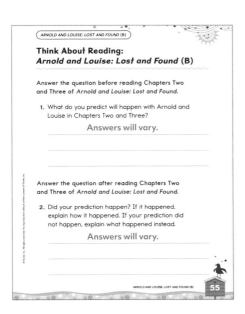

Arnold and Louise: Lost and Found (B)

Students will read Chapters Two and Three of *Arnold and Louise: Lost and Found* by Erica S. Perl. Encourage them to reread their favorite passages.

Reflect: *Arnold and Louise: Lost and Found* (B)

Students will confirm the prediction they made before reading Chapters Two and Three by completing Question 2 on Think About Reading: *Arnold and Louise: Lost and Found* (B) in *English Language Arts 2 Activity Book 1*.

LEARNING COACH CHECK-IN Help students read Question 2 on the activity page. Be sure not to state that a prediction was right or wrong. Readers make the best predictions they can with the information they have at the time. They can then confirm a prediction by saying whether it happened.

LEARN   Describing Characters

Students will explore pictures and text from *Arnold and Louise: Lost and Found* to describe the characters Arnold and Louise.

TRY IT   Describe Arnold and Louise

Students will complete Describe Arnold and Louise in *English Language Arts 2 Activity Book 1*.

LEARNING COACH CHECK-IN   As needed, help students read the activity page. It may be helpful for students to say their answers aloud before writing them.

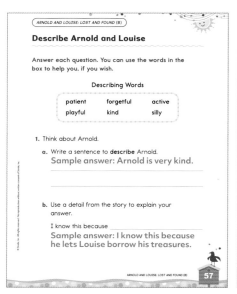

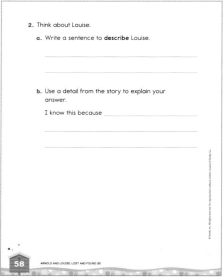

TRY IT   Practice: Spelling List 3

Students will practice the spelling patterns for Spelling List 3.

• In *English Language Arts 2 Activity Book 1*, students will complete Practice: Spelling List 3.

• Online, students will answer questions that require them to reflect on the spelling patterns.

NOTE   Students will need their cutouts from the Spelling List 3 activity page to complete Practice: Spelling List 3.

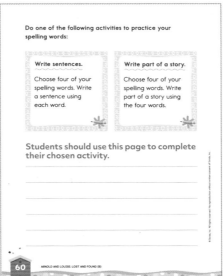

Practice: Spelling List 3

Get your spelling cutouts. Set up the headings, and sort the spelling words again.

Look at your sort, and write down each spelling word under the correct heading on the chart.

/ŏ/ box	/ō/ bone	oddball
hop	close	both
nod	cone	come
off	home	
rock	hope	
spot		

Do one of the following activities to practice your spelling words:

Write sentences.

Choose four of your spelling words. Write a sentence using each word.

Write part of a story.

Choose four of your spelling words. Write part of a story using the four words.

Students should use this page to complete their chosen activity.

WRAP-UP

Questions About *Arnold and Louise: Lost and Found* (B)

Students will answer questions to show that they understand the reading and spelling skills they learned in this lesson.

Handwriting

Students should gather their handwriting materials and begin where they left off. Remind students to form letters carefully and correctly.

TIP   Set a timer to help students stay focused during handwriting practice.

Go Read!

Students will read for pleasure. They should choose a book or a magazine that interests them, or they may choose a selection from the digital library, linked in the online lesson.

- Have students read aloud a few paragraphs of their selection.

- Then have students read silently for the rest of the time.

SUPPORT   Students should make no more than five errors in decoding when they read aloud a few paragraphs of their Go Read! selection. If students struggle or make more than five errors, they need to select a different (and easier) text for the Go Read! activity.

TIP   Have students select something to read ahead of time to help them stay focused.

Arnold and Louise: Lost and Found (C)

Lesson Overview

ACTIVITY	ACTIVITY TITLE	TIME	ONLINE/OFFLINE
GET READY	Introduction: *Arnold and Louise: Lost and Found* (C)	**1** minute	🖥️
	Segmenting Phonemes	**5** minutes	🖥️
	Review Words to Know from *Arnold and Louise: Lost and Found*	**10** minutes	🖥️
ALL ABOUT ME	Brain Break	**1** minute	🖥️ or 📄
READ	Think About Reading: *Arnold and Louise: Lost and Found* (C) **LEARNING COACH CHECK-IN**	**10** minutes	📄
	Arnold and Louise: Lost and Found (C)	**20** minutes	🖥️ and 📄
	Reflect: *Arnold and Louise: Lost and Found* (C) **LEARNING COACH CHECK-IN**	**10** minutes	📄
LEARN	It's All in the Voice	**20** minutes	🖥️
ALL ABOUT ME	Brain Break	**1** minute	🖥️ or 📄
TRY IT	Apply: Spelling List 3 **LEARNING COACH CHECK-IN**	**20** minutes	🖥️ and 📄
WRAP-UP	Questions About *Arnold and Louise: Lost and Found* (C)	**2** minutes	🖥️
	Handwriting	**10** minutes	📄
	Go Read!	**10** minutes	🖥️ or 📄

Content Background

Students will continue a series of lessons centered around the book *Arnold and Louise: Lost and Found* by Erica S. Perl. In this lesson, they will learn how hearing a story read aloud can help them understand characters.

Reading Foundations   Students will continue to develop their **phonemic awareness**, the ability to hear, identify, and manipulate sounds in spoken words. They will hear a spoken word, and then orally **segment**, or break apart, the individual sounds in the word—for example, students will be asked, "What are the sounds of the word *bug*?" Students are expected to separate the word into its individual sounds and say, "/b/ /ŭ/ /g/."

Reading   Hearing a story read aloud is a different experience than reading it silently to yourself. Students will learn that the expression in a speaker's voice conveys certain things about characters—in particular, their emotions. For example, when a speaker stresses words and uses expression to read Arnold's line, "So you *did* lose my treasure," listeners can hear that Arnold is angry.

Advance Preparation

Gather students' cutouts from the Spelling List 3 activity page from *Arnold and Louise: Lost and Found* (A). They will use the cutouts during Try It: Apply: Spelling List 3.

If students have removed My Speed Sort Times from the activity book, have them gather this activity page. They will use this activity page in Try It: Apply: Spelling List 3.

During the Go Read! activity, students will have the option of using the digital library. Allow extra time for students to make their reading selection, or have students make a selection before beginning the lesson.

MATERIALS

Supplied

- *Arnold and Louise: Lost and Found* by Erica S. Perl
- *English Language Arts 2 Activity Book 1*
  - Think About Reading: *Arnold and Louise: Lost and Found* (C)
  - Apply: Spelling List 3
  - My Speed Sort Times
- handwriting workbook

Also Needed

- Spelling List 3 activity page cutouts from *Arnold and Louise: Lost and Found* (A)
- reading material for Go Read!

Arnold and Louise: Lost and Found, Chapter Four Synopsis

Arnold thanks Louise for giving him the treasure of a good feeling. But, Arnold's good feeling about the baby birds using his treasure disappears quickly when he learns that Louise did indeed lose his treasure. As Arnold storms away from Louise, she tries to get him to stop by telling him that she has found new items for his collection. When Arnold does not respond, Louise finally admits that she loses things even though she doesn't mean to. But, she doesn't want to lose her best friend.

Lesson Goals

- Segment words into individual phonemes.
- Review new vocabulary.
- Read Chapter Four of *Arnold and Louise: Lost and Found*.
- Make and confirm a prediction about reading.
- Identify details about story characters conveyed by how a speaker reads a story aloud.
- Identify reasons for when and how to use certain spelling patterns.
- Develop letter formation fluency.
- Read independently to develop fluency.

Introduction: *Arnold and Louise: Lost and Found* (C)

Students will get a glimpse of what they will learn about in the lesson.

Segmenting Phonemes

In this oral activity, students will hear a one-syllable word, and then segment the word into its individual sounds.

Review Words to Know from *Arnold and Louise: Lost and Found*

Students will answer questions about the vocabulary words from the reading selection.

READ

Think About Reading: *Arnold and Louise: Lost and Found* (C)

Students will complete Question 1 on Think About Reading: *Arnold and Louise: Lost and Found* (C) in *English Language Arts 2 Activity Book 1*.

NOTE   In this activity, students will make a prediction about Chapter Four of *Arnold and Louise: Lost and Found*. Students will come back to the activity page to confirm their prediction after they complete the reading.

LEARNING COACH CHECK-IN   As needed, help students read the activity page.

ARNOLD AND LOUISE: LOST AND FOUND (C)

Think About Reading:
Arnold and Louise: Lost and Found (C)

Answer the question before reading Chapter Four of *Arnold and Louise: Lost and Found*.

1. What do you predict will happen with Arnold and Louise in Chapter Four?

    Answers will vary.

Answer the question after reading Chapter Four of *Arnold and Louise: Lost and Found*.

2. Did your prediction happen? If it happened, explain how it happened. If your prediction did not happen, explain what happened instead.

    Answers will vary.

ARNOLD AND LOUISE: LOST AND FOUND (C)   **61**

Arnold and Louise: Lost and Found (C)

Students will read Chapter Four of *Arnold and Louise: Lost and Found* by Erica S. Perl on their own. Encourage them to reread their favorite passages.

Reflect: *Arnold and Louise: Lost and Found* (C)

Students will confirm the prediction they made before reading Chapter Four by completing Question 2 on Think About Reading: *Arnold and Louise: Lost and Found* (C) in *English Language Arts 2 Activity Book 1*.

LEARNING COACH CHECK-IN   As needed, help students read the activity page.

LEARN AND TRY IT

LEARN   It's All in the Voice

Students will listen to passages read aloud from the reading. They will identify what the speaker's voice can convey about characters.

TRY IT   Apply: Spelling List 3

Students will apply what they have learned about the spelling patterns for Spelling List 3.

- In an online activity, students will complete a word sort and answer reflection questions.

- In *English Language Arts 2 Activity Book 1*, students will complete Apply: Spelling List 3.

NOTE   Students will need their cutouts from the Spelling List 3 activity page to complete the word sort.

TIP   Have students record the speed sort times on the My Speed Sort Times activity page, which is located at the back of the activity book. It can be motivating for students to see their progress as their ability to complete speed sorts should improve over time.

SUPPORT   For the offline task, students may benefit from having the letters they will use to build words written on small pieces of paper. It will allow them to physically move the letters into place and test where letters can be placed to make new words.

LEARNING COACH CHECK-IN   As needed, help students read the activity page.

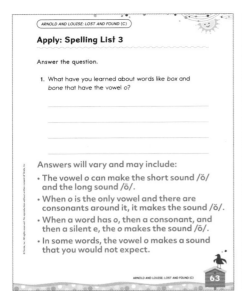

WRAP-UP

Questions About *Arnold and Louise: Lost and Found* (C)

Students will answer the questions to show that they understand the spelling skills they learned in this lesson.

Handwriting

Students should gather their handwriting materials and begin where they left off. Remind students to form letters carefully and correctly.

TIP　Set a timer to help students stay focused during handwriting practice.

Go Read!

Students will read for pleasure. They should choose a book or a magazine that interests them, or they may choose a selection from the digital library, linked in the online lesson.

- Have students read aloud a few paragraphs of their selection.

- Then have students read silently for the rest of the time.

SUPPORT　Students should make no more than five errors in decoding when they read aloud a few paragraphs of their Go Read! selection. If students struggle or make more than five errors, they need to select a different (and easier) text for the Go Read! activity.

TIP　Have students select something to read ahead of time to help them stay focused.

Arnold and Louise: Lost and Found (D)

Lesson Overview

ACTIVITY	ACTIVITY TITLE	TIME	ONLINE/OFFLINE
GET READY	Introduction: *Arnold and Louise: Lost and Found* (D)	**1** minute	🖥
	Words to Know: *Arnold and Louise: Lost and Found* (D)	**10** minutes	🖥
READ	Think About Reading: *Arnold and Louise: Lost and Found* (D) **LEARNING COACH CHECK-IN**	**5** minutes	📄
	Arnold and Louise: Lost and Found (D)	**15** minutes	🖥 and 📄
	Reflect: *Arnold and Louise: Lost and Found* (D) **LEARNING COACH CHECK-IN**	**5** minutes	📄
LEARN	A Story's Events	**10** minutes	🖥
ALL ABOUT ME	Brain Break	**1** minute	🖥 or 📄
LEARN AND **TRY IT**	Irregular Plural Nouns	**10** minutes	🖥
	Use an Irregular Plural Noun **LEARNING COACH CHECK-IN**	**15** minutes	📄
WRAP-UP	Questions About *Arnold and Louise: Lost and Found* (D)	**2** minutes	🖥
ALL ABOUT ME	Brain Break	**1** minute	🖥 or 📄
QUIZ	Spelling List 3	**25** minutes	🖥
WRAP-UP	Read and Record	**10** minutes	🖥
	Handwriting	**10** minutes	📄

Content Background

Students will conclude a series of lessons centered around the book *Arnold and Louise: Lost and Found* by Erica S. Perl. In this lesson, they will learn about the story element of plot and explore irregular plural nouns.

Vocabulary   Students will explore these words from the story: *admit*, *realize*, and *examine*. These definitions of the words are used in *Arnold and Louise: Lost and Found*:

- **admit** (verb) – to say that something is true but not be happy about it

- **realize** (verb) – to understand or become aware of something

- **examine** (verb) – to look at something closely or carefully

Reading   A story consists of **story structure elements**. Those elements include character, setting, plot, problem, and solution. The **plot** is what happens in a story, the story's events. Students will learn that when we describe the plot of a story, we describe the most important events in sequence, or the order in which they happen.

Writing Skills   A **noun** is a word that names a person, place, or thing. Nouns are essential parts of most sentences.

> **Example:** The **ranger** works at **Shenandoah National Park**.

A **plural noun** names more than one person, place, or thing. Most plural nouns end in *–s* or *–es*. But, an *irregular plural noun* has a spelling that must be learned. Common irregular plural nouns include *feet*, *mice*, *geese*, *children*, *men*, *women*, *teeth*, and *people*.

> **Example:** The **children** all brushed their **teeth**.

Arnold and Louise: Lost and Found, Chapter Five Synopsis

Arnold finally stops walking away from Louise after she says that she doesn't want to lose her best friend. Arnold realizes that Louise is more important to him than any item he could collect. He promises Louise that she will never lose him as a friend.

Lesson Goals

- Learn new vocabulary.
- Read Chapter Five of *Arnold and Louise: Lost and Found*.
- Make and confirm a prediction about reading.
- Describe important plot events of a story.
- Use irregular plural nouns.
- Take a spelling quiz.
- Read aloud to practice fluency.
- Develop letter formation fluency.

MATERIALS

Supplied
- *Arnold and Louise: Lost and Found* by Erica S. Perl
- *English Language Arts 2 Activity Book 1*
  - Think About Reading: *Arnold and Louise: Lost and Found* (D)
  - Use an Irregular Plural Noun
- handwriting workbook

KEYWORDS

noun – a word that names a person, place, thing, or idea
Examples: *nurses, Pennsylvania, phone, happiness*

plot – what happens in a story; the sequence of events

plural noun – a word that names more than one person, place, thing, or idea
Examples: *men, mountains, books, freedoms*

setting – when and where a story takes place

story structure elements – components of a story; they include character, setting, plot, problem, and solution

GET READY

Introduction: *Arnold and Louise: Lost and Found* (D)

Students will get a glimpse of what they will learn about in the lesson.

Words to Know: *Arnold and Louise: Lost and Found* (D)

Students will preview and answer a question about three vocabulary words from the reading selection.

READ

Think About Reading: *Arnold and Louise: Lost and Found* (D)

Students will complete Question 1 on Think About Reading: *Arnold and Louise: Lost and Found* (D) in *English Language Arts 2 Activity Book 1*.

NOTE   In this activity, students will make a prediction about Chapter Five of *Arnold and Louise: Lost and Found*. Students will come back to the activity page to confirm their prediction after they complete the reading.

LEARNING COACH CHECK-IN   As needed, help students read the activity page.

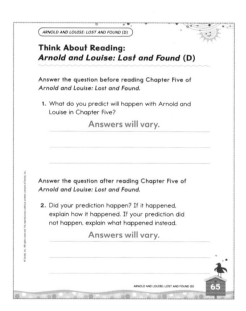

Arnold and Louise: Lost and Found (D)

Students will read Chapter Five of *Arnold and Louise: Lost and Found* by Erica S. Perl. Encourage them to reread their favorite passages.

Reflect: *Arnold and Louise: Lost and Found* (D)

Students will confirm the prediction they made before reading Chapter Five by completing Question 2 on Think About Reading: *Arnold and Louise: Lost and Found* (D) in *English Language Arts 2 Activity Book 1*.

LEARNING COACH CHECK-IN   As needed, help students read the activity page.

LEARN AND TRY IT

LEARN   A Story's Events

Students will learn that a story's plot consists of the events that happen in the story. They will identify important events that happen in the beginning, middle, and end of *Arnold and Louise: Lost and Found*.

LEARN   Irregular Plural Nouns

Through guided exploration of sentences from *Arnold and Louise: Lost and Found*, students will learn how to identify, form, and use irregular plural nouns.

NOTE   Some nouns have multiple correct plural forms. For example, both *fish* and *fishes* are correct plural forms of *fish* according to *Merriam-Webster Dictionary* at the time of this writing. In general, the first plural listed in a dictionary entry is the more widely used English form, but usage may vary regionally. Students will not be asked to differentiate between two correct plural forms.

TRY IT   Use an Irregular Plural Noun

Students will complete Use an Irregular Plural Noun in *English Language Arts 2 Activity Book 1*.

LEARNING COACH CHECK-IN   As needed, help students read the activity page. It may be helpful for students to say their answers to Questions 6 and 7 aloud before writing them.

ARNOLD AND LOUISE: LOST AND FOUND (D)

Use an Irregular Plural Noun

A **noun** shows a person, place, or thing.
A **singular noun** shows one person, place, or thing.
A **plural noun** shows *more than one*.
An **irregular plural noun** has a special spelling.

Circle the word that correctly completes each sentence.

1. There are two (childs/**children**) in my family.
2. Lexi drew a picture of four (**mice**/mouses).
3. Some (gooses/**geese**) just flew over the building.
4. There was only one (**man**/men) at the store.
5. How many (**feet**/foots) tall is the tree?

67

For each singular noun,
- Form the plural noun.
- Use the plural noun in a sentence.
- Read the sentence aloud.

6. tooth
   a. plural: teeth
   b. sentence:
      Sample answer: Joe lost his two front teeth.

7. fish
   a. plural: fish
   b. sentence:
      Sample answer: There are lots of fish in that creek.

68   ARNOLD AND LOUISE: LOST AND FOUND (D)

WRAP-UP

Questions About *Arnold and Louise: Lost and Found* (D)

Students will answer questions to show that they understand the reading and writing skills they learned in this lesson.

QUIZ

Spelling List 3

Students will take the Spelling List 3 quiz.

WRAP-UP

Read and Record

Good readers read quickly, smoothly, and with expression. This is called *fluency*. Students will record themselves reading aloud. They will listen to their recording and think about how quick, smooth, and expressive they sound.

TIP   Encourage students to rerecord as needed.

Handwriting

Students should gather their handwriting materials and begin where they left off. Remind students to form letters carefully and correctly.

TIP   Set a timer to help students stay focused during handwriting practice.

"Bears in Danger" (A)

Lesson Overview

ACTIVITY	ACTIVITY TITLE	TIME	ONLINE/OFFLINE
GET READY	Introduction: "Bears in Danger" (A)	**1** minute	🖥
	Book Walk: "Bears in Danger" (A)	**15** minutes	🖥
	Words to Know: "Bears in Danger" (A)	**10** minutes	🖥
READ	Think About Reading: "Bears in Danger" (A) **LEARNING COACH CHECK-IN**	**8** minutes	📄
ALL ABOUT ME	Brain Break	**1** minute	🖥 or 📄
READ	"Bears in Danger" (A)	**25** minutes	🖥 or 📄
	Check-In: "Bears in Danger" (A)	**5** minutes	🖥
LEARN	Confirming Predictions	**12** minutes	🖥
	Reflect: "Bears in Danger" (A) **LEARNING COACH CHECK-IN**	**5** minutes	📄
ALL ABOUT ME	Brain Break	**1** minute	🖥 or 📄
LEARN	Spelling List 4 **LEARNING COACH CHECK-IN**	**25** minutes	🖥 and 📄
WRAP-UP	Questions About "Bears in Danger" (A)	**2** minutes	🖥
	Handwriting	**10** minutes	📄

Content Background

Students will begin a series of lessons centered around the article "Bears in Danger" from the magazine *K12 World: Astounding Animals*. In this lesson, they will learn about using nonfiction text features and making and confirming predictions.

Book Walk   Students will be introduced to **nonfiction text features** and their purposes by exploring the magazine *K12 World: Astounding Animals*.

- Readers find a **table of contents** at the beginning of the magazine. The table of contents lists the titles of the magazine's articles and the page each article begins on.

- The **title** of an article lets readers know the article's topic.

- A **heading** is like a title, but it applies only to one section of an article. The heading tells readers what that particular section is about.

- A word in **bold print** indicates that the word is important and is defined in the magazine's glossary.

- A **glossary** is a list of important words and their meanings. Readers usually find it at the back of a nonfiction text.

- A **photograph** provides visual information, and its caption gives more information about that photograph.

Vocabulary   Students will explore these words from the article: *exist*, *active*, *seldom*, and *capture*. These are the definitions of the words as used in "Bears in Danger":

- **exist** (verb) – to be real; to continue to live

- **active** (adjective) – being busy or moving around a lot

- **seldom** (adverb) – not often; almost never

- **capture** (verb) – to catch someone or something

Reading   Students will learn that making a prediction involves connecting information from text with their background knowledge. Background knowledge comes from the things you have read, seen, and experienced in the past. For example, if the title of a book were *Let's Go for a Ride* and you have background knowledge related to riding a bike, you could make a prediction that the book *Let's Go for a Ride* is about bike riding.

Readers confirm predictions by finding that what they predicted is in the text. If the information is not in the text, they cannot confirm the prediction. Predictions shouldn't be described as right or wrong. Readers make the best prediction possible, based on the information they have.

When readers cannot confirm a prediction, they can gather new information from the text and modify, or change, their prediction. For example, if readers begin to read the book *Let's Go for a Ride* and find pictures and text about riding horses, they cannot confirm the original prediction that the book is about bike riding. Readers can take the new text information and modify their prediction. Their prediction may now be that the text will be about places to ride horses.

MATERIALS

Supplied

- *K12 World: Astounding Animals*
  - "Bears in Danger"
- *English Language Arts 2 Activity Book 1*
  - Think About Reading: "Bears in Danger" (A)
  - Spelling List 4
- handwriting workbook

Also Needed

- scissors
- envelope or baggie to store spelling cutouts

KEYWORDS

fact – something that can be proven true

nonfiction – writings about true things

text feature – part of a text that helps a reader locate information and determine what is most important; some examples are the title, table of contents, headings, pictures, and glossary

topic – the subject of a text

Spelling   Students will learn about spelling patterns that represent the sounds of short u, /ŭ/, and long u, /ū/. Students will sort words under these headings: **/ŭ/ *bus***, **/ū/ *cube***, **oddball**.

In this lesson, students will learn the following symbols and spelling patterns:

- The short u sound, /ŭ/, is found in words with a consonant-vowel-consonant (CVC) pattern. Students will learn that when the vowel *u* is the only vowel in a word and it is surrounded by consonants, the sound of the vowel *u* is usually /ŭ/. When students sort the spelling words, words with the sound /ŭ/ and a CVC spelling pattern will go under the heading **/ŭ/ *bus***.

- The long u sound, /ū/, is found in words with a vowel-consonant-silent e (VCe) pattern. Students will learn that when the vowel *u* is followed by a consonant and then silent e, the sound of the *u* is usually /ū/. When students sort the spelling words, words with the sound /ū/ and a VCe spelling pattern will go under the heading **/ū/ *cube***.

- In some words, the vowel sound is /ŭ/ or /ū/; however, the spelling is irregular and does not follow a CVC or a VCe pattern. For example, the word *does* has the short u sound, /ŭ/. However, it does not have a CVC spelling pattern. So, the word *does* is considered an oddball and would be placed under the **oddball** heading when students sort the spelling words.

"Bears in Danger" Synopsis

This informational text describes five types of bears that are listed as either vulnerable or endangered under the Endangered Species Act. The article provides background information on each type of bear such as where it lives, what it eats, and the dangers it faces. The article also describes a conservation plan that has helped grizzly bear numbers increase in Yellowstone National Park.

Lesson Goals

- Learn new vocabulary.
- Learn about and identify information that nonfiction text features provide.
- Read "Bears in Danger."
- Make and confirm predictions about nonfiction text.
- Sort words by sound and spelling pattern.
- Develop letter formation fluency.

Introduction: "Bears in Danger" (A)

Students will get a glimpse of what they will learn about in the lesson.

Book Walk: "Bears in Danger" (A)

Students will preview the major features of the new reading selection, a nonfiction article. They will be introduced to nonfiction text features typically found in informational text and learn how these features can be used to make predictions about information they will find in the article. This activity is designed to help students anticipate text content and connect to the selection.

TIP   Have students follow along with the book walk using their own copy of the magazine.

Words to Know: "Bears in Danger" (A)

Students will preview and answer a question about four vocabulary words from the reading selection.

READ

Think About Reading: "Bears in Danger" (A)

Students will complete Questions 1 and 2 on Think About Reading: "Bears in Danger" (A) in *English Language Arts 2 Activity Book 1*.

LEARNING COACH CHECK-IN   Students will make a prediction about information they may find in "Bears in Danger." As needed, help students read Questions 1 and 2 on the activity page. If they struggle to make a prediction, ask them guiding questions such as, "Do you think the article will tell you where bears live?" or "Do you think you will learn why bears are in danger?" Students will come back to the activity page after they complete the reading to indicate if they can confirm their prediction.

"Bears in Danger" (A)

Students will read the article "Bears in Danger" in the magazine *K12 World: Astounding Animals*. Encourage them to look closely at the nonfiction text features as they read.

Check-In: "Bears in Danger" (A)

Students will answer questions to demonstrate their comprehension of "Bears in Danger."

LEARN

Confirming Predictions

Students will learn about and practice making, confirming, and changing predictions.

Reflect: "Bears in Danger" (A)

Students will complete Questions 3 and 4 on Think About Reading: "Bears in Danger" (A) in *English Language Arts 2 Activity Book 1*.

LEARNING COACH CHECK-IN As needed, help students read Questions 3 and 4 on the activity page. Help them locate information in the text that confirms the prediction they made. For example, if students predicted that the article would explain what bears eat, help them locate a sentence that states what one of the types of bears eats.

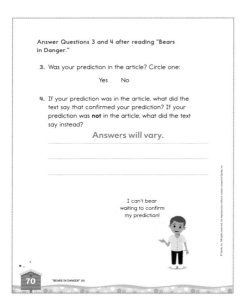

Spelling List 4

Students will learn and sort words with sounds and spelling patterns for short u and long u.

- In an online activity, students will learn about the spelling patterns and the sounds they represent. They will learn how to sort words according to those sounds and patterns. They will also complete a word sort.

- In *English Language Arts 2 Activity Book 1*, students will complete Spelling List 4.

NOTE Students will need scissors to cut out the spelling words on the activity page. Have students store their cutouts in a safe place, such as an envelope.

LEARNING COACH CHECK-IN As needed, help students read the activity page.

This is the complete list of words students will work with to learn the spelling patterns for short u and long u.

short u	long u	oddball
cub	cute	does
hunt	fume	pull
much	huge	
sun	mule	
us		

Questions About "Bears in Danger" (A)

Students will answer questions to show that they understand the reading and spelling skills they learned in this lesson.

Handwriting

Students should gather their handwriting materials and begin where they left off. Remind students to form letters carefully and correctly.

TIP Set a timer to help students stay focused during handwriting practice.

"Bears in Danger" (B)

Lesson Overview

ACTIVITY	ACTIVITY TITLE	TIME	ONLINE/OFFLINE
GET READY	Introduction: "Bears in Danger" (B)	**1** minute	🖥️
	Counting Phonemes	**15** minutes	🖥️
	Words to Know: "Bears in Danger" (B)	**15** minutes	🖥️
ALL ABOUT ME	Brain Break	**1** minute	🖥️ or 📄
LEARN AND **TRY IT**	Learning to Compare and Contrast	**15** minutes	🖥️
	Exploring Text Features	**15** minutes	🖥️
	Compare and Contrast Bears **LEARNING COACH CHECK-IN**	**15** minutes	📄
ALL ABOUT ME	Brain Break	**1** minute	🖥️ or 📄
TRY IT	Practice: Spelling List 4 **LEARNING COACH CHECK-IN**	**20** minutes	🖥️ and 📄
WRAP-UP	Questions About "Bears in Danger" (B)	**2** minutes	🖥️
	Handwriting	**10** minutes	📄
	Go Read!	**10** minutes	🖥️ or 📄

Content Background

Students will continue a series of lessons centered around the article "Bears in Danger" from the magazine *K12 World: Astounding Animals*. In this lesson, students will learn about compare-and-contrast text structure and explore text features. They will also compare and contrast types of bears.

Reading Foundations   Students will continue to develop their **phonemic awareness**, the ability to hear, identify, and manipulate sounds in spoken words.

Students will count the number of phonemes in a one-syllable word. They will hear a word. They will then need to segment the word into its individual sounds to count the sounds—for example, the word *den* has three phonemes, or sounds. Students will need to segment *den* into its individual sounds—/d/ /ĕ/ /n/—to count the phonemes.

Vocabulary   Students will explore these words from the article: *rare*, *law*, and *protect*. These are the definitions of the words as used in "Bears in Danger":

- **rare** (adjective) – not common

- **law** (noun) – a rule or set of rules made by the government of a town, city, state, or country

- **protect** (verb) – to keep someone or something from being hurt or damaged

Reading   Students will be introduced to common text structures found in nonfiction text. **Text structure** indicates how the information in a text is organized. Common text structures include:

- **sequence** – Information is organized in the order in which events happen.

- **cause and effect** – Text is organized to explain how an event or action causes another event or action to happen.

- **descriptive** – The author describes a topic by providing characteristics and examples.

Students will then compare and contrast characteristics of the types of bears described in the article "Bears in Danger."

To **compare** is to say how things are alike. For example, if we compare sun bears and Andean bears, we find that they are alike because both types of bears spend a lot of time in trees.

To **contrast** is to say how things are different. For example, if we contrast polar bears and giant pandas, we find that they are different because polar bears live near the North Pole, while giant pandas live in the mountains of China.

Advance Preparation

Gather students' cutouts from the Spelling List 4 activity page from "Bears in Danger" (A). They will use the cutouts during Try It: Practice: Spelling List 4.

During the Go Read! activity, students will have the option of using the digital library. Allow extra time for students to make their reading selection, or have students make a selection before beginning the lesson.

MATERIALS

Supplied
- *K12 World: Astounding Animals*
  - "Bears in Danger"
- *English Language Arts 2 Activity Book 1*
  - Compare and Contrast Bears
  - Practice: Spelling List 4
- handwriting workbook

Also Needed
- Spelling List 4 activity page cutouts from "Bears in Danger" (A)
- crayons or markers (optional)
- reading material for Go Read!

KEYWORDS

compare – to explain how two or more things are alike

contrast – to explain how two or more things are different

text structure – the organizational pattern of a text, such as cause and effect, compare and contrast, and chronological order

Lesson Goals

- Count the number of phonemes in a one-syllable word.
- Learn new vocabulary.
- Identify the text structure of a passage.
- Identify the purposes of specific nonfiction text features.
- Answer questions with information provided by nonfiction text features.
- Answer questions about nonfiction text that is read aloud.
- Compare and contrast information from a nonfiction text.
- Identify and write spelling patterns that stand for sounds within words.
- Develop letter formation fluency.
- Read independently to develop fluency.

GET READY

Introduction: "Bears in Danger" (B)
Students will get a glimpse of what they will learn about in the lesson.

Counting Phonemes
In this oral activity, students will identify how many sounds they hear in a one-syllable word.

Words to Know: "Bears in Danger" (B)
Students will preview and answer questions about three vocabulary words from the reading selection.

LEARN AND TRY IT

LEARN   Learning to Compare and Contrast
Students will learn one way that nonfiction text, or informational text, is structured is to compare and contrast. They will also answer questions comparing and contrasting types of bears.

LEARN   Exploring Text Features
Students will explore the nonfiction text features in "Bears in Danger." They will identify the purposes of the text features.

TRY IT   Compare and Contrast Bears

Students will complete Compare and Contrast Bears in *English Language Arts 2 Activity Book 1*.

LEARNING COACH CHECK-IN   As needed, help students read the instructions and sentence frames on the activity page. Help them locate information in the text to fill in the blanks.

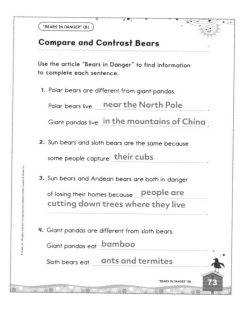

TRY IT   Practice: Spelling List 4

Students will practice the spelling patterns for Spelling List 4.

- In *English Language Arts 2 Activity Book 1*, students will complete Practice: Spelling List 4.

- Online, students will answer questions that require them to reflect on the spelling patterns.

NOTE   Students will need their cutouts from the Spelling List 4 activity page to complete Practice: Spelling List 4.

NOTE   Students may wish to use crayons or markers to draw their pictures or comic strip.

LEARNING COACH CHECK-IN   As needed, help students read the activity page.

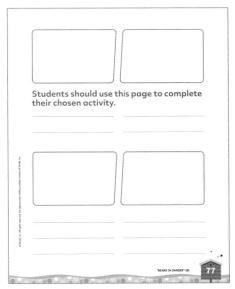

Practice: Spelling List 4

Get your spelling cutouts. Set up the headings, and sort the spelling words again.

Look at your sort, and write down each spelling word under the correct heading on the chart.

/ŭ/ bus	/ū/ cube	oddball
cub	cute	does
hunt	fume	pull
much	huge	
sun	mule	
us		

Do one of the following activities to practice your spelling words:

Draw and label.

Choose four of your spelling words. Draw a picture for each word. Then write the word under the picture.

Create a comic strip.

Create four panels of a comic strip. Draw pictures and write text with four or more of your spelling words.

Students should use this page to complete their chosen activity.

WRAP-UP

Questions About "Bears in Danger" (B)

Students will answer questions to show that they understand the reading and spelling skills they learned in this lesson.

Handwriting

Students should gather their handwriting materials and begin where they left off. Remind students to form letters carefully and correctly.

TIP Set a timer to help students stay focused during handwriting practice.

Go Read!

Students will read for pleasure. They should choose a book or a magazine that interests them, or they may choose a selection from the digital library, linked in the online lesson.

- Have students read aloud a few paragraphs of their selection.

- Then have students read silently for the rest of the time.

SUPPORT Students should make no more than five errors in decoding when they read aloud a few paragraphs of their Go Read! selection. If students struggle or make more than five errors, they need to select a different (and easier) text for the Go Read! activity.

TIP Have students select something to read ahead of time to help them stay focused.

"Bears in Danger" (C)

Lesson Overview

ACTIVITY	ACTIVITY TITLE	TIME	ONLINE/OFFLINE
GET READY	Introduction: "Bears in Danger" (C)	**1** minute	🖥️
	Substituting Sounds	**10** minutes	🖥️
READ	"Bears in Danger" (C)	**15** minutes	🖥️ or 📄
ALL ABOUT ME	Brain Break	**1** minute	🖥️ or 📄
LEARN AND TRY IT	Paragraphs	**10** minutes	🖥️
	Plan a Paragraph	**10** minutes	🖥️
	Plan Your Paragraph **LEARNING COACH CHECK-IN**	**30** minutes	📄
ALL ABOUT ME	Brain Break	**1** minute	🖥️ or 📄
TRY IT	Apply: Spelling List 4 **LEARNING COACH CHECK-IN**	**20** minutes	🖥️ and 📄
WRAP-UP	Questions About "Bears in Danger" (C)	**2** minutes	🖥️
	Read and Record	**10** minutes	🖥️
	Handwriting	**10** minutes	📄

Content Background

Students will conclude a series of lessons centered around the article "Bears in Danger" from the magazine *K12 World: Astounding Animals*. In this lesson, they will explore the parts of a paragraph and begin planning a paragraph.

Reading Foundations   Students will continue to develop their **phonemic awareness**, the ability to hear, identify, and manipulate sounds in spoken words.

The highest level of phonemic awareness is the ability to substitute one sound for another in a word.

We can change the initial sound in a one-syllable word. For example, in the word *fun*, change the /f/ to /s/. What's the new word? *sun*

We can change the final sound in a word. For example, in the word *him*, change the /m/ to /t/. What's the new word? *hit*

We can change the medial, or middle, vowel sound in a word. For example, in the word *hop*, change the /ŏ/ to /ĭ/. What's the new word? *hip*

Reading   Students will continue to learn about nonfiction text features. They will be introduced to a **sidebar**. A sidebar is a short text within a longer text. A sidebar provides information that is relevant to the main topic of the nonfiction text. But, the sidebar is not necessary for understanding the main content of the article.

The text with the heading "Road to Recovery" is a sidebar in the article "Bears in Danger." This sidebar provides information on what has been done to help grizzly bears come back from the brink of extinction. However, this information is not necessary for understanding the main content of the article about the types of bears that are in danger.

Another characteristic that identifies text as a sidebar is the print itself. The text in a sidebar is usually printed in a different font than the main body text. It identifies that the sidebar is something in addition to the main body text.

Writing Skills   A **paragraph** is a group of related sentences that are organized logically. A paragraph begins with a **topic sentence**, which tells what the paragraph is about. The topic sentence is followed by **supporting details**, which tell more about the main idea of the paragraph. Finally, a **concluding sentence** sums up what the paragraph is about.

As writers become more skilled, they may purposely adjust this structure, adding elements such as transitional sentences at the beginning and end of paragraphs, forgoing the topic sentence for effect, or setting off a single sentence as a paragraph. In this course, students will focus on writing paragraphs that follow the basic structure of topic sentence, supporting details, and concluding sentence.

Students will begin working on a paragraph about something they know a lot about. They will complete this assignment over the course of several lessons by following the writing process.

Writing Process

1 Prewriting	2 Drafting	3 Revising	4 Proofreading	5 Publishing

The writing process is a series of steps that writers use to plan, write, and refine their work. Even though the process is shown as linear, expert writers adjust the process as needed, often repeating, combining, or skipping steps. Through self-monitoring strategies, students can effectively apply and adjust the writing process so that it serves their particular needs.

MATERIALS

Supplied
- *K12 World: Astounding Animals*
  - "Bears in Danger"
- *English Language Arts 2 Activity Book 1*
  - Model Paragraph
  - Plan Your Paragraph
  - Apply: Spelling List 4
  - My Speed Sort Times
- handwriting workbook

Also Needed
- folder for organizing paragraph assignment pages
- Spelling List 4 activity page cutouts from "Bears in Danger" (A)

During **prewriting**, writers choose a topic and create a plan for their writing assignment. To choose a topic, writers often **brainstorm**, or come up with and evaluate several ideas. Brainstorming techniques include listing, freewriting, drawing, and talking.

Another important aspect of prewriting is planning. Planning techniques include filling out an outline or using a graphic organizer or other visual plan.

Advance Preparation

Gather a folder that students can use to keep all activity pages related to their paragraph.

Gather students' cutouts from the Spelling List 4 activity page from "Bears in Danger" (A). They will use the cutouts during Try It: Apply: Spelling List 4.

If students have removed My Speed Sort Times from the activity book, have them gather this activity page. They will use this activity page in Try It: Apply: Spelling List 4.

Lesson Goals

- Substitute sounds in one-syllable words.

- Reread "Bears in Danger."

- Learn about the parts of a paragraph.

- Plan your paragraph.

- Identify reasons for when and how to use certain spelling patterns.

- Read aloud to practice fluency.

- Develop letter formation fluency.

GET READY

Introduction: "Bears in Danger" (C)
Students will get a glimpse of what they will learn about in the lesson.

Substituting Sounds
In this oral activity, students will substitute one sound for another in one-syllable words.

READ

"Bears in Danger" (C)

Students will reread the article "Bears in Danger" in the magazine *K12 World: Astounding Animals*.

LEARN AND TRY IT

LEARN   Paragraphs

Through guided exploration, students will learn about the parts of a paragraph.

LEARN   Plan a Paragraph

Students will learn about choosing a writing topic and using a graphic organizer to plan a paragraph.

TRY IT   Plan Your Paragraph

Students will complete Plan Your Paragraph in *English Language Arts 2 Activity Book 1*.

LEARNING COACH CHECK-IN   As needed, help students read the activity page. Make sure the topic they have chosen (Question 2) is something that they are excited to write about and that they can write about without doing research.

TIP   Read the Model Paragraph together with students to ensure that they understand the assignment before they choose a topic.

NOTE   Have students put the Model Paragraph and their completed Plan Your Paragraph activity page into a folder for safe keeping.

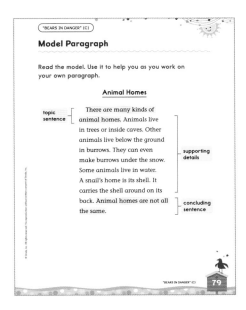

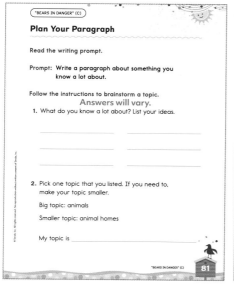

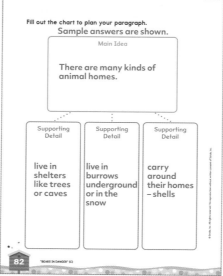

TRY IT   Apply: Spelling List 4

Students will apply what they have learned about the spelling patterns for Spelling List 4.

- In an online activity, students will complete a word sort and answer reflection questions.

- In *English Language Arts 2 Activity Book 1*, students will complete Apply: Spelling List 4.

NOTE   Students will need their cutouts from the Spelling List 4 activity page to complete the word sort.

TIP   Have students record their speed sort times on the My Speed Sort Times activity page, which is located at the back of the activity book. It can be motivating for students to see their progress as their ability to complete speed sorts should improve over time.

LEARNING COACH CHECK-IN   As needed, help students read the activity page.

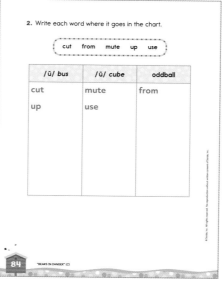

Questions About "Bears in Danger" (C)

Students will answer questions to show that they understand the reading, writing, and spelling skills they learned in this lesson.

Read and Record

Good readers read quickly, smoothly, and with expression. This is called *fluency*. Students will record themselves reading aloud. They will listen to their recording and think about how quick, smooth, and expressive they sound.

> **TIP** Encourage students to rerecord as needed.

Handwriting

Students should gather their handwriting materials and begin where they left off. Remind students to form letters carefully and correctly.

> **TIP** Set a timer to help students stay focused during handwriting practice.

Bears Everywhere (A)

Lesson Overview

ACTIVITY	ACTIVITY TITLE	TIME	ONLINE/OFFLINE
GET READY	Introduction: Bears Everywhere (A)	**1** minute	🖥️
READ	Bears Everywhere (A)	**20** minutes	🖥️
ALL ABOUT ME	Brain Break	**1** minute	🖥️ or 📄
LEARN AND **TRY IT**	The Writing Process	**10** minutes	🖥️
	Draft a Paragraph	**10** minutes	🖥️
	Draft Your Paragraph **LEARNING COACH CHECK-IN**	**50** minutes	📄
WRAP-UP	Question About Bears Everywhere (A)	**2** minutes	🖥️
ALL ABOUT ME	Brain Break	**1** minute	🖥️ or 📄
QUIZ	Spelling List 4	**25** minutes	🖥️

Content Background

Students will focus on writing in this lesson.

Writing Skills   Students will continue working on a **paragraph** about something they know a lot about. They will complete this assignment over the course of several lessons by following the writing process.

Writing Process

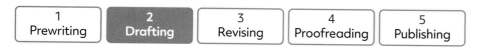

During **drafting**, writers use their prewriting work to write a complete first version of a piece. Writers create drafts to get all their ideas fleshed out and in order, from beginning to end.

MATERIALS

Supplied
- *English Language Arts 2 Activity Book 1*
  - Draft Your Paragraph
- Drafting Paper (printout)

Also Needed
- folder in which students are storing paragraph assignment pages

KEYWORDS

drafting – the step in which a writer first writes a piece

Advance Preparation

Gather the folder that students are using to keep all activity pages related to their paragraph:

- Model Paragraph from "Bears in Dangers" (C)

- Students' completed Plan Your Paragraph activity page from "Bears in Dangers" (C)

Lesson Goals

- Read nonfiction text about bears or chipmunks.

- Learn about the writing process.

- Draft your paragraph.

- Take a spelling quiz.

GET READY

Introduction: Bears Everywhere (A)

Students will get a glimpse of what they will learn about in the lesson.

READ

Bears Everywhere (A)

Students will choose and read a nonfiction text about either bears or chipmunks.

NOTE The reading selections for this activity are located in the digital library, which is linked in the online lesson.

LEARN AND TRY IT

LEARN The Writing Process

Students will learn about the writing process.

LEARN Draft a Paragraph

Students will learn about using work completed during prewriting to write a first draft.

TRY IT Draft Your Paragraph

Students will complete Draft Your Paragraph in *English Language Arts 2 Activity Book 1*. Make sure students have the Model Paragraph and their completed Plan Your Paragraph activity page to refer to as they work.

LEARNING COACH CHECK-IN As needed, help students read the activity page. Ensure that they are using their completed graphic organizer to help them write their draft.

NOTE Have students add their completed Draft Your Paragraph activity page to the folder they are using to store their paragraph assignment pages.

NOTE Additional sheets of Drafting Paper are available online.

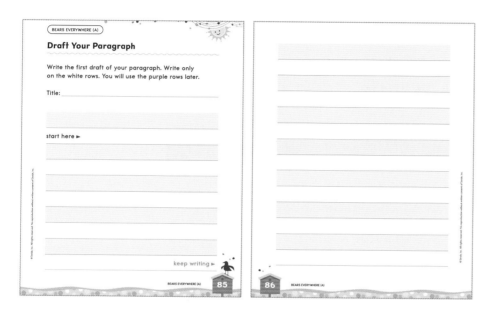

Question About Bears Everywhere (A)

Students will answer a question to show that they understand the writing skills they learned in this lesson.

Spelling List 4

Students will complete the Spelling List 4 quiz.

Bears Everywhere (B)

Lesson Overview

ACTIVITY	ACTIVITY TITLE	TIME	ONLINE/OFFLINE
GET READY	Introduction: Bears Everywhere (B)	**1** minute	🛜
READ	Bears Everywhere (B)	**15** minutes	🛜
ALL ABOUT ME	Brain Break	**1** minute	🖥 or 📄
LEARN AND **TRY IT**	Revise and Proofread a Paragraph	**15** minutes	🛜
	Revise and Proofread Your Paragraph **LEARNING COACH CHECK-IN**	**40** minutes	📄
ALL ABOUT ME	Brain Break	**1** minute	🖥 or 📄
LEARN	Spelling List 5 **LEARNING COACH CHECK-IN**	**25** minutes	🖥 and 📄
WRAP-UP	Questions About Bears Everywhere (B)	**2** minutes	🛜
	Read and Record	**10** minutes	🛜
	More Language Arts Practice	**10** minutes	🛜

Content Background

Students will focus on writing in this lesson.

Writing Skills   Students will revise and proofread their **paragraph** about something they know a lot about.

Writing Process

1 Prewriting	2 Drafting	**3 Revising**	**4 Proofreading**	5 Publishing

During **revising**, writers look back at their work and find ways to improve it. They focus on ideas and organization, not punctuation, grammar, and spelling. Punctuation, grammar, and spelling are what writers review during **proofreading**. Since the paragraph is a short writing assignment, students will use a single checklist to revise and proofread.

Proofreading is sometimes called *editing*.

MATERIALS

Supplied
- *English Language Arts 2 Activity Book 1*
  - Revise and Proofread Your Paragraph
  - Spelling List 5
- Paragraph: Feedback Sheet (printout)

Also Needed
- folder in which students are storing paragraph assignment pages
- scissors
- envelope or baggie to store spelling cutouts

Spelling   Students will learn about spelling patterns that represent the sound /k/ at the end of a word. Students will sort words under these headings: **–k *book***, **–ck *duck***, **–ke *bike***.

Students will learn that the spelling of the final sound /k/ is directly related to the vowel that comes before it. Words in which the vowel sound is represented by a vowel team, such as *oo* or *ea*, end with the single letter *k*. The words *look* and *cheek* are examples of words in which a vowel team is followed by the letter *k*.

Words in which the vowel has a short sound end with the letters *–ck*. The words *luck* and *snack* are examples of words with a short vowel sound that ends with the letters *–ck*.

Words in which the vowel sound is long due to the VCe pattern end with the letters *–ke*. The words *woke* and *spike* are examples.

Advance Preparation

Gather the folder that students are using to keep all activity pages related to their paragraph:

- Model Paragraph from "Bears in Dangers" (C)

- Students' completed Plan Your Paragraph activity page from "Bears in Dangers" (C)

- Students' completed draft from Bears Everywhere (A)

Prior to Try It: Revise and Proofread Your Paragraph, read students' draft and complete the Paragraph: Feedback Sheet.

> ### Lesson Goals
> - Read nonfiction text about bears or chipmunks.
> - Revise and proofread your paragraph.
> - Sort words by sound and spelling pattern.
> - Read aloud to practice fluency.

Introduction: Bears Everywhere (B)
Students will get a glimpse of what they will learn about in the lesson.

READ

Bears Everywhere (B)

Students will choose and read a nonfiction text about either bears or chipmunks.

NOTE   The reading selections for this activity are located in the digital library, which is linked in the online lesson.

LEARN AND TRY IT

LEARN   Revise and Proofread a Paragraph

Students will learn about using a checklist to revise and proofread.

TRY IT   Revise and Proofread Your Paragraph

Students will revise and proofread their paragraph using Revise and Proofread Your Paragraph in *English Language Arts 2 Activity Book 1*, which is a checklist. They will need their draft from Bears Everywhere (A).

LEARNING COACH CHECK-IN   Guide students through the revising and proofreading process using the Paragraph: Feedback Sheet that you completed.

TIP   Have students read their paragraph aloud to identify missing or extra words, incomplete sentences, and other potential areas for improvement.

NOTE   Have students put their revised and edited draft into the folder they are using to store their paragraph assignment pages.

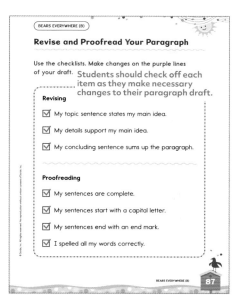

LEARN   Spelling List 5

Students will learn and sort words with spelling patterns that represent the sound /k/ at the end of a word.

- In an online activity, students will learn about the spelling patterns and the sounds they represent. They will learn how to sort words according to those sounds and patterns. They will also complete a word sort.

- In *English Language Arts 2 Activity Book 1*, students will complete Spelling List 5.

NOTE   Students will need scissors to cut out the spelling words on the activity page. Have students store their cutouts in a safe place, such as an envelope.

LEARNING COACH CHECK-IN   As needed, help students read the activity page.

This is the complete list of words students will work with to learn the spelling patterns for the sound /k/.

words ending in –k	words ending in –ck	words ending in –ke
brook	knock	broke
cheek	lick	snake
look	luck	spike
speak	snack	woke

Questions About Bears Everywhere (B)

Students will answer questions to show that they understand the writing and spelling skills they learned in this lesson.

Read and Record

Good readers read quickly, smoothly, and with expression. This is called *fluency*. Students will record themselves reading aloud. They will listen to their recording and think about how quick, smooth, and expressive they sound.

TIP   Encourage students to rerecord as needed.

More Language Arts Practice

Students will practice skills according to their individual needs.

Goldilocks (A)

Lesson Overview

ACTIVITY	ACTIVITY TITLE	TIME	ONLINE/OFFLINE
GET READY	Introduction: Goldilocks (A)	**1** minute	🖥️
	Letters and Sounds	**5** minutes	🖥️
	Words to Know: *Goldilocks and the Three Bears*	**10** minutes	🖥️
READ	Think About Reading: Goldilocks (A) **LEARNING COACH CHECK-IN**	**10** minutes	📄
	Goldilocks (A)	**10** minutes	🖥️ or 📄
LEARN AND TRY IT	5Ws + H	**15** minutes	🖥️
	Use Details to Answer Questions	**10** minutes	🖥️
ALL ABOUT ME	Brain Break	**1** minute	🖥️ or 📄
LEARN AND TRY IT	Publish a Paragraph	**5** minutes	🖥️
	Publish Your Paragraph **LEARNING COACH CHECK-IN**	**30** minutes	📄
ALL ABOUT ME	Brain Break	**1** minute	🖥️ or 📄
TRY IT	Practice: Spelling List 5 **LEARNING COACH CHECK-IN**	**20** minutes	🖥️ and 📄
WRAP-UP	Questions About Goldilocks (A)	**2** minutes	🖥️

Content Background

Students will begin a series of lessons centered around the book *Goldilocks and the Three Bears* retold by Jan Brett. In this lesson, they will check their understanding of what they've read by using story details to answer questions. They will also publish their paragraph.

Reading Foundations   Students will transition from developing the foundational reading skill of **phonemic awareness** to **phonics**. Phonics is the study of the sounds of spoken language and how letters represent those sounds in written language. Students will be asked to listen to a sound and then choose the letter that matches the sound.

Vocabulary   Students will explore these words from the story: *latch*, *tempting*, and *shrill*. These are the definitions of the words as used in *Goldilocks and the Three Bears*:

- **latch** (noun) – a fastener found on items such as a door or cabinet that can be opened and closed

- **tempting** (adjective) – causing you to want to do something, even though you know you shouldn't

- **shrill** (adjective) – having a sharp, high-pitched sound

Reading   Students will learn that one way to check that they understand what they've read is by answering questions that begin with the question words *who*, *what*, *where*, *when*, *why*, and *how*.

Some questions require **literal recall**, the ability to recall information stated directly in a text. An example of a question that requires literal recall would be, "What is the name of the girl who goes into the three bears' home?" Students can put their finger right on the answer in the text.

Some questions require inferential thinking. To answer these questions, students must use their background knowledge combined with text information to make an inference. An example of a question that requires inferential thinking would be, "Why does Goldilocks go into the bears' home?" From Goldilocks's actions, we can infer that she is curious.

Writing Skills   Students will finish their **paragraph** about something they know a lot about.

Writing Process

1 Prewriting	2 Drafting	3 Revising	4 Proofreading	**5 Publishing**

During **publishing**, writers create a clean copy of their piece. They incorporate the changes they made during the previous two steps of the process.

Note that often writers revise drafts and incorporate changes multiple times before proofreading and publishing. Many factors influence how writers apply the writing process to particular pieces.

MATERIALS

Supplied
- *Goldilocks and the Three Bears* retold by Jan Brett
- *English Language Arts 2 Activity Book 1*
  - Think About Reading: Goldilocks (A)
  - Publish Your Paragraph
  - Practice: Spelling List 5
- Writing Paper (printout)

Also Needed
- folder in which students are storing paragraph assignment pages
- Spelling List 5 activity page cutouts from Bears Everywhere (B)

KEYWORDS

literal recall – the ability to describe information stated directly in a text

publishing – the step in which a writer makes a clean copy of the piece and shares it

Advance Preparation

Gather the folder that students are using to keep all activity pages related to their paragraph:

- Model Paragraph from "Bears in Dangers" (C)

- Students' completed Plan Your Paragraph activity page from "Bears in Dangers" (C)

- Students' revised and edited draft from Bears Everywhere (B)

Gather students' cutouts from the Spelling List 5 activity page from Bears Everywhere (B). They will use the cutouts during Try It: Practice: Spelling List 5.

Goldilocks and the Three Bears Synopsis

Jan Brett retells and illustrates this traditional version of the Goldilocks story. After the three bears leave their home for a walk, Goldilocks enters. She tries out the bears' porridge, chairs, and beds, falling asleep in the small bear's bed. When the bears arrive home, they discover that somebody has been there. They search and find Goldilocks. She wakes up and runs away.

Lesson Goals

- Identify letters that represent spoken sounds.

- Learn new vocabulary.

- Read *Goldilocks and the Three Bears*.

- Answer questions that require literal level and inferential thinking.

- Publish your paragraph.

- Identify and write spelling patterns that stand for sounds within words.

GET READY

Introduction: Goldilocks (A)
Students will get a glimpse of what they will learn about in the lesson.

Letters and Sounds
In this phonics activity, students will match letters to the sounds they represent.

Words to Know: *Goldilocks and the Three Bears*

Students will preview and answer questions about three vocabulary words from the reading selection.

Think About Reading: Goldilocks (A)

Students will complete Think About Reading: Goldilocks (A) in *English Language Arts 2 Activity Book 1*.

LEARNING COACH CHECK-IN   As needed, help students read the activity page.

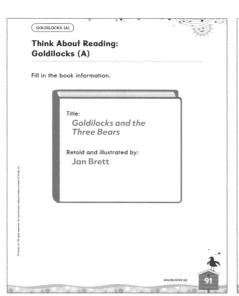

Goldilocks (A)

Students will listen to *Goldilocks and the Three Bears* retold by Jan Brett. Students may choose to read the story on their own. Encourage them to reread their favorite passages.

LEARN AND TRY IT

LEARN   5Ws + H

Students will learn about using details from a story to answer questions. It is a way that students can check their understanding of what they've read.

TRY IT   Use Details to Answer Questions

Students will answer questions about *Goldilocks and the Three Bears* to demonstrate their recollection and understanding of the story.

LEARN   Publish a Paragraph

Students will learn about publishing a piece of writing.

TRY IT   Publish Your Paragraph

Students will complete Publish Your Paragraph in *English Language Arts 2 Activity Book 1*. They should gather their draft and write a clean copy of their paragraph that incorporates the changes they made during revising and proofreading.

LEARNING COACH CHECK-IN   As needed, help students read the activity page and ensure that they are using their revised and edited draft to create their final copy. Otherwise, they should work independently.

NOTE   Additional sheets of Writing Paper are available online.

NOTE   Students will turn in this assignment to their teacher in Bears Wrap-Up (A).

TRY IT   Practice: Spelling List 5

Students will practice the spelling patterns for Spelling List 5.

- In *English Language Arts 2 Activity Book 1*, students will complete Practice: Spelling List 5.

- Online, students will answer questions that require them to reflect on the spelling patterns.

NOTE   Students will need their cutouts from the Spelling List 5 activity page to complete Practice: Spelling List 5.

LEARNING COACH CHECK-IN   As needed, help students read the activity page.

Practice: Spelling List 5

Get your spelling cutouts. Set up the headings, and sort the spelling words again.

Look at your sort, and write down each spelling word under the correct heading on the chart.

–k book	–ck duck	–ke bike
brook	knock	broke
cheek	lick	snake
look	luck	spike
speak	snack	woke

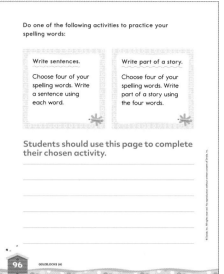

Do one of the following activities to practice your spelling words:

Write sentences.

Choose four of your spelling words. Write a sentence using each word.

Write part of a story.

Choose four of your spelling words. Write part of a story using the four words.

Students should use this page to complete their chosen activity.

WRAP-UP

Questions About Goldilocks (A)

Students will answer questions to show that they understand the reading, writing, and spelling skills they learned in this lesson.

Goldilocks (B)

Lesson Overview

ACTIVITY	ACTIVITY TITLE	TIME	ONLINE/OFFLINE
GET READY	Introduction: Goldilocks (B)	**1** minute	🖥️
	Blends and Digraphs	**5** minutes	🖥️
	Review Words to Know from *Goldilocks and the Three Bears*	**15** minutes	🖥️
ALL ABOUT ME	Brain Break	**1** minute	🖥️ or 📄
READ	Goldilocks (B)	**25** minutes	📄
LEARN	Characters' Actions	**20** minutes	🖥️
ALL ABOUT ME	Brain Break	**1** minute	🖥️ or 📄
TRY IT	Apply: Spelling List 5 **LEARNING COACH CHECK-IN**	**20** minutes	🖥️ and 📄
WRAP-UP	Questions About Goldilocks (B)	**2** minutes	🖥️
	Handwriting	**10** minutes	📄
	Go Read!	**20** minutes	🖥️ or 📄

Content Background

Students will continue a series of lessons centered around the book *Goldilocks and the Three Bears* retold by Jan Brett. In this lesson, students will focus on characters, how to describe them, and how their actions develop the story's theme.

Reading Foundations   Students will learn about consonant blends and digraphs.

A **consonant blend** is when two or more consonants are together in a word and the sound of each consonant is heard. The letters *f-l* in the word *flat* are a consonant blend. When you say the word *flat*, you can hear the sound of both consonants, *f* and *l*.

A **digraph** is when two consonants together make one sound. The letters *c-h* in the word *chop* form a digraph. The most common digraphs are *ch*, *sh*, and *th*.

Reading   Students will focus on characters and their actions. Details about characters and their actions help us describe characters. Descriptions of characters can be found directly in text. For example, the size of each bear is described directly in the story of Goldilocks.

Characters' actions affect the direction of a story when those actions lead to other events. For example, Goldilocks breaks the small bear's chair. When the bears find the broken chair, this leads them to search the rest of their home and find Goldilocks.

Characters' actions also develop a story's **theme**. For example, Goldilocks's actions develop the theme that it's important to respect people and the things that belong to them.

Advance Preparation

Gather students' cutouts from the Spelling List 5 activity page from Bears Everywhere (B). They will use the cutouts during Try It: Apply: Spelling List 5.

If students have removed My Speed Sort Times from the activity book, have them gather this activity page. They will use this activity page in the Try It: Apply: Spelling List 5.

During the Go Read! activity, students will have the option of using the digital library. Allow extra time for students to make their reading selection, or have students make a selection before beginning the lesson.

MATERIALS

Supplied
- *Goldilocks and the Three Bears* retold by Jan Brett
- *English Language Arts 2 Activity Book 1*
  - Apply: Spelling List 5
  - My Speed Sort Times
- handwriting workbook

Also Needed
- Spelling List 5 activity page cutouts from Bears Everywhere (B)
- reading material for Go Read!

KEYWORDS

theme – the author's message or big idea

GET READY

Introduction: Goldilocks (B)
Students will get a glimpse of what they will learn about in the lesson.

Blends and Digraphs
Students will identify words that contain consonant blends and digraphs.

Review Words to Know from *Goldilocks and the Three Bears*
Students will answer questions about the vocabulary words from the reading selection.

READ

Goldilocks (B)
Students will read *Goldilocks and the Three Bears* retold by Jan Brett.

LEARN AND TRY IT

LEARN   Characters' Actions
Students will describe characters and identify how characters' actions affect the story. They will learn how a character's actions develop a story's theme.

TRY IT   Apply: Spelling List 5

Students will apply what they have learned about the spelling patterns for Spelling List 5.

- In an online activity, students will complete a word sort and answer reflection questions.

- In *English Language Arts 2 Activity Book 1*, students will complete Apply: Spelling List 5.

NOTE   Students will need their cutouts from the Spelling List 5 activity page to complete the word sort.

TIP   Have students record their speed sort times on the My Speed Sort Times activity page, which is located at the back of the activity book. It can be motivating for students to see their progress as their ability to complete speed sorts should improve over time.

LEARNING COACH CHECK-IN   As needed, help students read the activity page.

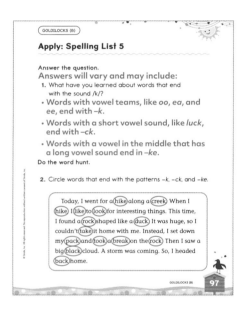

WRAP-UP

Questions About Goldilocks (B)

Students will answer questions to show that they understand the reading and spelling skills they learned in this lesson.

Handwriting

Students should gather their handwriting materials and begin where they left off. Remind students to form letters carefully and correctly.

TIP   Set a timer to help students stay focused during handwriting practice.

Go Read!

Students will read for pleasure. They should choose a book or a magazine that interests them, or they may choose a selection from the digital library, linked in the online lesson.

• Have students read aloud a few paragraphs of their selection.

• Then have students read silently for the rest of the time.

SUPPORT   Students should make no more than five errors in decoding when they read aloud a few paragraphs of their Go Read! selection. If students struggle or make more than five errors, they need to select a different (and easier) text for the Go Read! activity.

TIP   Have students select something to read ahead of time to help them stay focused.

Goldilocks (C)

Lesson Overview

ACTIVITY	ACTIVITY TITLE	TIME	ONLINE/OFFLINE
GET READY	Introduction: Goldilocks (C)	**1** minute	🖥️
	Word Families	**15** minutes	📶
READ	*Goatilocks and the Three Bears*	**30** minutes	📶
ALL ABOUT ME	Brain Break	**1** minute	📶 or 📄
LEARN	Goldilocks vs. Goatilocks	**25** minutes	🖥️
WRAP-UP	Question About Goldilocks (C)	**2** minutes	📶
ALL ABOUT ME	Brain Break	**1** minute	📶 or 📄
QUIZ	Spelling List 5	**25** minutes	📶
WRAP-UP	Read and Record	**10** minutes	🖥️
	Handwriting	**10** minutes	📄

Content Background

Students will conclude a series of lessons centered around the book *Goldilocks and the Three Bears* retold by Jan Brett. In this lesson, students read another book, *Goatilocks and the Three Bears* by Erica S. Perl. They will compare and contrast those two versions of the Goldilocks tale.

Reading Foundations   A **word family** is a group of words that rhyme and have the same spelling pattern at the end of the word. To determine a word's word family, we must look at the vowel and the consonants that come after it. The word *tell* belongs to the *–ell* word family. The words *bell* and *shell* also belong to the *–ell* word family.

Reading   We can compare and contrast characters in stories, describing how they are alike and how they are different. We can also compare and contrast characters' **perspectives**, or what they think and believe.

MATERIALS

Supplied
- *Goldilocks and the Three Bears* retold by Jan Brett
- *Goatilocks and the Three Bears* by Erica S. Perl (link is in online lesson)
- handwriting workbook

KEYWORDS

perspective – what a character thinks or believes

Goatilocks and the Three Bears Synopsis

In this twist on the traditional Goldilocks tale, a goat named Goatilocks is the main character. Goatilocks not only tries out the bears' porridge, chairs, and beds, she also eats baby bear's spoon, chair, and bed. When the bears return home, Goatilocks runs away. But, the next day, she wakes up feeling bad about her actions. She returns to the bears' home and offers them a basket of flowers to apologize.

Lesson Goals

- Identify the word family a word belongs to.
- Read *Goatilocks and the Three Bears*.
- Compare and contrast characters and their perspectives in two versions of the same story.
- Take a spelling quiz.
- Read aloud to practice fluency.
- Develop letter formation fluency.

GET READY

Introduction: Goldilocks (C)
Students will get a glimpse of what they will learn about in the lesson.

Word Families
Students will learn about some of the more common word families. Then they will answer questions that require them to identify the word family a word belongs to.

READ

Goatilocks and the Three Bears
Students will read *Goatilocks and the Three Bears* by Erica S. Perl.

NOTE   The reading selection for this activity is linked in the online lesson.

Goldilocks vs. Goatilocks

Students will explore how characters in the stories *Goldilocks and the Three Bears* and *Goatilocks and the Three Bears* are alike and different.

WRAP-UP

Question About Goldilocks (C)

Students will answer a question to show that they understand the reading skills they learned in this lesson.

QUIZ

Spelling List 5

Students will complete the Spelling List 5 quiz.

WRAP-UP

Read and Record

Good readers read quickly, smoothly, and with expression. This is called *fluency*. Students will record themselves reading aloud. They will listen to their recording and think about how quick, smooth, and expressive they sound.

TIP   Encourage students to rerecord as needed.

Handwriting

Students should gather their handwriting materials and begin where they left off. Remind students to form letters carefully and correctly.

TIP   Set a timer to help students stay focused during handwriting practice.

Brownilocks (A)

Lesson Overview

ACTIVITY	ACTIVITY TITLE	TIME	ONLINE/OFFLINE
GET READY	Introduction: Brownilocks (A)	**1** minute	🖥
	Figuring Out Unknown Words	**20** minutes	🖥
ALL ABOUT ME	Brain Break	**1** minute	🖥 or 📄
READ	Brownilocks (A)	**25** minutes	🖥
	Check-In: Brownilocks (A)	**5** minutes	🖥
LEARN	Revisit Story Elements	**20** minutes	🖥
ALL ABOUT ME	Brain Break	**1** minute	🖥 or 📄
LEARN	Spelling List 6 **LEARNING COACH CHECK-IN**	**25** minutes	🖥 and 📄
WRAP-UP	Questions About Brownilocks (A)	**2** minutes	🖥
	Handwriting	**10** minutes	📄
	Go Read!	**10** minutes	🖥 or 📄

Content Background

Students will begin a series of lessons centered around the book *Brownilocks and the Three Bowls of Cornflakes* by Enid Richemont. In this lesson, they will revisit the story elements of characters, setting, and plot.

Reading Foundations   There are various strategies that can help readers determine the meaning of an unknown word.

- **Calling on background knowledge** – Background knowledge can help readers with the word *snapped* in this sentence from *Brownilocks and the Three Bowls of Cornflakes*: "Brownilocks was too heavy and Sam's chair snapped." Background knowledge gained from traditional *Goldilocks* stories is that Goldilocks breaks the small bear's chair. This background knowledge can be used to determine that the word *snapped* means "broke."

- **Using text features** – Text features such as illustrations can provide clues to the meaning of an unknown word. An illustration in *Brownilocks* provides a clue to the meaning of the word *snapped* in the sentence "Brownilocks was too heavy and Sam's chair snapped." The accompanying illustration shows Brownilocks on the floor and pieces of the broken chair flying around her. This illustration shows that *snapped* means "broke."

- **Using context clues** – Often context in the sentences around an unknown word can help readers figure out a word's meaning. These sentences from *Brownilocks* provide an example of using context clues: "But Brownilocks longed to be outside. She climbed out of the window and ran into the woods." Brownilocks *longed* to be outside. She then goes outside and runs into the woods. The context here helps readers determine that the word *longed* means "wanted."

Spelling   Words taught in this spelling lesson have the following consonant blends at the end: *–nd, –nk, –nt*. When the consonant *n* comes before another consonant, the sound can be difficult to hear. By focusing on consonant blends with the letter *n*, students will learn to listen carefully to distinguish the sound /n/ from other sounds. It should be noted that the consonant blends taught in this spelling list can never appear at the beginning of a word.

Advance Preparation

During the Go Read! activity, students will have the option of using the digital library. Allow extra time for students to make their reading selection, or have students make a selection before beginning the lesson.

Brownilocks and the Three Bowls of Cornflakes Synopsis

In this twist on the Goldilocks tale, a bear named Brownilocks is the main character. While Sam, Mom, and Dad take a walk in the woods, Brownilocks climbs into their home through a window to get at the cornflakes she smells. Brownilocks tries each family member's chair, breaking Sam's. She then tries all the beds and falls asleep in Sam's. When the family discovers Brownilocks, she runs away. But, Sam, Mom, and Dad make Brownilocks welcome the next day. Mom puts out a big bowl of cornflakes just for her. Dad finds a bean bag for her to sit in. Sam reads Brownilocks a story. Being a bear, Brownilocks wants to be outside and returns to the woods. But, she returns to visit day after day.

Supplied
- *Brownilocks and the Three Bowls of Cornflakes* by Enid Richemont (in digital library; link is in online lesson)
- *English Language Arts 2 Activity Book 1*
  - Spelling List 6
- handwriting workbook

Also Needed
- scissors
- envelope or baggie to store spelling cutouts
- reading material for Go Read!

context clue – a word or phrase in a text that helps you figure out the meaning of an unknown word

Lesson Goals

- Determine meanings of unknown words by using background knowledge, text features, and context clues.

- Read *Brownilocks and the Three Bowls of Cornflakes*.

- Describe the characters, setting, and plot of a story.

- Sort words by spelling pattern.

- Develop letter formation fluency.

- Read independently to develop fluency.

GET READY

Introduction: Brownilocks (A)

Students will get a glimpse of what they will learn about in the lesson.

Figuring Out Unknown Words

Students will learn and practice strategies for determining the meanings of unknown words.

READ

Brownilocks (A)

Students will read *Brownilocks and the Three Bowls of Cornflakes* by Enid Richemont.

NOTE   The reading selection for this activity is located in the digital library, which is linked in the online lesson.

Check-In: Brownilocks (A)

Students will answer questions to demonstrate their comprehension of *Brownilocks and the Three Bowls of Cornflakes*

LEARN

Revisit Story Elements

Students will explore the characters, setting, and plot of *Brownilocks and the Three Bowls of Cornflakes*.

Spelling List 6

Students will learn and sort words that end with the spelling patterns –nd, –nk, and –nd.

- In an online activity, students will learn about the spelling patterns and how to sort words according to those patterns. They will also complete a word sort.

- In *English Language Arts 2 Activity Book 1*, students will complete Spelling List 6.

NOTE   Students will need scissors to cut out the spelling words on the activity page. Have students store their cutouts in a safe place, such as an envelope.

LEARNING COACH CHECK-IN   As needed, help students read the activity page.

This is the complete list of words students will work with to learn the spelling patterns.

–nd	–nk	–nt
around	junk	front
pretend	stink	grunt
second	think	mount
wind	yank	went

Questions About Brownilocks (A)

Students will answer questions to show that they understand the reading and spelling skills they learned in this lesson.

Handwriting

Students should gather their handwriting materials and begin where they left off. Remind students to form letters carefully and correctly.

TIP Set a timer to help students stay focused during handwriting practice.

Go Read!

Students will read for pleasure. They should choose a book or a magazine that interests them, or they may choose a selection from the digital library, linked in the online lesson.

- Have students read aloud a few paragraphs of their selection.

- Then have students read silently for the rest of the time.

SUPPORT Students should make no more than five errors in decoding when they read aloud a few paragraphs of their Go Read! selection. If students struggle or make more than five errors, they need to select a different (and easier) text for the Go Read! activity.

TIP Have students select something to read ahead of time to help them stay focused.

Brownilocks (B)

Lesson Overview

ACTIVITY	ACTIVITY TITLE	TIME	ONLINE/OFFLINE
GET READY	Introduction: Brownilocks (B)	**1** minute	📶
	Multisyllabic Words	**10** minutes	📶
READ	Brownilocks (B)	**15** minutes	📶
LEARN	Retelling and Character's Perspective	**25** minutes	📶
ALL ABOUT ME	Brain Break	**1** minute	📶 or 📄
LEARN AND **TRY IT**	Irregular Past Tense Verbs	**10** minutes	📶
	Use an Irregular Past Tense Verb **LEARNING COACH CHECK-IN**	**15** minutes	📄
ALL ABOUT ME	Brain Break	**1** minute	📶 or 📄
TRY IT	Practice: Spelling List 6 **LEARNING COACH CHECK-IN**	**20** minutes	📶 and 📄
WRAP-UP	Questions About Brownilocks (B)	**2** minutes	📶
	Handwriting	**10** minutes	📄
	Go Read!	**10** minutes	📶 or 📄

Content Background

Students will continue a series of lessons centered around *Brownilocks and the Three Bowls of Cornflakes* by Enid Richemont. In this lesson, they will learn about retelling a story and about how to determine a character's perspective. They will also explore the past tense of irregular verbs.

Reading Foundations A multisyllabic word is a word with more than one syllable. The following strategies can help with decoding, or reading, a multisyllabic word:

- **Looking for familiar spelling patterns** – An example is using knowledge of the consonant-vowel-consonant (CVC) pattern in a word like *rabbit*. Both syllables have the CVC pattern, so both syllables have a short vowel sound.

- **Looking for a known word in a longer word** – An example is finding a base word such as *walk* within the longer word *walking*.

- **Looking for smaller words within a compound word** – An example is breaking down the compound word *outside* into its two smaller words *out* and *side*.

Reading **Retelling** is when you use your own words to tell a story that you have read. Retelling helps readers check that they remember what they have read. A retelling should include the following:

- Naming the characters and setting, which are typically introduced in the beginning of a story

- The most important events that happen in the beginning, middle, and end of the story, which should be described in the order they happen

A character's **perspective** is that character's thoughts and beliefs about something. Readers can often determine a character's perspective based on that character's actions. For example, the Brownilocks character runs away after Sam finds her in his bed. From this action, we can determine that Brownilocks's perspective is that Sam, Mom, and Dad are frightening.

Writing Skills A **verb** shows an action or links ideas. It is part of the predicate of a sentence. In the following example, *tasted* is an action verb, and *was* is a linking verb.

> **Example:** First she **tasted** the porridge of the great, huge bear, but it **was** too hot.

A verb in the **past tense** shows an action that already happened. The past tense of an **irregular verb** has a spelling that must be learned. Common irregular verbs in the past tense are *told*, *sat*, *hid*, *grew*, *ate*, *swam*, and *wrote*.

> **Example:** Yesterday, I **sat** for one hour and **wrote** a story.

Advance Preparation

Gather students' cutouts from the Spelling List 6 activity page from Brownilocks (A). They will use the cutouts during Try It: Practice: Spelling List 6.

During the Go Read! activity, students will have the option of using the digital library. Allow extra time for students to make their reading selection, or have students make a selection before beginning the lesson.

MATERIALS

Supplied
- *Brownilocks and the Three Bowls of Cornflakes* by Enid Richemont (in digital library; link is in online lesson)
- *English Language Arts 2 Activity Book 1*
  - Use an Irregular Past Tense Verb
  - Practice: Spelling List 6
- handwriting workbook

Also Needed
- Spelling List 6 activity page cutouts from Brownilocks (A)
- crayons or markers (optional)
- reading material for Go Read!

KEYWORDS

irregular verb – a verb that does not add *–d* or *–ed* to form the past and past participle
Examples: *ran, wore, knew*

past tense – the verb form that tells what already has happened
Examples: *walked, knew*

retelling – using your own words to tell a story that you have listened to or read

verb – a word that shows action or links ideas
Examples: *jump* (action), *is* (linking)

Lesson Goals

- Decode multisyllabic words.

- Reread *Brownilocks and the Three Bowls of Cornflakes.*

- Retell a story.

- Determine a character's perspective.

- Use the past tense of irregular verbs.

- Identify and write spelling patterns that stand for sounds within words.

- Develop letter formation fluency.

- Read independently to develop fluency.

GET READY

Introduction: Brownilocks (B)

Students will get a glimpse of what they will learn about in the lesson.

Multisyllabic Words

Students will learn and apply strategies for breaking down and decoding words with more than one syllable.

READ

Brownilocks (B)

Students will reread *Brownilocks and the Three Bowls of Cornflakes* by Enid Richemont.

NOTE   The reading selection for this activity is located in the digital library, which is linked in the online lesson.

LEARN AND TRY IT

LEARN   Retelling and Character's Perspective

Students will retell the beginning, middle, and end of a story. They will also determine a character's perspective based on that character's actions.

LEARN   Irregular Past Tense Verbs

Through guided exploration of sentences from *Brownilocks and the Three Bowls of Cornflakes*, students will learn how to form and use the past tense of irregular verbs.

NOTE   There is more than one correct way to form the past tense of some verbs. For example, both *dreamed* and *dreamt* are correct ways to form the past tense of *dream* according to *Merriam-Webster's Dictionary* at the time of this writing. In general, the first form listed in a dictionary entry is the more widely used American English form, but usage may vary regionally. Students will not be asked to differentiate between two correct ways to write the past tense.

TRY IT   Use an Irregular Past Tense Verb

Students will complete Use an Irregular Past Tense Verb in *English Language Arts 2 Activity Book 1*.

LEARNING COACH CHECK-IN   As needed, help students read the activity page. It may be helpful for students to say their answers to Questions 6 and 7 aloud before writing them.

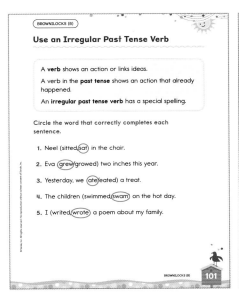
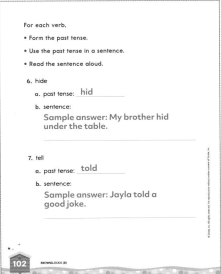

TRY IT   Practice: Spelling List 6

Students will practice the spelling patterns for Spelling List 6.

- In *English Language Arts 2 Activity Book 1*, students will complete Practice: Spelling List 6.

- Online, students will answer questions that require them to reflect on the spelling patterns.

NOTE   Students will need their cutouts from the Spelling List 6 activity page to complete Practice: Spelling List 6.

NOTE   Students may wish to use crayons or markers to draw their pictures or comic strip.

LEARNING COACH CHECK-IN   As needed, help students read the activity page.

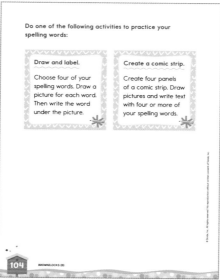

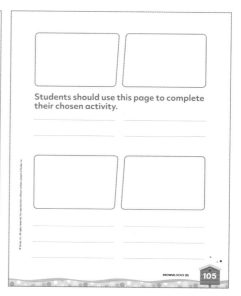

WRAP-UP

Questions About Brownilocks (B)

Students will answer questions to show that they understand the reading, writing, and spelling skills they learned in this lesson.

Handwriting

Students should gather their handwriting materials and begin where they left off. Remind students to form letters carefully and correctly.

TIP   Set a timer to help students stay focused during handwriting practice.

Go Read!

Students will read for pleasure. They should choose a book or a magazine that interests them, or they may choose a selection from the digital library, linked in the online lesson.

- Have students read aloud a few paragraphs of their selection.

- Then have students read silently for the rest of the time.

SUPPORT   Students should make no more than five errors in decoding when they read aloud a few paragraphs of their Go Read! selection. If students struggle or make more than five errors, they need to select a different (and easier) text for the Go Read! activity.

TIP   Have students select something to read ahead of time to help them stay focused.

Brownilocks (C)

Lesson Overview

ACTIVITY	ACTIVITY TITLE	TIME	ONLINE/OFFLINE
GET READY	Introduction: Brownilocks (C)	**1** minute	🖥
READ	Brownilocks (C)	**25** minutes	🖥
ALL ABOUT ME	Brain Break	**1** minute	🖥 or 📄
TRY IT	Think About Brownilocks	**15** minutes	🖥
	Comparing Goldilocks Stories **LEARNING COACH CHECK-IN**	**25** minutes	📄
ALL ABOUT ME	Brain Break	**1** minute	🖥 or 📄
TRY IT	Apply: Spelling List 6 **LEARNING COACH CHECK-IN**	**20** minutes	🖥 and 📄
WRAP-UP	Questions About Brownilocks (C)	**2** minutes	🖥
	Read and Record	**10** minutes	🖥
	More Language Arts Practice	**10** minutes	🖥
	Handwriting	**10** minutes	📄

Content Background

Students will continue a series of lessons centered around the book *Brownilocks and the Three Bowls of Cornflakes* by Enid Richemont. In this lesson, they will compare and contrast the main characters from two of the versions of Goldilocks they have read in this unit.

Advance Preparation

Gather students' cutouts from the Spelling List 6 activity page from Brownilocks (A). They will use the cutouts during Try It: Apply: Spelling List 6.

If students have removed My Speed Sort Times from the activity book, have them gather this activity page. They will use this activity page in Try It: Spelling List 6.

Lesson Goals

- Demonstrate understanding of a story by answering literal and inferential questions.

- Compare and contrast characters from different versions of the same story.

- Identify reasons for when and how to use certain spelling patterns.

- Read aloud to practice fluency.

- Develop letter formation fluency.

MATERIALS

Supplied

- *Brownilocks and the Three Bowls of Cornflakes* by Enid Richemont (in digital library; link is in online lesson)
- *Goatilocks and the Three Bears* by Erica S. Perl (link is in online lesson)
- *English Language Arts 2 Activity Book 1*
  - Comparing Goldilocks Stories
  - Apply: Spelling List 6
  - My Speed Sort Times
- handwriting workbook

Also Needed

- Spelling List 6 activity page cutouts from Brownilocks (A)

GET READY

Introduction: Brownilocks (C)

Students will get a glimpse of what they will learn about in the lesson.

READ

Brownilocks (C)

Students will reread *Brownilocks and the Three Bowls of Cornflakes* by Enid Richemont.

NOTE *Brownilocks and the Three Bowls of Cornflakes* is located in the digital library, which is linked in the online lesson.

TRY IT

Think About Brownilocks

Students will answer questions to demonstrate their knowledge of the characters, setting, and plot of *Brownilocks and the Three Bowls of Cornflakes*.

Comparing Goldilocks Stories

Students will complete Comparing Goldilocks Stories in *English Language Arts 2 Activity Book 1*.

LEARNING COACH CHECK-IN As needed, help students read the activity page and locate necessary information in *Brownilocks and the Three Bowls of Cornflakes* and *Goatilocks and the Three Bears*.

Apply: Spelling List 6

Students will apply what they have learned about the spelling patterns for Spelling List 6.

- In an online activity, students will complete a word sort and answer reflection questions.

- In *English Language Arts 2 Activity Book 1*, students will complete Apply: Spelling List 6.

NOTE Students will need their cutouts from the Spelling List 6 activity page to complete the word sort.

TIP Have students record their speed sort times on the My Speed Sort Times activity page, which is located at the back of the activity book. It can be motivating for students to see their progress as their ability to complete speed sorts should improve over time.

SUPPORT For the offline task, students may benefit from having the letters they will use to build words written on small pieces of paper. It will allow them to physically move the letters into place and test where letters can be placed to make new words.

LEARNING COACH CHECK-IN As needed, help students read the activity page.

WRAP-UP

Questions About Brownilocks (C)

Students will answer questions to show that they understand the reading and spelling skills they learned in this lesson.

Read and Record

Good readers read quickly, smoothly, and with expression. This is called *fluency*. Students will record themselves reading aloud. They will listen to their recording and think about how quick, smooth, and expressive they sound.

> **TIP** Encourage students to rerecord as needed.

More Language Arts Practice

Students will practice skills according to their individual needs.

Handwriting

Students should gather their handwriting materials and begin where they left off. Remind students to form letters carefully and correctly.

> **TIP** Set a timer to help students stay focused during handwriting practice.

Bears Wrap-Up (A)

Lesson Overview

ACTIVITY	ACTIVITY TITLE	TIME	ONLINE/OFFLINE
GET READY	Introduction: Bears Wrap-Up (A)	**1** minute	🖥️
QUIZ	Spelling List 6	**25** minutes	🖥️
ALL ABOUT ME	Brain Break	**1** minute	🖥️ or 📄
GET READY	Closed Syllables	**5** minutes	🖥️
REVIEW	Bears	**25** minutes	🖥️
ALL ABOUT ME	Brain Break	**1** minute	🖥️ or 📄
WRAP-UP	Theme Time: Bears **LEARNING COACH CHECK-IN**	**41** minutes	📄
	Your Choice Time	**20** minutes	🖥️ or 📄
	Turn In Your Paragraph	**1** minute	🖥️

Advance Preparation

During the Your Choice Time activity, students will be given the option to read something of their choice. If students are using the digital library, allow extra time for them to make their reading selection, or have them make a selection before beginning the lesson.

Gather students' completed Publish Your Paragraph activity page from Goldilocks (A). Students will turn in this page during Wrap-Up: Turn In Your Paragraph.

MATERIALS

Supplied
- *English Language Arts 2 Activity Book 1*
  - Theme Time: Bears

Also Needed
- reading material for Your Choice Time (optional)
- completed Publish Your Paragraph activity page from Goldilocks (A)

Lesson Goals

- Take a spelling quiz.
- Decode words with closed syllables.
- Review writing, vocabulary, and reading skills from the unit.
- Make connections among the texts in the unit.
- Submit your paragraph.

GET READY

Introduction: Bears Wrap-Up (A)

Students will get a glimpse of what they will do in the lesson.

QUIZ

Spelling List 6

Students will complete the Spelling List 6 quiz.

GET READY

Closed Syllables

Students will identify closed syllables and decode words comprising closed syllables.

NOTE A closed syllable has a consonant-vowel-consonant (CVC) pattern. The final consonant "closes" the syllable, causing the vowel in the syllable to make its short sound.

REVIEW

Bears

Students will answer questions to review the vocabulary, writing, and reading skills they learned in the unit.

WRAP-UP

Theme Time: Bears

Students will complete Theme Time: Bears in *English Language Arts 2 Activity Book 1*.

NOTE This activity page includes an optional ungraded project. Students may need additional materials to complete the project.

LEARNING COACH CHECK-IN As needed, help students read the activity page. Discuss students' responses. If students complete the optional project, ask to watch their retelling with stick puppets—or offer to play one of the characters!

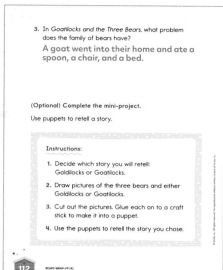

Theme Time: Bears

You have read about make-believe bears and real bears. Many of the bears had a problem. Answer the questions.

1. What is one of Arnold's problems in *Arnold and Louise: Lost and Found?*

   Possible answers: Louise often loses things that belong to Arnold; Louise loses Arnold's treasure and lies to him about it.

2. According to the article "Bears in Danger," polar bears are facing a problem. What is that problem?

   The sea ice that polar bears live on is melting.

3. In *Goatilocks and the Three Bears*, what problem does the family of bears have?

   A goat went into their home and ate a spoon, a chair, and a bed.

(Optional) Complete the mini-project.

Use puppets to retell a story.

Instructions:

1. Decide which story you will retell: Goldilocks or Goatilocks.

2. Draw pictures of the three bears and either Goldilocks or Goatilocks.

3. Cut out the pictures. Glue each on to a craft stick to make it into a puppet.

4. Use the puppets to retell the story you chose.

Your Choice Time

Students will choose among the following activities:

- Independent reading

- Independent writing

- Completing the optional project from the Theme Time: Bears activity page

- Completing their Publish Your Paragraph activity page

Turn In Your Paragraph

Students will submit their completed Publish Your Paragraph activity page to their teacher.

Bears Wrap-Up (B)

Lesson Overview

ACTIVITY	ACTIVITY TITLE	TIME	ONLINE/OFFLINE
GET READY	Introduction: Bears Wrap-Up (B)	**1** minute	🖥
QUIZ	Bears	**33** minutes	🖥
ALL ABOUT ME	Brain Break	**1** minute	🖥 or 📄
REFLECTION	Go Write! and Set a Goal **LEARNING COACH CHECK-IN**	**30** minutes	📄
WRAP-UP	Celebrate: Bears	**20** minutes	📄
	Discussion: My Best Sentence **LEARNING COACH CHECK-IN**	**15** minutes	🖥
	More Language Arts Practice	**10** minutes	🖥
	Your Choice Time	**10** minutes	🖥 or 📄

Advance Preparation

If students have removed the My Reading Log and My Badge Book activity pages from the activity book, have them gather these pages. They will use these activity pages in the Celebrate: Bears activity.

During the Your Choice Time activity, students will be given the option to read something of their choice. If they are using the digital library, allow extra time for them to make their reading selection, or have them make a selection before beginning the lesson.

Lesson Goals

- Take a quiz on the writing, vocabulary, and reading skills from the unit.
- Freewrite to develop fluency and reflect on learning.
- Set a goal for future learning.
- Celebrate accomplishments from the unit.
- Participate in a discussion.

MATERIALS

Supplied
- *English Language Arts 2 Activity Book 1*
  - Go Write! and Set a Goal
  - My Reading Log
  - My Badge Book

Also Needed
- crayons or markers
- reading material for Your Choice Time (optional)

GET READY

Introduction: Bears Wrap-Up (B)

Students will get a glimpse of what they will do in the lesson.

QUIZ

Bears

Students will complete the Bears quiz.

REFLECTION

Go Write! and Set a Goal

Students will complete Go Write! and Set a Goal in *English Language Arts 2 Activity Book 1*.

NOTE The Go Write! activity is intended to build writing fluency. Students should write for 10 minutes.

LEARNING COACH CHECK-IN As needed, help students read the activity page. Discuss their goal, including any steps they can take as well as support you can provide in helping them meet it.

A goal is something that you want to do.

You are getting ready to start a new unit. Choose one goal for yourself as a reader or writer. Or, write your own goal.

My GOAL!

- [ ] Read each book twice.
- [ ] Read for 10 minutes a day.
- [ ] Read to someone in my family.
- [ ] Write a paragraph on my own.
- [ ] _____

Write one thing you can do to help reach your goal.

I will _____

WRAP-UP

Celebrate: Bears

Students will celebrate accomplishments from the unit.

- They will record what they read this unit in their reading log.

- They will color the badge for this unit in their badge book. They may also color a badge to celebrate reading accomplishments.

  NOTE The My Reading Log and My Badge Book activity pages are located at the back of the activity book.

  NOTE Students will need crayons or markers to color in their badges.

Discussion: My Best Sentence

Students will respond to a discussion prompt.

LEARNING COACH CHECK-IN Students should discuss the questions shown on-screen with an adult. In some cases, teachers may facilitate a group discussion.

More Language Arts Practice

Students will practice skills according to their individual needs.

Your Choice Time

Students will choose among the following activities:

- Independent reading

- Independent writing

- Completing the optional project from the Theme Time: Bears activity page

Dinosaurs

Brontorina (A)

Lesson Overview

ACTIVITY	ACTIVITY TITLE	TIME	ONLINE/OFFLINE
GET READY	Introduction: *Brontorina* (A)	**1** minute	🖥️
	Words to Know: *Brontorina* (A)	**10** minutes	🖥️
READ	Think About Reading: *Brontorina* (A) **LEARNING COACH CHECK-IN**	**5** minutes	📄
	Brontorina (A)	**15** minutes	🖥️ and 📄
	Check-In: *Brontorina* (A)	**5** minutes	🖥️
	Reflect: *Brontorina* (A) **LEARNING COACH CHECK-IN**	**10** minutes	📄
ALL ABOUT ME	Brain Break	**1** minute	🖥️ or 📄
LEARN AND **TRY IT**	*And, Or, But*	**10** minutes	🖥️
	Use *And, Or, But* **LEARNING COACH CHECK-IN**	**15** minutes	📄
ALL ABOUT ME	Brain Break	**1** minute	🖥️ or 📄
LEARN	Spelling List 7 **LEARNING COACH CHECK-IN**	**25** minutes	🖥️ and 📄
WRAP-UP	Questions About *Brontorina* (A)	**2** minutes	🖥️
	Handwriting	**10** minutes	📄
	Go Read!	**10** minutes	🖥️ or 📄

Content Background

Students will begin a series of lessons centered around the book *Brontorina* by James Howe. In this lesson, they will make a prediction about the story and learn about common conjunctions.

Vocabulary   Students will explore these words from the story: *command*, *graceful*, and *downcast*. These are the definitions for how the words are used in *Brontorina*:

- **command** (verb) – to give an order; to tell someone in a forceful way to do something

- **graceful** (adjective) – moving in a smooth and controlled way that is pleasant to watch

- **downcast** (adjective) – feeling sad and without hope

Writing Skills   A **conjunction** is a joining word. There are different categories of conjunctions. This activity focuses on three common *coordinating conjunctions*: *and*, *or*, and *but*. Conjunctions are one tool that writers use to show the relationship between and among ideas.

The conjunction *and* joins things that are alike or in a pair.
    Example: We ate rice **and** beans for dinner.

The conjunction *or* joins choices.
    Example: Roy **or** Mia, could one of you wash the dishes?

The conjunction *but* joins things that contrast.
    Example: I want to help **but** feel so tired.

Coordinating conjunctions like *and*, *or*, and *but* can be used in both simple and compound sentences. Students will explore how these conjunctions function in simple sentences only. In a later lesson, they will explore coordinating conjunctions in compound sentences.

Spelling   Students will learn about spelling patterns that represent the long i sound, /ī/. They will sort words under these headings: **īCC mind**, **igh *high***, **y *fly***, and **oddball**.

In this lesson, students will learn the following symbols and spelling patterns:

- The long i sound, /ī/, is found in words with an i-consonant-consonant (īCC) pattern. Students will learn that the vowel *i* in the spelling patterns *–ild* and *–ind* has the sound /ī/. When students sort the spelling words, words with the sound /ī/ and the spelling patterns of *–ild* and *–ind* will go under the heading **īCC mind**.

- Students will learn that the vowel team *igh* represents the long i sound, /ī/. Any combination of letters that represents a vowel sound is called a vowel team, even if letters in that combination are consonants. Words with the sound /ī/ and the vowel team *igh* will go under the heading **igh *high***.

- The letter *y* at the end of a word represents the long i sound, /ī/. Words in which the sound /ī/ is made by the letter *y* will go under the heading **y *fly***.

- Some words have the sound /ī/, but the sound is not represented by the patterns īCC, *igh*, or *y*. These words will be sorted under the **oddball** heading.

MATERIALS

Supplied
- *Brontorina* by James Howe
- *English Language Arts 2 Activity Book 1*
  - Think About Reading: *Brontorina* (A)
  - Use *And*, *Or*, *But*
  - Spelling List 7
- handwriting workbook

Also Needed
- scissors
- envelope or baggie to store spelling cutouts
- reading material for Go Read!

KEYWORDS

conjunction – a word that joins parts of a sentence Examples: *and, but, or, although, because*

Advance Preparation

During the Go Read! activity, students will have the option of using the digital library. Allow extra time for students to make their reading selection, or have students make a selection before beginning the lesson.

Brontorina Synopsis

Brontorina, a dinosaur, dreams of dancing ballet. When Brontorina comes to Madame Lucille's Dance Academy, some students say that Brontorina is too big. But, Madame Lucille gives Brontorina a chance and finds that, even though she is a dinosaur, she is quite graceful. Dancing inside Madame Lucille's studio is a problem for Brontorina because of her size. Madame Lucille determines that she needs a bigger studio for Brontorina to dance in. When she cannot find a large enough space, Madame Lucille establishes an outdoor studio with room enough for everyone (and everything!) that wants to dance.

Lesson Goals

- Learn new vocabulary.
- Make and confirm a prediction about the reading selection.
- Listen to a read-aloud of *Brontorina*.
- Write simple sentences using the conjunctions *and*, *or*, and *but*.
- Sort words by sound and spelling pattern.
- Develop letter formation fluency.
- Read independently to develop fluency.

GET READY

Introduction: *Brontorina* (A)

Students will get a glimpse of what they will learn about in the lesson.

Words to Know: *Brontorina* (A)

Students will preview and answer questions about three vocabulary words from the reading selection.

Think About Reading: *Brontorina* (A)

Students will complete the book information and Question 1 on Think About Reading: *Brontorina* (A) in *English Language Arts 2 Activity Book 1*.

NOTE Encourage students to preview the reading selection by completing a book walk on their own. Previewing the story will help them make a prediction about the story's content.

NOTE In this activity, students will make a prediction about *Brontorina*. They will come back to the activity page to confirm their prediction after the read-along.

LEARNING COACH CHECK-IN As needed, help students read the activity page.

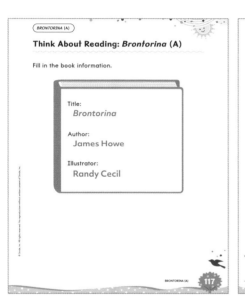

Brontorina (A)

Students will listen to and read along with *Brontorina* by James Howe. They may choose to read the story on their own. Encourage them to reread their favorite passages.

Check-In: *Brontorina* (A)

Students will answer questions to demonstrate their comprehension of *Brontorina*.

Reflect: *Brontorina* (A)

Students complete Question 2 on Think About Reading: *Brontorina* (A) in *English Language Arts 2 Activity Book 1*.

LEARNING COACH CHECK-IN As needed, help students read the activity page. Students will confirm the prediction they made before the read-along of *Brontorina*. Be sure not to state that a prediction was right or wrong. Readers make the best predictions they can with the information they have at the time. They can then confirm a prediction by saying whether it happened.

LEARN *And, Or, But*

Through guided exploration of sentences about *Brontorina*, students will learn how the conjunctions *and*, *or*, and *but* can be used to write and expand sentences.

SUPPORT   Swap *and* for *or* in a sentence, and vice versa. For example, change "I ate peanut butter and jelly" to "I ate peanut butter or jelly." Talk about how the meaning of the sentence changes.

TRY IT Use *And, Or, But*

Students will complete Use *And, Or, But* in *English Language Arts 2 Activity Book 1*.

LEARNING COACH CHECK-IN   As needed, help students read the activity page. It may be helpful for students to say their answers to Questions 4–7 aloud before writing them.

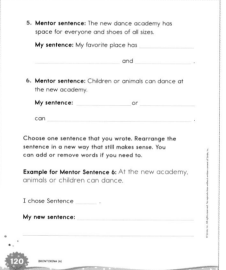

LEARN Spelling List 7

Students will learn and sort words with spelling patterns for the sound of long i.

- In an online activity, students will learn about the spelling patterns and the sounds they represent. They will learn how to sort words according to those sounds and patterns. They will also complete a word sort.

- In *English Language Arts 2 Activity Book 1*, students will complete Spelling List 7.

NOTE   Students will need scissors to cut out the spelling words on the activity page. Have students store their cutouts in a safe place, such as an envelope.

LEARNING COACH CHECK-IN   As needed, help students read the activity page.

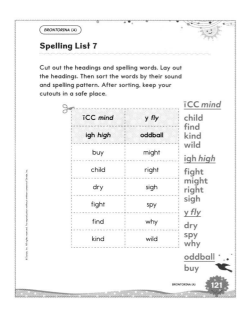

This is the complete list of words students will work with to learn the spelling patterns.

īCC	igh	y	oddball
child	fight	dry	buy
find	might	spy	
kind	right	why	
wild	sigh		

WRAP-UP

Questions About *Brontorina* (A)

Students will answer questions to show that they understand the writing and spelling skills they learned in this lesson.

Handwriting

Students should gather their handwriting materials and begin where they left off. Remind students to form letters carefully and correctly.

TIP Set a timer to help students stay focused during handwriting practice.

Go Read!

Students will read for pleasure. They should choose a book or a magazine that interests them, or they may choose a selection from the digital library, linked in the online lesson.

- Have students read aloud a few paragraphs of their selection.

- Then have students read silently for the rest of the time.

SUPPORT Students should make no more than five errors in decoding when they read aloud a few paragraphs of their Go Read! selection. If students struggle or make more than five errors, they need to select a different (and easier) text for the Go Read! activity.

TIP Have students select something to read ahead of time to help them stay focused.

Brontorina (B)

Lesson Overview

ACTIVITY	ACTIVITY TITLE	TIME	ONLINE/OFFLINE
GET READY	Introduction: *Brontorina* (B)	**1** minute	🖥️
READ	*Brontorina* (B)	**30** minutes	🖥️ and 📄
LEARN	Characters and Theme	**20** minutes	🖥️
ALL ABOUT ME	Brain Break	**1** minute	🖥️ or 📄
TRY IT	Solve a Problem **LEARNING COACH CHECK-IN**	**25** minutes	📄
ALL ABOUT ME	Brain Break	**1** minute	🖥️ or 📄
TRY IT	Practice: Spelling List 7 **LEARNING COACH CHECK-IN**	**20** minutes	🖥️ and 📄
WRAP-UP	Questions About *Brontorina* (B)	**2** minutes	🖥️
	Read and Record	**10** minutes	🖥️
	Handwriting	**10** minutes	📄

Content Background

Students will conclude a series of lessons centered around the book *Brontorina* by James Howe. In this lesson, they will learn how a character's perspective influences that character's actions. They will also learn about a story's theme.

Reading A character's **perspective** is that character's thoughts and beliefs about something. For example, in *Brontorina*, Brontorina believes that she is a dancer. It is her perspective.

A character's perspective influences that character's actions, which affects the story's plot. For example, Brontorina's perspective that she is a dancer influences her actions. It causes her to go to Madame Lucille's Dance Academy to take lessons.

A story's **theme** is a message the author conveys. A story can have more than one theme.

MATERIALS

Supplied
- *Brontorina* by James Howe
- *English Language Arts 2 Activity Book 1*
  - Solve a Problem
  - Practice: Spelling List 7
- handwriting workbook

Also Needed
- crayons or markers
- Spelling List 7 activity page cutouts from *Brontorina* (A)

Characters' actions develop a story's theme. For example, Madame Lucille welcomes Brontorina to her dance studio for lessons, even though Brontorina is a large dinosaur. Madame Lucille's actions help develop the theme that people should be accepted as they are, no matter their size or shape.

KEYWORDS

theme – the author's message or big idea

Advance Preparation

Gather students' cutouts from the Spelling List 7 activity page from *Brontorina* (A). They will use the cutouts during Try It: Practice: Spelling List 7.

Lesson Goals

- Listen to a read-aloud of *Brontorina*.
- Identify how characters' perspectives influence their actions.
- Determine a story's theme.
- Identify details that support the theme of a story.
- Identify reasons for when and how to use certain spelling patterns.
- Read aloud to develop fluency.
- Develop letter formation fluency.

GET READY

Introduction: *Brontorina* (B)

Students will get a glimpse of what they will learn about in the lesson.

READ

Brontorina (B)

Students will listen to and read along with *Brontorina* by James Howe. They may choose to read the story on their own. Encourage them to reread their favorite passages.

LEARN AND TRY IT

LEARN   Characters and Theme

Students will explore how a character's perspective influences that character's actions and how that character's actions help develop a story's theme. They will then answer questions about characters' perspectives and *Brontorina*'s theme.

TRY IT   Solve a Problem

Students will complete Solve a Problem in *English Language Arts 2 Activity Book 1*.

NOTE   Students will need crayons or markers to complete this activity page.

LEARNING COACH CHECK-IN   As needed, help students read the activity page. This activity page contains an open-ended question. It may be helpful for you to brainstorm possible answers with students.

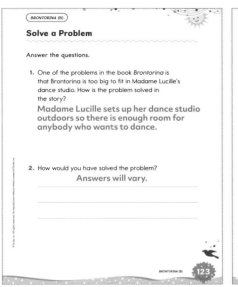 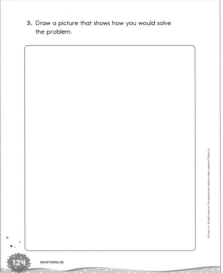

TRY IT   Practice: Spelling List 7

Students will practice the spelling patterns for Spelling List 7.

- In *English Language Arts 2 Activity Book 1*, students will complete Practice: Spelling List 7.

- Online, students will answer questions that require them to reflect on the spelling patterns.

NOTE   Students will need their cutouts from the Spelling List 7 activity page to complete Practice: Spelling List 7.

LEARNING COACH CHECK-IN   As needed, help students read the activity page.

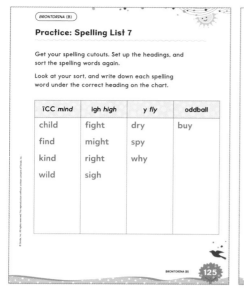

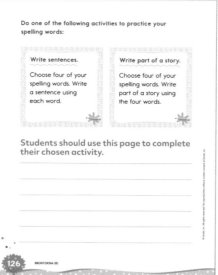

WRAP-UP

Questions About *Brontorina* (B)

Students will answer questions to show that they understand the reading and spelling skills they learned in this lesson.

Read and Record

Good readers read quickly, smoothly, and with expression. This is called *fluency*. Students will record themselves reading aloud. They will listen to their recording and think about how quick, smooth, and expressive they sound.

TIP Encourage students to rerecord as needed.

Handwriting

Students should gather their handwriting materials and begin where they left off. Remind students to form letters carefully and correctly.

TIP Set a timer to help students stay focused during handwriting practice.

If the Dinosaurs Came Back (A)

Lesson Overview

ACTIVITY	ACTIVITY TITLE	TIME	ONLINE/OFFLINE
GET READY	Introduction: *If the Dinosaurs Came Back* (A)	**1** minute	📶
	Open Syllables	**10** minutes	📶
	Words to Know: *If the Dinosaurs Came Back* (A)	**5** minutes	📶
READ	Think About Reading: *If the Dinosaurs Came Back* (A) **LEARNING COACH CHECK-IN**	**15** minutes	📄
	If the Dinosaurs Came Back (A)	**20** minutes	🖥 or 📄
	Check-In: *If the Dinosaurs Came Back* (A)	**5** minutes	📶
ALL ABOUT ME	Brain Break	**1** minute	📶 or 📄
TRY IT	What If? **LEARNING COACH CHECK-IN**	**20** minutes	📄
ALL ABOUT ME	Brain Break	**1** minute	📶 or 📄
TRY IT	Apply: Spelling List 7 **LEARNING COACH CHECK-IN**	**20** minutes	📶 and 📄
WRAP-UP	Question About *If the Dinosaurs Came Back* (A)	**2** minutes	📶
	Handwriting	**10** minutes	📄
	Go Read!	**10** minutes	📶 or 📄

Content Background

Students will begin a series of lessons centered around the book *If the Dinosaurs Came Back* by Bernard Most. In this lesson, they will answer comprehension questions about the reading selection and write sentences modeled off of those in the story.

Reading Foundations   An **open syllable** is a syllable that ends with a vowel. It is called an open syllable because the syllable is not closed by a consonant. In an open syllable, the vowel represents its long sound. The one-syllable word *so* is an open syllable. In the two-syllable word *begin*, the syllable *be–* is an open syllable. You can tell that *so* and *be–* are open syllables because they end with a vowel and the vowel makes its long sound.

Vocabulary   Students will explore these words from the book: *lawn mower*, *plow*, *skyscraper*, and *ski slope*. These are the definitions for how the words are used in *If the Dinosaurs Came Back*:

- **lawn mower** (noun) – a machine with a small motor that is used to cut grass

- **plow** (noun) – a piece of equipment that farmers use in their fields to get it ready for planting seeds

- **plow** (verb) – to dig into the soil and turn it over

- **skyscraper** (noun) – a very tall building, often found in large cities

- **ski slope** (noun) – an area on a mountain that people can ski down

Writing Skills   The majority of sentences in the story *If the Dinosaurs Came Back* have the same structure:

> **Examples:** "**If the dinosaurs came back,** we wouldn't need any more lawn mowers."
>
> "**If the dinosaurs came back,** they could help build big skyscrapers."

These sentences are examples of *complex sentences*. They contain two complete thoughts, or *clauses*. One of the clauses begins with a *subordinating conjunction* (in this case, *if*). Since the clause that begins with a subordinating conjunction begins the sentence, it is followed by a comma.

Students will **not** be introduced to the terminology *complex sentence*, *clause*, or *subordinating conjunction*. However, they will learn that sentences that begin with *if* or similar starter words (*after*, *when*, etc.) usually contain two complete thoughts and a comma.

By imitating various sentence structures, students gain experience that they can apply to their own authentic writing.

Advance Preparation

Gather students' cutouts from the Spelling List 7 activity page from *Brontorina* (A). They will use the cutouts during Try It: Apply: Spelling List 7.

If students removed My Speed Sort Times from the activity book, have them gather this activity page. They will use this activity page in Try It: Apply: Spelling List 7.

During the Go Read! activity, students will have the option of using the digital library. Allow extra time for students to make their reading selection, or have students make a selection before beginning the lesson.

If the Dinosaurs Came Back Synopsis

In *If the Dinosaurs Came Back*, Bernard Most has created humorous and imaginative scenarios in which dinosaurs could help people if the dinosaurs were to return.

Lesson Goals

- Identify and decode words with open syllables.
- Learn new vocabulary.
- Read *If the Dinosaurs Came Back*.
- Write sentences that begin with *if* and similar words.
- Identify reasons for when and how to use certain spelling patterns.
- Develop letter formation fluency.
- Read independently to develop fluency.

GET READY

Introduction: *If the Dinosaurs Came Back* (A)
Students will get a glimpse of what they will learn about in the lesson.

Open Syllables
Students will identify and decode words with open syllables.

Words to Know: *If the Dinosaurs Came Back* (A)
Students will preview vocabulary words from the reading selection.

READ

Think About Reading: *If the Dinosaurs Came Back* (A)
Students will complete Think About Reading: *If the Dinosaurs Came Back* (A) in *English Language Arts 2 Activity Book 1*.

LEARNING COACH CHECK-IN   As needed, help students read the activity page.

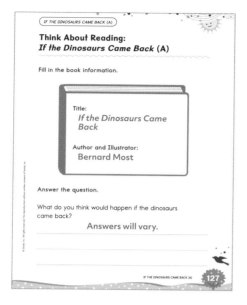

If the Dinosaurs Came Back (A)

Students will read *If the Dinosaurs Came Back* by Bernard Most. Encourage them to reread their favorite passages.

Check-In: *If the Dinosaurs Came Back* (A)

Students will answer questions to demonstrate their comprehension of *If the Dinosaurs Came Back*.

TRY IT

What If?

Students will complete What If? in *English Language Arts 2 Activity Book 1*.

LEARNING COACH CHECK-IN   As needed, help students read the activity page. When students read aloud the sentences in Questions 1 and 2, help them connect the comma to a short pause in reading.

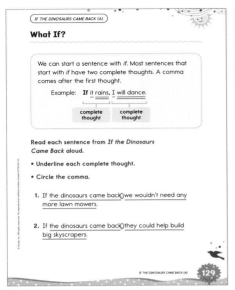

What If?

We can start a sentence with *if*. Most sentences that start with *if* have two complete thoughts. A comma comes after the first thought.

Example: **If** it rains, I will dance.
complete thought   complete thought

Read each sentence from *If the Dinosaurs Came Back* aloud.

• Underline each complete thought.

• Circle the comma.

1. If the dinosaurs came back we wouldn't need any more lawn mowers.

2. If the dinosaurs came back they could help build big skyscrapers.

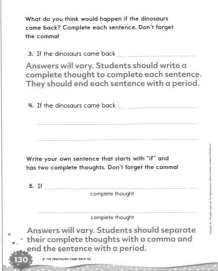

What do you think would happen if the dinosaurs came back? Complete each sentence. Don't forget the comma!

3. If the dinosaurs came back _____

Answers will vary. Students should write a complete thought to complete each sentence. They should end each sentence with a period.

4. If the dinosaurs came back _____

_____

_____

Write your own sentence that starts with "if" and has two complete thoughts. Don't forget the comma!

5. If _____
complete thought

_____
complete thought

Answers will vary. Students should separate their complete thoughts with a comma and end the sentence with a period.

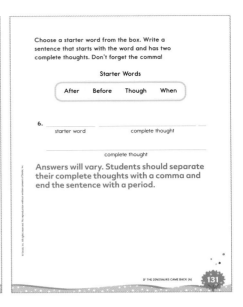

Choose a starter word from the box. Write a sentence that starts with the word and has two complete thoughts. Don't forget the comma!

Starter Words

After	Before	Though	When

6. _____
starter word   complete thought

_____
complete thought

Answers will vary. Students should separate their complete thoughts with a comma and end the sentence with a period.

Apply: Spelling List 7

Students will apply what they have learned about the spelling patterns for Spelling List 7.

• In an online activity, students will complete a word sort and answer reflection questions.

• In *English Language Arts 2 Activity Book 1*, students will complete Apply: Spelling List 7.

NOTE   Students will need their cutouts from the Spelling List 7 activity page to complete the word sort.

TIP   Have students record their speed sort times on the My Speed Sort Times activity page, which is located at the back of the activity book. It can be motivating for students to see their progress as their ability to complete speed sorts should improve over time.

LEARNING COACH CHECK-IN   As needed, help students read the activity page.

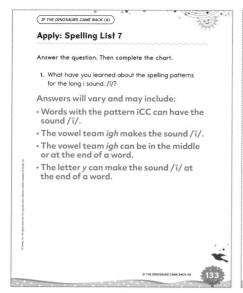
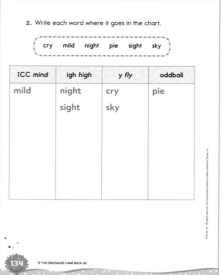

IF THE DINOSAURS CAME BACK (A)

Apply: Spelling List 7

Answer the question. Then complete the chart.

1. What have you learned about the spelling patterns for the long i sound, /ī/?

Answers will vary and may include:

- Words with the pattern īCC can have the sound /ī/.
- The vowel team *igh* makes the sound /ī/.
- The vowel team *igh* can be in the middle or at the end of a word.
- The letter *y* can make the sound /ī/ at the end of a word.

2. Write each word where it goes in the chart.

cry   mild   night   pie   sight   sky

īCC *mind*	igh *high*	y *fly*	oddball
mild	night	cry	pie
	sight	sky	

WRAP-UP

Question About *If the Dinosaurs Came Back* (A)

Students will answer a question to show that they understand the spelling skills they learned in this lesson.

Handwriting

Students should gather their handwriting materials and begin where they left off. Remind students to form letters carefully and correctly.

TIP   Set a timer to help students stay focused during handwriting practice.

Go Read!

Students will read for pleasure. They should choose a book or a magazine that interests them, or they may choose a selection from the digital library, linked in the online lesson.

- Have students read aloud a few paragraphs of their selection.

- Then have students read silently for the rest of the time.

SUPPORT   Students should make no more than five errors in decoding when they read aloud a few paragraphs of their Go Read! selection. If students struggle or make more than five errors, they need to select a different (and easier) text for the Go Read! activity.

TIP   Have students select something to read ahead of time to help them stay focused.

If the Dinosaurs Came Back (B)

Lesson Overview

ACTIVITY	ACTIVITY TITLE	TIME	ONLINE/OFFLINE
GET READY	Introduction: *If the Dinosaurs Came Back* (B)	**1** minute	🖥️
	More Open Syllables	**15** minutes	🖥️
READ	*If the Dinosaurs Came Back* (B)	**20** minutes	🖥️ or 📄
ALL ABOUT ME	Brain Break	**1** minute	🖥️ or 📄
LEARN AND TRY IT	The Narrator's Perspective	**15** minutes	🖥️
	A Dinosaur's Perspective **LEARNING COACH CHECK-IN**	**25** minutes	📄
ALL ABOUT ME	Brain Break	**1** minute	🖥️ or 📄
TRY IT	More Practice: Spelling List 7 **LEARNING COACH CHECK-IN**	**20** minutes	🖥️ and 📄
WRAP-UP	Questions About *If the Dinosaurs Came Back* (B)	**2** minutes	🖥️
	Read and Record	**10** minutes	🖥️
	Handwriting	**10** minutes	📄

Content Background

Students will conclude a series of lessons centered around the book *If the Dinosaurs Came Back* by Bernard Most. In this lesson, they will identify the narrator's perspective in a story.

Reading   The **narrator** is who is telling a story. The author writes a story. The narrator tells the story. A narrator can be inside a story or outside a story.

A narrator inside a story is a character in the story who is taking part in the action. When a narrator is inside the story, the text often uses first-person pronouns such as *I*, *me*, *my*, or *we*.

When a narrator is outside a story, it's as if somebody is watching and describing what is happening in the story but is not taking part in it. When a narrator is outside the story, the text often uses third-person pronouns such as *he*, *she*, or *they*.

MATERIALS

Supplied
- *If the Dinosaurs Came Back* by Bernard Most
- *English Language Arts 2 Activity Book 1*
  - A Dinosaur's Perspective
  - More Practice: Spelling List 7
  - My Speed Sort Times
- handwriting workbook

Also Needed
- crayons or markers
- Spelling List 7 activity page cutouts from *Brontorina* (A)

Somebody's **perspective** is that person's thoughts and beliefs about something. For example, in *If the Dinosaurs Came Back*, the narrator's perspective on dinosaurs is that they could help people in many ways if they were to come back.

KEYWORDS

narrator – the teller of a story

Advance Preparation

Gather students' cutouts from the Spelling List 7 activity page from *Brontorina* (A). They will use the cutouts during Try It: More Practice: Spelling List 7.

If students removed My Speed Sort Times from the activity book, have them gather this activity page. They will use this activity page in Try It: Apply: Spelling List 7.

Lesson Goals

- Identify and decode words with open syllables.
- Reread *If the Dinosaurs Came Back*.
- Identify the narrator of a story.
- Identify a character's perspective.
- Identify and write spelling patterns that stand for sounds within words.
- Read aloud to develop fluency.
- Develop letter formation fluency.

GET READY

Introduction: *If the Dinosaurs Came Back* (B)
Students will get a glimpse of what they will learn about in the lesson.

More Open Syllables
Students will identify open syllables and decode more words with open syllables.

READ

If the Dinosaurs Came Back (B)
Students will reread *If the Dinosaurs Came Back* by Bernard Most.

LEARN   The Narrator's Perspective

Students will identify the story's narrator and the narrator's perspective on dinosaurs.

TRY IT   A Dinosaur's Perspective

Students will complete A Dinosaur's Perspective in *English Language Arts 2 Activity Book 1*.

NOTE   Students will need crayons or markers to complete this activity page.

LEARNING COACH CHECK-IN   As needed, help students read the activity page.

TRY IT   More Practice: Spelling List 7

Students will continue to practice the spelling patterns for Spelling List 7 to increase automatic recognition of the patterns.

- In an online activity, students will practice the spelling words and patterns.

- In *English Language Arts 2 Activity Book 1*, students will complete More Practice: Spelling List 7.

NOTE   Students will need their cutouts from the Spelling List 7 activity page to complete the word sort.

TIP   Have students record their speed sort times on the My Speed Sort Times activity page, which is located at the back of the activity book. It can be motivating for students to see their progress as their ability to complete speed sorts should improve over time.

LEARNING COACH CHECK-IN   As needed, help students read the activity page.

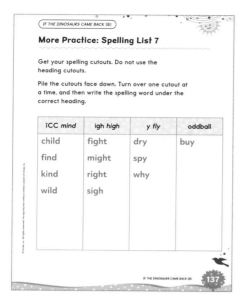

WRAP-UP

Questions About *If the Dinosaurs Came Back* (B)

Students will answer questions to show that they understand the reading skills they learned in this lesson.

Read and Record

Good readers read quickly, smoothly, and with expression. This is called *fluency*. Students will record themselves reading aloud. They will listen to their recording and think about how quick, smooth, and expressive they sound.

TIP   Encourage students to rerecord as needed.

Handwriting

Students should gather their handwriting materials and begin where they left off. Remind students to form letters carefully and correctly.

TIP   Set a timer to help students stay focused during handwriting practice.

Truth or Lie: Dinosaurs! (A)

Lesson Overview

ACTIVITY	ACTIVITY TITLE	TIME	ONLINE/OFFLINE
GET READY	Introduction: *Truth or Lie: Dinosaurs!* (A)	**1** minute	🖥
	Words to Know: *Truth or Lie: Dinosaurs!* (A)	**10** minutes	🖥
	Before You Read: Fiction vs. Nonfiction	**5** minutes	🖥
	Author's Purpose	**8** minutes	🖥
READ	Think About Reading: *Truth or Lie: Dinosaurs!* (A) LEARNING COACH CHECK-IN	**7** minutes	📄
	Truth or Lie: Dinosaurs! (A)	**15** minutes	🖥 and 📄
	Reflect: *Truth or Lie: Dinosaurs!* (A) LEARNING COACH CHECK-IN	**5** minutes	📄
ALL ABOUT ME	Brain Break	**1** minute	🖥 or 📄
LEARN AND TRY IT	Three Truths and a Lie	**10** minutes	🖥
	Start Researching an Animal LEARNING COACH CHECK-IN	**20** minutes	🖥 and 📄
WRAP-UP	Questions About *Truth or Lie: Dinosaurs!* (A)	**2** minutes	🖥
ALL ABOUT ME	Brain Break	**1** minute	🖥 or 📄
QUIZ	Spelling List 7	**25** minutes	🖥
WRAP-UP	Handwriting	**10** minutes	📄
	Go Read!	**10** minutes	🖥 or 📄

Content Background

Students will begin a series of lessons centered around the book *Truth or Lie: Dinosaurs!* by Erica S. Perl. In this lesson, they will learn how to distinguish fiction from nonfiction. They will build background knowledge on author's purpose. They will also begin researching an animal.

Vocabulary Students will explore these words from the story: *sleuth, lack,* and *vulnerable.* These are the definitions for how the words are used in *Truth or Lie: Dinosaurs!*:

- **sleuth** (noun) – someone who looks for information; someone who acts as a detective

- **lack** (verb) – to not have something; to not have enough of something

- **vulnerable** (adjective) – capable of being easily hurt or injured

Writing Skills Students will begin working on the **short research assignment**, Three Truths and a Lie. They will complete this assignment over the course of several lessons by following the writing process.

Writing Process

| 1 Prewriting | 2 Drafting | 3 Revising | 4 Proofreading | 5 Publishing |

Research is gathering information from **sources**. Sources of research can include books, articles, videos, and interviews. During research, it is important to record key information about the source. For this assignment, students will use a single book as a source, and they will record the title and author. In future courses, they will be expected to cite and format source information, which is not an expectation of this course.

It is also important that writers do not plagiarize, or copy, their research. In this lesson, students are not introduced to the term *plagiarize*, but they are taught the importance of putting ideas found in research into their own words. In future courses, students will learn about synthesizing information from multiple sources and well as using direct quotations; those concepts are beyond the scope of this assignment.

Advance Preparation

Gather a folder that students can use to keep all activity pages related to their short research assignment.

During the Go Read! activity, students will have the option of using the digital library. Allow extra time for students to make their reading selection, or have students make a selection before beginning the lesson.

Truth or Lie: Dinosaurs! Synopsis

In this nonfiction text, readers act as sleuths to determine which statements about dinosaurs are true and which ones are lies.

Lesson Goals

- Learn new vocabulary.
- Distinguish fiction text from nonfiction text.
- Identify the author's purpose for writing a text.
- Identify the topic of a text.
- Listen to a read-aloud of *Truth or Lie: Dinosaurs!*
- Begin researching an animal.
- Take a spelling quiz.
- Develop letter formation fluency.
- Read independently to develop fluency.

GET READY

Introduction: *Truth or Lie: Dinosaurs!* (A)

Students will get a glimpse of what they will learn about in the lesson.

Words to Know: *Truth or Lie: Dinosaurs!* (A)

Students will preview and answer questions about three vocabulary words from the reading selection.

Before You Read: Fiction vs. Nonfiction

Students will learn how to distinguish fiction texts from nonfiction texts.

Author's Purpose

Students will build background knowledge on author's purpose, the reasons why an author writes a text.

READ

Think About Reading: *Truth or Lie: Dinosaurs!* (A)

Students will complete Questions 1 and 2 on Think About Reading: *Truth or Lie: Dinosaurs!* (A) in *English Language Arts 2 Activity Book 1*.

NOTE In this activity, students will identify the topic of the book and what they already know about the topic. They will come back to this activity page to write what they learned about the topic after the read-along.

LEARNING COACH CHECK-IN As needed, help students read the activity page. If students are unsure about the term *topic*, remind them that the topic of a text is what the text is mostly about.

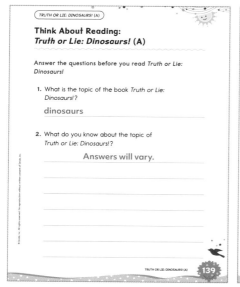

Truth or Lie: Dinosaurs! (A)

Students will listen to and read along with *Truth or Lie: Dinosaurs!* by Erica S. Perl. They may choose to read the story on their own. Encourage them to reread their favorite passages.

Reflect: *Truth or Lie: Dinosaurs!* (A)

Students will complete Question 3 on Think About Reading: *Truth or Lie: Dinosaurs!* in *English Language Arts 2 Activity Book 1*.

LEARNING COACH CHECK-IN   As needed, help students read the activity page.

LEARN AND TRY IT

LEARN   Three Truths and a Lie

Students will learn the steps they will take to research and write three truths and a lie about an animal of their choice. The steps include selecting and reading a book about an animal from the digital library, recording research in a graphic organizer, and then writing their research as three truths and a lie.

TRY IT   Start Researching an Animal

Students will select and read a book from the Amazing Animals series. The series can be found on the digital bookshelf that is linked in the online lesson.

After they read their selected book, students will begin My Animal Research in *English Language Arts 2 Activity Book 1*. They will have additional time to complete this activity page in *Truth or Lie: Dinosaurs!* (B).

LEARNING COACH CHECK-IN   Ensure that students select and read a book from the Amazing Animal series before they begin the My Animal Research activity page. As needed, help students read the book and the activity page.

TIP   Read the Model Three Truths and a Lie together to ensure that students understand the assignment before they choose a topic.

NOTE   Have students put the Model Three Truths and a Lie and their in-progress My Animal Research activity page into a folder for safe keeping.

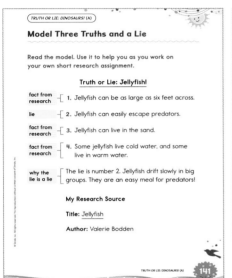

WRAP-UP

Questions About *Truth or Lie: Dinosaurs!* (A)

Students will answer questions to show that they understand the reading and writing skills they learned in this lesson.

QUIZ

Spelling List 7

Students will complete the Spelling List 7 quiz.

Handwriting

Students should gather their handwriting materials and begin where they left off. Remind students to form letters carefully and correctly.

TIP Set a timer to help students stay focused during handwriting practice.

Go Read!

Students will read for pleasure. They should choose a book or a magazine that interests them, or they may choose a selection from the digital library, linked in the online lesson.

• Have students read aloud a few paragraphs of their selection.

• Then have students read silently for the rest of the time.

SUPPORT Students should make no more than five errors in decoding when they read aloud a few paragraphs of their Go Read! selection. If students struggle or make more than five errors, they need to select a different (and easier) text for the Go Read! activity.

TIP Have students select something to read ahead of time to help them stay focused.

Truth or Lie: Dinosaurs! (B)

Lesson Overview

ACTIVITY	ACTIVITY TITLE	TIME	ONLINE/OFFLINE
GET READY	Introduction: *Truth or Lie: Dinosaurs!* (B)	**1** minute	📶
	Words to Know: *Truth or Lie: Dinosaurs!* (B)	**10** minutes	📶
READ	*Truth or Lie: Dinosaurs!* (B)	**10** minutes	📶 and 📄
LEARN	Clearing Up Confusion	**20** minutes	📶
ALL ABOUT ME	Brain Break	**1** minute	📶 or 📄
TRY IT	Finish Researching an Animal **LEARNING COACH CHECK-IN**	**30** minutes	📶 and 📄
ALL ABOUT ME	Brain Break	**1** minute	📶 or 📄
LEARN	Spelling List 8 **LEARNING COACH CHECK-IN**	**25** minutes	📶 and 📄
WRAP-UP	Questions About *Truth or Lie: Dinosaurs!* (B)	**2** minutes	📶
	Handwriting	**10** minutes	📄
	Go Read!	**10** minutes	📶 or 📄

Content Background

Students will continue a series of lessons centered around the book *Truth or Lie: Dinosaurs!* by Erica S. Perl. In this lesson, they will learn about strategies that help them monitor and clarify comprehension of text. They will also finish researching the animal they chose.

Vocabulary   Students will explore these words from the story: *armor*, *provide*, and *exposed*. These are the definitions for how the words are used in *Truth or Lie: Dinosaurs!*:

- **armor** (noun) – a hard covering that protects something

- **provide** (verb) – to supply something

- **exposed** (adjective) – not protected or covered

Reading   The goal of reading is to understand. Certain reading strategies help readers check their understanding of what they've read and can help them clear up confusion if they're unsure about their **comprehension**.

Asking a question and then using **text features**, such as illustrations, to answer the question is one method for checking or clarifying understanding.

Identifying a point of confusion and then rereading is a strategy that can help readers clarify meaning.

Writing Skills   Students will continue working on the **short research assignment**, Three Truths and a Lie. They will complete this assignment over the course of several lessons by following the writing process.

Writing Process

1 Prewriting	2 Drafting	3 Revising	4 Proofreading	5 Publishing

Students will finish researching the animal that they chose.

Advance Preparation

Gather the folder that students are using to keep all activity pages related to their short research assignment.

- Model Three Truths and a Lie from *Truth or Lie: Dinosaurs!* (A)

- Students' in-progress My Animal Research activity page from *Truth or Lie: Dinosaurs!* (A)

During the Go Read! activity, students will have the option of using the digital library. Allow extra time for students to make their reading selection, or have students make a selection before beginning the lesson.

Lesson Goals

- Learn new vocabulary.
- Reread part of *Truth or Lie: Dinosaurs!*
- Use reading strategies to monitor and clarify comprehension.
- Finish researching an animal.
- Sort words by sound and spelling pattern.
- Develop letter formation fluency.
- Read independently to develop fluency.

Introduction: *Truth or Lie: Dinosaurs!* (B)
Students will get a glimpse of what they will learn about in the lesson.

Words to Know: *Truth or Lie: Dinosaurs!* (B)
Students will preview and answer questions about three vocabulary words from the reading selection.

READ

Truth or Lie: Dinosaurs! (B)
Students will reread pages 6–9 of *Truth or Lie: Dinosaurs!* by Erica S. Perl.

LEARN AND TRY IT

LEARN   Clearing Up Confusion
Students will learn strategies for checking and clarifying comprehension when they read.

TRY IT   Finish Researching an Animal
Students will complete My Animal Research in *English Language Arts 2 Activity Book 1*. They will use the book they selected from the Amazing Animals series. This series can be found on the digital bookshelf that is linked in the online lesson.

LEARNING COACH CHECK-IN   Ensure that students are using the book that they selected from the Amazing Animals series, found online, to complete the My Animal Research activity page. As needed, help students read the activity page.

NOTE   Have students put their completed My Animal Research activity page in the folder they are using to store their short research assignment pages.

LEARN Spelling List 8

Students will learn and sort words with spelling patterns for the sounds of short e and long e.

- In an online activity, students will learn about the spelling patterns and the sounds they represent. They will learn how to sort words according to those sounds and patterns. They will also complete a word sort.

- In *English Language Arts 2 Activity Book 1*, students will complete Spelling List 8.

NOTE Students will need scissors to cut out the spelling words on the activity page. Have students store their cutouts in a safe place, such as an envelope.

LEARNING COACH CHECK-IN As needed, help students read the activity page.

This is the complete list of words students will work with to learn the spelling patterns.

/ĕ/ bed	/ē/ feet	/ē/ eat	oddball
best	green	mean	been
check	meet	meat	feather
	sleep	pea	
	teeth	read	

Questions About *Truth or Lie: Dinosaurs!* (B)

Students will answer questions to show that they understand the reading, writing, and spelling skills they learned in this lesson.

Handwriting

Students should gather their handwriting materials and begin where they left off. Remind students to form letters carefully and correctly.

TIP Set a timer to help students stay focused during handwriting practice.

Go Read!

Students will read for pleasure. They should choose a book or a magazine that interests them, or they may choose a selection from the digital library, linked in the online lesson.

- Have students read aloud a few paragraphs of their selection.

- Then have students read silently for the rest of the time.

SUPPORT Students should make no more than five errors in decoding when they read aloud a few paragraphs of their Go Read! selection. If students struggle or make more than five errors, they need to select a different (and easier) text for the Go Read! activity.

TIP Have students select something to read ahead of time to help them stay focused.

Truth or Lie: Dinosaurs! (C)

Lesson Overview

ACTIVITY	ACTIVITY TITLE	TIME	ONLINE/OFFLINE
GET READY	Introduction: *Truth or Lie: Dinosaurs!* (C)	**1** minute	🖥️
	Digging Into a Dictionary	**10** minutes	🖥️
	Words to Know: *Truth or Lie: Dinosaurs!* (C)	**10** minutes	🖥️
READ	*Truth or Lie: Dinosaurs!* (C)	**10** minutes	🖥️ and 📄
LEARN	Nonfiction Text Features	**15** minutes	🖥️
ALL ABOUT ME	Brain Break	**1** minute	🖥️ or 📄
TRY IT	Draft Your Three Truths and a Lie LEARNING COACH CHECK-IN	**40** minutes	📄
ALL ABOUT ME	Brain Break	**1** minute	🖥️ or 📄
TRY IT	Practice: Spelling List 8 LEARNING COACH CHECK-IN	**20** minutes	🖥️ and 📄
WRAP-UP	Questions About *Truth or Lie: Dinosaurs!* (C)	**2** minutes	🖥️
	Read and Record	**10** minutes	🖥️

Content Background

Students will conclude a series of lessons centered around the book *Truth or Lie: Dinosaurs!* by Erica S. Perl. In this lesson, they will learn about dictionaries and nonfiction text features. They will also use the information they have gathered about an animal to write a draft.

Reading Foundations   A dictionary entry provides the following information about a word: spelling, pronunciation, part of speech, definition.

Vocabulary   Students will explore these words from the story: *term*, *scent*, and *habit*. These are the definitions for how the words are used in *Truth or Lie: Dinosaurs!*:

- **term** (noun) – a word or phrase that has an exact meaning

- **scent** (noun) – a smell

- **habit** (noun) – a usual way of behaving or doing something

Reading   Nonfiction text features are all the features that appear in addition to the body text. Some help readers locate information, such as a **table of contents** or a **heading** that lets readers know what a section of text is about.

Some text features provide visual information, such as a graph, photograph, or **illustration**. Visual features often give information beyond what is provided in the text. For example, the body text may tell some details about a dinosaur, but an illustration can go further and show readers what the dinosaur looked like.

Writing Skills   Students will continue working on their **short research assignment**, Three Truths and a Lie. They will complete this assignment over the course of several lessons by following the writing process.

Writing Process

1 Prewriting	2 Drafting	3 Revising	4 Proofreading	5 Publishing

Students will write their complete draft.

Advance Preparation

Gather the folder that students are using to keep all activity pages related to their short research assignment.

- Model Three Truths and a Lie from *Truth or Lie: Dinosaurs!* (A)

- Students' completed My Animal Research activity page from *Truth or Lie: Dinosaurs!* (B)

Gather students' cutouts from the Spelling List 8 activity page from *Truth or Lie: Dinosaurs!* (B). They will use the cutouts during Try It: Practice: Spelling List 8.

Lesson Goals

- Identify information in a dictionary entry.

- Learn new vocabulary.

- Listen to a read-aloud of *Truth or Lie: Dinosaurs!*

- Identify information in and determine the purpose of an image in an informational text.

- Use text features to locate information in an informational text.

- Draft your Three Truths and a Lie.

- Identify and write spelling patterns that stand for sounds within words.

- Read aloud to practice fluency.

MATERIALS

Supplied
- *Truth or Lie: Dinosaurs!* by Erica S. Perl
- *English Language Arts 2 Activity Book 1*
  - Draft Your Three Truths and a Lie
  - Practice: Spelling List 8
- Drafting Paper (printout)

Also Needed
- folder in which students are storing short research assignment pages
- Spelling List 8 activity page cutouts from *Truth or Lie: Dinosaurs!* (B)
- crayons or markers (optional)

KEYWORDS

heading – a title within the body of a text that tells the reader something important about a section of the text

illustration – a drawing

table of contents – a list at the start of a book that gives the titles of the book's stories, poems, articles, chapters, or nonfiction pieces and the pages where they can be found

Introduction: *Truth or Lie: Dinosaurs!* (C)
Students will get a glimpse of what they will learn about in the lesson.

Digging Into a Dictionary
Students will learn the basic features of a dictionary and the parts of a dictionary entry.

Words to Know: *Truth or Lie: Dinosaurs!* (C)
Students will preview and answer questions about three vocabulary words from the reading selection.

READ

Truth or Lie: Dinosaurs! (C)
Students will listen to and read along with *Truth or Lie: Dinosaurs!* by Erica S. Perl again. They may choose to reread the story on their own.

LEARN AND TRY IT

LEARN   Nonfiction Text Features
Students will learn how some nonfiction text features help with locating information, while visual features provide information beyond the body text and can help readers better understand the topic of a text.

TRY IT   Draft Your Three Truths and a Lie
Students will complete Draft Your Three Truths and a Lie in *English Language Arts 2 Activity Book 1*. Make sure students have their completed My Animal Research activity page and Model Three Truths and a Lie to refer to as they work.

LEARNING COACH CHECK-IN   As needed, help students read the activity page. Ensure that students understand what to do.

- Use their research to write four statements about their chosen animal: three facts and one lie. They can put these statements in any order.

- Identify the lie and write at least one statement that explains why the lie is false.

Finally, remind students to use their own words (not copy sentences from their research source).

NOTE   Have students add their completed Draft Your Three Truths and a Lie activity page to the folder they are using to store their short research assignment pages.

NOTE   Additional sheets of Drafting Paper are available online.

Draft Your Three Truths and a Lie

Write the first draft of your three truths and a lie.

☐ Choose three facts from your research. Write them in your own words.

☐ Write one lie about your animal.

☐ Write which statement is a lie, and explain why.

Write only on the white rows. You will use the purple rows later.

Title: **Truth or Lie:** _____ !

start here ▶

keep writing ▶

keep writing ▶

keep writing ▶

TRY IT   Practice: Spelling List 8

Students will practice the spelling patterns for Spelling List 8.

- In *English Language Arts 2 Activity Book 1*, students will complete Practice: Spelling List 8.

- Online, students will answer questions that require them to reflect on the spelling patterns.

NOTE   Students will need their cutouts from the Spelling List 8 activity page to complete Practice: Spelling List 8.

NOTE   Students may wish to use crayons or markers to draw their pictures or comic strip.

LEARNING COACH CHECK-IN   As needed, help students read the activity page.

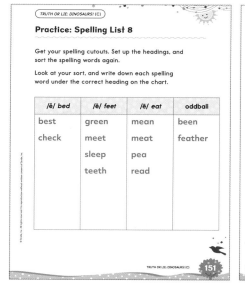

Practice: Spelling List 8

Get your spelling cutouts. Set up the headings, and sort the spelling words again.

Look at your sort, and write down each spelling word under the correct heading on the chart.

/ē/ bed	/ē/ feet	/ē/ eat	oddball
best	green	mean	been
check	meet	meat	feather
	sleep	pea	
	teeth	read	

TRUTH OR LIE: DINOSAURS! (C) **151**

Do one of the following activities to practice your spelling words:

Draw and label.

Choose four of your spelling words. Draw a picture for each word. Then write the word under the picture.

Create a comic strip.

Create four panels of a comic strip. Draw pictures and write text with four or more of your spelling words.

152 TRUTH OR LIE: DINOSAURS! (C)

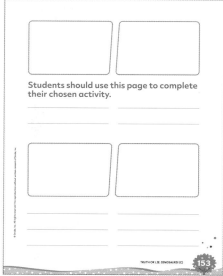

Students should use this page to complete their chosen activity.

TRUTH OR LIE: DINOSAURS! (C) **153**

WRAP-UP

Questions About *Truth or Lie: Dinosaurs!* (C)

Students will answer questions to show that they understand the reading, writing, and spelling skills they learned in this lesson.

Read and Record

Good readers read quickly, smoothly, and with expression. This is called *fluency*. Students will record themselves reading aloud. They will listen to their recording and think about how quick, smooth, and expressive they sound.

TIP Encourage students to rerecord as needed.

Digging Into Dinosaurs (A)

Lesson Overview

ACTIVITY	ACTIVITY TITLE	TIME	ONLINE/OFFLINE
GET READY	Introduction: Digging Into Dinosaurs (A)	**1** minute	📶
READ	Digging Into Dinosaurs (A)	**25** minutes	📶
ALL ABOUT ME	Brain Break	**1** minute	📶 or 📄
LEARN AND TRY IT	Revise Your Three Truths and a Lie LEARNING COACH CHECK-IN	**30** minutes	📄
	Use a Dictionary to Check Spelling	**10** minutes	📶
	Proofread Your Three Truths and a Lie LEARNING COACH CHECK-IN	**30** minutes	📄
ALL ABOUT ME	Brain Break	**1** minute	📶 or 📄
TRY IT	Apply: Spelling List 8 LEARNING COACH CHECK-IN	**20** minutes	📶 and 📄
WRAP-UP	Questions About Digging Into Dinosaurs (A)	**2** minutes	📶

Content Background

Students will focus on writing in this lesson.

Writing Skills   Students will continue working on the **short research assignment**, Three Truths and a Lie. They will complete this assignment over the course of several lessons by following the writing process.

Writing Process

Writers often use **references** to help them revise and proofread. A dictionary can be used to check spelling. Simply look up the potentially misspelled word, read the definition to confirm you've looked up the correct word, and then check the dictionary spelling against the spelling in your draft.

To check the spelling of a plural noun, look up the singular noun. In most dictionaries, the spelling of the plural noun will be part of that entry (rather than its own entry). The same process is true for checking the spelling of a verb form, such as the past form: Look up the base form, and then find the spelling of other verb forms in the entry.

A learner's dictionary is a dictionary written for children. It has fewer entries than a standard dictionary, and the definitions are written with children in mind. Some learner's dictionaries include pictures.

Advance Preparation

Gather the folder that students are using to keep all activity pages related to their short research assignment.

- Model Three Truths and a Lie from *Truth or Lie: Dinosaurs!* (A)

- Students' completed My Animal Research activity page from *Truth or Lie: Dinosaurs!* (B)

- Students' completed draft from *Truth or Lie: Dinosaurs!* (C)

Prior to Try It: Revise Your Three Truths and a Lie, read students' draft and complete the Three Truths and a Lie: Feedback Sheet.

Gather students' cutouts from the Spelling List 8 activity page from *Truth or Lie: Dinosaurs!* (B). They will use the cutouts during Try It: Apply: Spelling List 8.

If students have removed My Speed Sort Times from the activity book, have them gather this activity page. They will use this activity page in Try It: Apply: Spelling List 8.

Lesson Goals

- Read about dinosaurs.
- Revise and proofread your Three Truths and a Lie.
- Use a dictionary to check spelling.
- Identify reasons for when and how to use certain spelling patterns.

GET READY

Introduction: Digging Into Dinosaurs (A)

Students will get a glimpse of what they will learn about in the lesson.

READ

Digging Into Dinosaurs (A)

Students will read nonfiction texts about dinosaurs.

NOTE The reading selections for this activity are located in the digital library, which is linked in the online lesson.

LEARN AND TRY IT

TRY IT   Revise Your Three Truths and a Lie

Students will revise their Three Truths and a Lie using Revise and Proofread Your Three Truths and a Lie in *English Language Arts 2 Activity Book 1*. They should use only the **revising checklist** found on the page.

They will need their draft from *Truth or Lie: Dinosaurs!* (C).

LEARNING COACH CHECK-IN Guide students through the revising process using the revising part of the Three Truths and a Lie: Feedback Sheet that you completed.

NOTE Have students put their revised draft into the folder they are using to store their writing assignment pages.

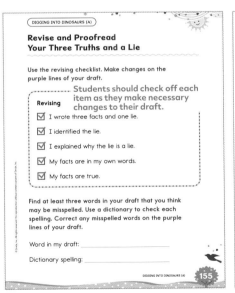
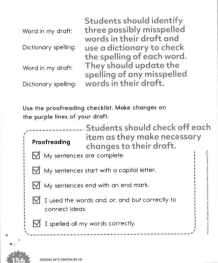

LEARN   Use a Dictionary to Check Spelling

Students will learn how to use a dictionary to check the spelling of a word.

TRY IT   Proofread Your Three Truths and a Lie

Students will proofread their Three Truths and a Lie using Revise and Proofread Your Three Truths and a Lie in *English Language Arts 2 Activity Book 1*. They should complete the **guided dictionary section** and then use the **proofreading checklist** found on the page.

They will need their revised draft from the Revise Your Three Truths and a Lie activity. They will also need a learner's dictionary.

LEARNING COACH CHECK-IN   Guide students through the proofreading process using the proofreading part of the Three Truths and a Lie: Feedback Sheet that you completed.

TIP   To find a learner's dictionary online, search "learner's dictionary."

OPTIONAL   Have students exchange drafts with a peer and use the checklists from the activity book to give each other feedback.

NOTE   Have students add their revised and edited draft to the folder they are using to store their short research assignment pages.

TRY IT   Apply: Spelling List 8

Students will apply what they have learned about the spelling patterns for Spelling List 8.

- In an online activity, students will complete a word sort and answer reflection questions.

- In *English Language Arts 2 Activity Book 1*, students will complete Apply: Spelling List 8.

NOTE   Students will need their cutouts from the Spelling List 8 activity page to complete the word sort.

TIP   Have students record their speed sort times on the My Speed Sort Times activity page, which is at the back of the activity book. It can be motivating for students to see their progress as their ability to complete speed sorts should improve over time.

SUPPORT   For the offline task, students may benefit from having the letters they will use to build words written on small pieces of paper. It will allow them to physically move the letters into place and test where letters can be placed to make new words.

LEARNING COACH CHECK-IN   As needed, help students read the activity page.

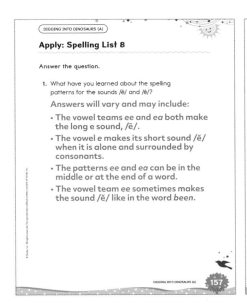

Apply: Spelling List 8

Answer the question.

1. What have you learned about the spelling patterns for the sounds /ĕ/ and /ē/?

   Answers will vary and may include:

   - The vowel teams *ee* and *ea* both make the long e sound, /ē/.
   - The vowel *e* makes its short sound /ĕ/ when it is alone and surrounded by consonants.
   - The patterns *ee* and *ea* can be in the middle or at the end of a word.
   - The vowel team *ee* sometimes makes the sound /ĕ/ like in the word *been*.

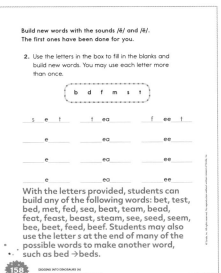

Build new words with the sounds /ĕ/ and /ē/. The first ones have been done for you.

2. Use the letters in the box to fill in the blanks and build new words. You may use each letter more than once.

   | b | d | f | m | s | t |

   s e t   t ea   f ee t

   _ e _   _ ea _   _ ee _

   _ e _   _ ea _   _ ee _

   _ e _   _ ea _   _ ee _

With the letters provided, students can build any of the following words: bet, test, bed, met, fed, sea, beat, team, bead, feat, feast, beast, steam, see, seed, seem, bee, beet, feed, beef. Students may also use the letter *s* at the end of many of the possible words to make another word, such as bed →beds.

WRAP-UP

Questions About Digging into Dinosaurs (A)

Students will answer questions to show that they understand the writing and spelling skills they learned in this lesson.

Digging Into Dinosaurs (B)

Lesson Overview

ACTIVITY	ACTIVITY TITLE	TIME	ONLINE/OFFLINE
GET READY	Introduction: Digging Into Dinosaurs (B)	**1** minute	🖥️
READ	Digging Into Dinosaurs (B)	**30** minutes	🖥️
ALL ABOUT ME	Brain Break	**1** minute	🖥️ or 📄
TRY IT	Publish Your Three Truths and a Lie **LEARNING COACH CHECK-IN**	**45** minutes	📄
ALL ABOUT ME	Brain Break	**1** minute	🖥️ or 📄
TRY IT	More Practice: Spelling List 8 **LEARNING COACH CHECK-IN**	**20** minutes	🖥️ and 📄
WRAP-UP	Question About Digging Into Dinosaurs (B)	**2** minutes	🖥️
	Read and Record	**20** minutes	🖥️
	More Language Arts Practice	**10** minutes	🖥️

Content Background

Students will focus on writing in this lesson.

Writing Skills Students will finish their **short research assignment**, Three Truths and a Lie.

Writing Process

1 Prewriting	2 Drafting	3 Revising	4 Proofreading	**5 Publishing**

Advance Preparation

Gather the folder that students are using to keep all activity pages related to their short research assignment.

- Model Three Truths and a Lie from *Truth or Lie: Dinosaurs!* (A)

- Students' completed My Animal Research activity page from *Truth or Lie: Dinosaurs!* (B)

- Students' revised and edited draft from Digging Into Dinosaurs (A)

MATERIALS

Supplied
- *English Language Arts 2 Activity Book 1*
  - Publish Your Three Truths and a Lie
  - More Practice: Spelling List 8
  - My Speed Sort Times
- Writing Paper (printout)

Also Needed
- folder in which students are storing short research assignment pages
- crayons or markers (optional)
- Spelling List 8 activity page cutouts from *Truth or Lie: Dinosaurs!* (B)

Gather students' cutouts from the Spelling List 8 activity page from *Truth or Lie: Dinosaurs!* (B). They will use the cutouts during Try It: More Practice: Spelling List 8.

If students have removed My Speed Sort Times from the activity book, have them gather this activity page. They will use this activity page in Try It: Apply: Spelling List 8.

Lesson Goals

- Read about dinosaurs.
- Publish your Three Truths and a Lie.
- Identify and write spelling patterns that stand for sounds within words.

GET READY

Introduction: Digging Into Dinosaurs (B)

Students will get a glimpse of what they will learn about in the lesson.

READ

Digging Into Dinosaurs (B)

Students will read nonfiction texts about dinosaurs.

NOTE The reading selections for this activity are located in the digital library, which is linked in the online lesson.

TRY IT

Publish Your Three Truths and a Lie

Students will complete Publish Your Three Truths and a Lie in *English Language Arts 2 Activity Book 1*. They should gather their draft and write a clean copy of their three truths and a lie that incorporates the changes they made during revising and proofreading.

NOTE Additional sheets of Writing Paper are available online.

NOTE Students will not turn in this assignment for grading.

NOTE Students may wish to use crayons or markers to draw a picture to go with their lie.

LEARNING COACH CHECK-IN As needed, help students read the activity page and ensure that they are using their revised and edited draft to create their final copy. Provide feedback on their final copy, focusing on their writing growth.

Publish Your Three Truths and a Lie

Write a clean copy of your three truths and a lie.
At the end, write the title and author of your
research source.

Title: Truth or Lie: _____ !

_____

_____

_____

_____

_____

_____

_____

_____

_____

_____

_____

_____

_____

_____

_____

_____

_____

_____

_____

_____

_____

_____

_____

_____

_____

_____

_____

My Research Source

Title: _____

Author: _____

(Optional) Draw a funny picture to go with your lie.

More Practice: Spelling List 8

Students will continue to practice the spelling patterns for Spelling List 8 to increase automatic recognition of the patterns.

- In an online activity, students will practice the spelling words and patterns.

- In *English Language Arts 2 Activity Book 1*, students will complete More Practice: Spelling List 8.

NOTE   Students will need their cutouts from the Spelling List 8 activity page to complete More Practice: Spelling List 8.

TIP   Have students record their speed sort times on the My Speed Sort Times activity page, which is at the back of the activity book. It can be motivating for students to see their progress as their ability to complete speed sorts should improve over time.

LEARNING COACH CHECK-IN   As needed, help students read the activity page.

WRAP-UP

Question About Digging Into Dinosaurs (B)
Students will answer a question to show that they understand the writing skills they learned in this lesson.

Read and Record
Good readers read quickly, smoothly, and with expression. This is called *fluency*. Students will record themselves reading aloud. They will listen to their recording and think about how quick, smooth, and expressive they sound.

TIP   Encourage students to rerecord as needed.

More Language Arts Practice
Students will practice skills according to their individual needs.

Dinosaurs Wrap-Up (A)

Lesson Overview

ACTIVITY	ACTIVITY TITLE	TIME	ONLINE/OFFLINE
GET READY	Introduction: Dinosaurs Wrap-Up (A)	**1** minute	🖥️
QUIZ	Spelling List 8	**25** minutes	🖥️
ALL ABOUT ME	Brain Break	**1** minute	🖥️ or 📄
REVIEW	Dinosaurs	**25** minutes	🖥️
ALL ABOUT ME	Brain Break	**1** minute	🖥️ or 📄
WRAP-UP	Theme Time: Dinosaurs **LEARNING COACH CHECK-IN**	**47** minutes	📄
	Your Choice Time	**10** minutes	🖥️ or 📄

Advance Preparation

During the Your Choice Time activity, students will be given the option to read something of their choice. If students are using the digital library, allow extra time for them to make their reading selection, or have them make a selection before beginning the lesson.

Lesson Goals

- Take a spelling quiz.
- Review vocabulary, writing, and reading skills from the unit.
- Make connections among the texts in the unit.

GET READY

Introduction: Dinosaurs Wrap-Up (A)

Students will get a glimpse of what they will do in the lesson.

QUIZ

Spelling List 8

Students will complete the Spelling List 8 quiz.

REVIEW

Dinosaurs

Students will answer questions to review the vocabulary, writing, and reading skills they learned in the unit.

WRAP-UP

Theme Time: Dinosaurs

Students will complete Theme Time: Dinosaurs in *English Language Arts 2 Activity Book 1*.

NOTE This activity page includes an optional ungraded project. Students may need additional materials to complete the project.

LEARNING COACH CHECK-IN As needed, help students read the activity page. Discuss students' responses.

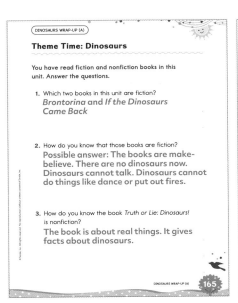

Your Choice Time

Students will choose among the following activities:

- Independent reading

- Independent writing

- Completing the optional project from the Theme Time: Dinosaurs activity page

Dinosaurs Wrap-Up (B)

Lesson Overview

ACTIVITY	ACTIVITY TITLE	TIME	ONLINE/OFFLINE
GET READY	Introduction: Dinosaurs Wrap-Up (B)	**1** minute	🖥️
QUIZ	Dinosaurs	**33** minutes	🖥️
ALL ABOUT ME	Brain Break	**1** minute	🖥️ or 📄
REFLECTION	Go Write! and Set a Goal **LEARNING COACH CHECK-IN**	**30** minutes	📄
WRAP-UP	Celebrate: Dinosaurs	**20** minutes	📄
	Discussion: Share Your Research **LEARNING COACH CHECK-IN**	**15** minutes	🖥️
	More Language Arts Practice	**10** minutes	🖥️
	Your Choice Time	**10** minutes	🖥️ or 📄

Advance Preparation

If students have removed the My Reading Log and My Badge Book activity pages from the activity book, have them gather these activity pages. They will use these activity pages in the Celebrate: Dinosaurs activity.

Gather students' completed Publish Your Three Truths and a Lie activity page from Digging Into Dinosaurs (B). Students will use this activity page in the Discussion: Share Your Research activity.

During the Your Choice Time activity, students will be given the option to read something of their choice. If students are using the digital library, allow extra time for them to make their reading selection, or have them make a selection before beginning the lesson.

MATERIALS

Supplied
- *English Language Arts 2 Activity Book 1*
  - Go Write! and Set a Goal
  - My Reading Log
  - My Badge Book

Also Needed
- crayons or markers
- students' completed Publish Your Three Truths and a Lie activity page from Digging Into Dinosaurs (B)
- reading material for Your Choice Time (optional)

Lesson Goals

- Take a quiz on the writing, vocabulary, and reading skills from the unit.
- Freewrite to develop fluency and reflect on learning.
- Set a goal for future learning.
- Celebrate accomplishments from the unit.
- Participate in a discussion.

GET READY

Introduction: Dinosaurs Wrap-Up (B)

Students will get a glimpse of what they will do in the lesson.

QUIZ

Dinosaurs

Students will complete the Dinosaurs quiz.

REFLECTION

Go Write! and Set a Goal

Students will complete Go Write! and Set a Goal in *English Language Arts 2 Activity Book 1*.

NOTE   The Go Write! activity is intended to build writing fluency. Students should write for 10 minutes.

LEARNING COACH CHECK-IN   As needed, help students read the activity page. Discuss their goal, including any steps they can take as well as support you can provide in helping them meet it.

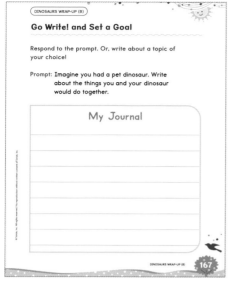

WRAP-UP

Celebrate: Dinosaurs

Students will celebrate accomplishments from the unit.

- They will record what they read this unit in their reading log.

- They will color the badge for this unit in their badge book. They may also color a badge to celebrate reading accomplishments.

NOTE My Reading Log and My Badge Book are located at the back of the activity book.

NOTE Students will need crayons or markers to color in their badges.

Discussion: Share Your Research

Students will respond to a discussion prompt. They will need their completed short research assignment, Three Truths and a Lie.

LEARNING COACH CHECK-IN Students should discuss the questions shown on-screen with an adult. In some cases, teachers may facilitate a group discussion.

More Language Arts Practice

Students will practice skills according to their individual needs.

Your Choice Time

Students will choose among the following activities:

- Independent reading

- Independent writing

- Completing the optional project from the Theme Time: Dinosaurs activity page

Insects

"The Life of a Butterfly" (A)

Lesson Overview

ACTIVITY	ACTIVITY TITLE	TIME	ONLINE/OFFLINE
GET READY	Introduction: "The Life of a Butterfly" (A)	**1** minute	🖥️
	Think About Reading: "The Life of a Butterfly" (A)	**5** minutes	📄
	Words to Know: "The Life of a Butterfly" (A)	**10** minutes	🖥️
ALL ABOUT ME	Brain Break	**1** minute	🖥️ or 📄
READ	"The Life of a Butterfly" (A)	**25** minutes	🖥️ or 📄
	Reflect: "The Life of a Butterfly" (A)	**10** minutes	📄
LEARN	Identify a Topic and a Main Idea	**20** minutes	🖥️
ALL ABOUT ME	Brain Break	**1** minute	🖥️ or 📄
LEARN	Spelling List 9	**25** minutes	🖥️ and 📄
WRAP-UP	Questions About "The Life of a Butterfly" (A)	**2** minutes	🖥️
	Handwriting	**10** minutes	📄
	Go Read!	**10** minutes	🖥️ or 📄

Content Background

Students will begin a series of lessons centered around the article "The Life of a Butterfly" from the magazine *K12 World: Invaluable Insects*. In this lesson, they will learn to identify a topic and main ideas.

Vocabulary   Students will explore these words from the article: *creature*, *female*, and *cycle*. These are the definitions of the words as used in "The Life of a Butterfly":

- **creature** (noun) – an animal

- **female** (adjective) – having to do with an animal that can lay eggs or birth newborn animals

- **cycle** (noun) – steps or events that happen over and over in the same way or order

Reading   The **topic** of an informational text is what the text is mainly about. The **main idea** supports the topic and provides more information about the topic. There is one topic in a text, but there is usually more than one main idea.

Spelling   In this lesson, students will learn the following symbols and spelling patterns:

- The long o sound, /ō/, is the sound of the letter o in the word *bone*.

- The vowel-consonant-e (VCe) pattern comes at the end of a word and ends with a silent e, as in the word *nose*. Students will learn that the silent e in the VCe pattern signals that the vowel o has its long o sound, /ō/.

- The vowel team *oa* has two letters that make one vowel sound, the long o sound, /ō/, which is the vowel sound in the word *load*.

- The vowel team *ow* has two letters that make one vowel sound, the long o sound, /ō/, which is the vowel sound in the word *grow*.

Students will sort words into groups. For a word to fit into a group, it must match both the target sound and the spelling pattern.

- Words in which the VCe spelling pattern makes the sound /ō/ will go under the heading **oCe bone**.

- Words in which the vowel team *oa* makes the sound /ō/ will go under the heading **oa coat**.

- Words in which the vowel team *ow* makes the sound /ō/ will go under the heading **ow snow**.

- The words *goes* and *move* go under the heading **oddball**. The word *goes* has the long o sound but not a typical long o spelling pattern. The word *move* has the VCe spelling pattern but not the long o sound.

Advance Preparation

During the Go Read! activity, students will have the option of using the digital library. Allow extra time for students to make their reading selection, or have students make a selection before beginning the lesson.

"The Life of a Butterfly" Synopsis

This article explains the life cycle of a butterfly. It emphasizes how the butterfly changes as it develops from an egg, to a larva, to a pupa in a chrysalis, and finally into a butterfly. Female butterflies lay eggs on plants. A caterpillar, or larva, hatches from each egg. The caterpillar grows and sheds its skin until it becomes a chrysalis. The pupa inside the chrysalis forms wings and emerges as a butterfly.

MATERIALS

Supplied
- *K12 World: Invaluable Insects*
  - "The Life of a Butterfly"
- *English Language Arts 2 Activity Book 1*
  - Think About Reading: "The Life of a Butterfly" (A)
  - Reflect: "The Life of a Butterfly" (A)
  - Spelling List 9
- handwriting workbook

Also Needed
- crayons or markers (optional)
- scissors
- envelope or baggie to store spelling cutouts
- reading material for Go Read!

KEYWORDS

inference – a guess you make using the clues in a text and what you already know

main idea – the most important idea in a paragraph or text

topic – the subject of a text

Lesson Goals

- Learn new vocabulary.

- Read "The Life of a Butterfly."

- Identify the topic and the main idea of a text.

- Sort words by sound and spelling pattern.

- Develop letter formation fluency.

- Read independently to develop fluency.

GET READY

Introduction: "The Life of a Butterfly" (A)

Students will get a glimpse of what they will learn about in the lesson.

Think About Reading: "The Life of a Butterfly" (A)

Students will complete Think About Reading: "The Life of a Butterfly" (A) in *English Language Arts 2 Activity Book 1*.

NOTE Students may wish to use crayons or markers to draw their picture.

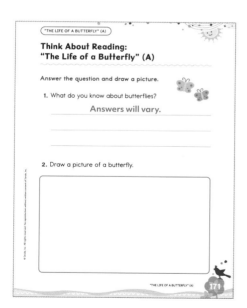

Words to Know: "The Life of a Butterfly" (A)

Students will preview and answer questions about three vocabulary words from the reading selection.

"The Life of a Butterfly" (A)

Students will read "The Life of a Butterfly" in *K12 World: Invaluable Insects*. Encourage them to reread their favorite passages.

Reflect: "The Life of a Butterfly" (A)

Students will complete Reflect: "The Life of a Butterfly" (A) in *English Language Arts 2 Activity Book 1*. They will make an inference.

TIP Students may require help in making an inference. An inference is something that is implied but not actually stated in the text. Guide them through the concept of *reading between the lines*.

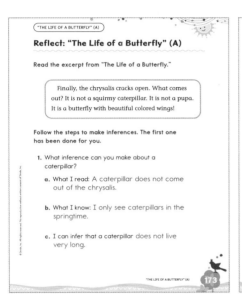

LEARN

Identify a Topic and a Main Idea

Students will learn how to identify the topic of an informational text. They will learn how to find the main idea of a paragraph and how it differs from the topic of the article. They will also learn how the main idea supports the topic by adding additional information.

Spelling List 9

Students will learn and sort words with the sound and spelling patterns for long o.

- In an online activity, students will learn about the spelling patterns and the sounds they represent. They will learn how to sort words according to those sounds and patterns. They will also complete a word sort.

- In *English Language Arts 2 Activity Book 1*, students will complete Spelling List 9.

NOTE Students will need scissors to cut out the spelling words on the activity page. Have students store their cutouts in a safe place, such as an envelope.

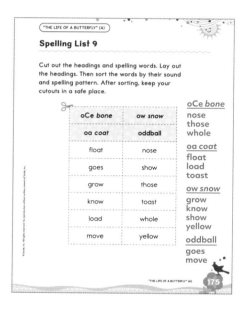

This is the complete list of words students will work with to learn the spelling patterns for the sound of long o.

oCe *bone*	oa *coat*	ow *snow*	oddball
nose	float	grow	goes
those	load	know	move
whole	toast	show	
		yellow	

Questions About "The Life of a Butterfly" (A)

Students will answer questions to show that they understand the reading and spelling skills they learned in this lesson.

Handwriting

Students should gather their handwriting materials and begin where they left off. Remind students to form letters carefully and correctly.

NOTE Set a timer to help students stay focused during handwriting practice.

Go Read!

Students will read for pleasure. They should choose a book or a magazine that interests them, or they may choose a selection from the digital library, linked in the online lesson.

- Have students read aloud a few paragraphs of their selection.

- Then have students read silently for the rest of the time.

SUPPORT Students should make no more than five errors in decoding when they read aloud a few paragraphs of their Go Read! selection. If students struggle or make more than five errors, they need to select a different (and easier) text for the Go Read! activity.

TIP Have students select something to read ahead of time to help them stay focused.

"The Life of a Butterfly" (B)

Lesson Overview

ACTIVITY	ACTIVITY TITLE	TIME	ONLINE/OFFLINE
GET READY	Introduction: "The Life of a Butterfly" (B)	**1** minute	🖥️
	Compound Words	**10** minutes	🖥️
	Words to Know: "The Life of a Butterfly" (B)	**10** minutes	🖥️
ALL ABOUT ME	Brain Break	**1** minute	🖥️ or 📄
LEARN AND **TRY IT**	Key Details	**20** minutes	🖥️
	It's All in the Details **LEARNING COACH CHECK-IN**	**25** minutes	📄
ALL ABOUT ME	Brain Break	**1** minute	🖥️ or 📄
TRY IT	Practice: Spelling List 9	**20** minutes	🖥️ and 📄
WRAP-UP	Questions About "The Life of a Butterfly" (B)	**2** minutes	🖥️
	More Language Arts Practice	**10** minutes	🖥️
	Handwriting	**10** minutes	📄
	Go Read!	**10** minutes	🖥️ or 📄

Content Background

Students will continue a series of lessons centered around the article "The Life of a Butterfly" from the magazine *K12 World: Invaluable Insects*. In this lesson, they will learn about key details and compound words.

Vocabulary   Students will explore these words from the article: *settle*, *firm*, and *energy*. These definitions of the words are used in "The Life of a Butterfly":

- **settle** (verb) – stop moving and stay still on something

- **firm** (adjective) – hard or stiff

- **energy** (noun) – strength to do something with your body or mind

Reading   The key **details** in an informational text support the main idea. They provide additional information about the main idea. **Text features** help readers identify key details. These features include headings, captions, and bold print.

Advance Preparation

Gather students' cutouts from the Spelling List 9 activity page from "The Life of a Butterfly" (A). They will use the cutouts during Try It: Practice: Spelling List 9.

During the Go Read! activity, students will have the option of using the digital library. Allow extra time for students to make their reading selection, or have students make a selection before beginning the lesson.

Lesson Goals

- Use structural analysis, spelling, and word meanings to identify and define compound words.
- Learn new vocabulary.
- Identify key details and use text features to locate key facts.
- Identify and write spelling patterns that stand for sounds within words.
- Read independently to develop fluency.
- Develop letter formation fluency.

GET READY

Introduction: "The Life of a Butterfly" (B)
Students will get a glimpse of what they will learn about in the lesson.

Compound Words
Students will identify and define compound words with the help of text features and by using structural analysis, spelling, and word meanings.

Words to Know: "The Life of a Butterfly" (B)
Students will preview and answer questions about three vocabulary words from the reading selection.

LEARN AND TRY IT

LEARN   Key Details
Students will identify key details and learn how they support the main idea. They will learn how text features can help them identify key details.

MATERIALS

Supplied
- *K12 World: Invaluable Insects*
  - "The Life of a Butterfly"
- *English Language Arts 2 Activity Book 1*
  - It's All in the Details
  - Practice: Spelling List 9
- handwriting workbook

Also Needed
- Spelling List 9 activity page cutouts from "The Life of a Butterfly" (A)
- reading material for Go Read!

KEYWORDS

bold type – type that is darker than the surrounding text that draws attention to a word or phrase

caption – writing under a picture that describes the picture

compound word – a word made from two smaller words

detail – a fact or description that tells more about a topic

heading – a title within the body of a text that tells the reader something important about a section of the text

text feature – part of a text that helps a reader locate information and determine what is most important; some examples are the title, table of contents, headings, pictures, and glossary

TRY IT   It's All in the Details

Students will complete It's All in the Details in *English Language Arts 2 Activity Book 1*.

LEARNING COACH CHECK-IN Have students read their paragraph aloud to you. Work together to identify the main idea and key details. Have students explain why something is a main idea or detail.

SUPPORT If students are struggling to get started, have them describe their paragraph aloud before writing it. Students may also benefit from working together with you to create a rough outline.

TRY IT   Practice: Spelling List 9

Students will practice the spelling patterns for Spelling List 9.

• In *English Language Arts 2 Activity Book 1*, students will complete Practice: Spelling List 9.

• Online, students will answer questions that require them to reflect on the spelling patterns.

NOTE Students will need their cutouts from the Spelling List 9 activity page to complete the Practice: Spelling List 9.

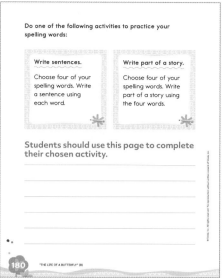

WRAP-UP

Questions About "The Life of a Butterfly" (B)

Students will answer questions to show that they understand the reading and spelling skills they learned in this lesson.

More Language Arts Practice

Students will practice skills according to their individual needs.

Handwriting

Students should gather their handwriting materials and begin where they left off. Remind students to form letters carefully and correctly.

TIP   Set a timer to help students stay focused during handwriting practice.

Go Read!

Students will read for pleasure. They should choose a book or a magazine that interests them, or they may choose a selection from the digital library, linked in the online lesson.

- Have students read aloud a few paragraphs of their selection.

- Then have students read silently for the rest of the time.

SUPPORT   Students should make no more than five errors in decoding when they read aloud a few paragraphs of their Go Read! selection. If students struggle or make more than five errors, they need to select a different (and easier) text for the Go Read! activity.

TIP   Have students select something to read ahead of time to help them stay focused.

"The Life of a Butterfly" (C)

Lesson Overview

ACTIVITY	ACTIVITY TITLE	TIME	ONLINE/OFFLINE
GET READY	Introduction: "The Life of a Butterfly" (C)	**1** minute	🖥
	More Compound Words	**10** minutes	🖥
	Words to Know: "The Life of a Butterfly" (C)	**10** minutes	🖥
LEARN AND **TRY IT**	Sequence of Events	**20** minutes	🖥
	Life Cycle of a Butterfly	**10** minutes	🖥
ALL ABOUT ME	Brain Break	**1** minute	🖥 or 📄
LEARN AND **TRY IT**	Reflexive Pronouns	**10** minutes	🖥
	Use a Reflexive Pronoun LEARNING COACH CHECK-IN	**15** minutes	📄
ALL ABOUT ME	Brain Break	**1** minute	🖥 or 📄
TRY IT	Apply: Spelling List 9	**20** minutes	🖥 and 📄
WRAP-UP	Questions About "The Life of a Butterfly" (C)	**2** minutes	🖥
	Read and Record	**10** minutes	🖥
	Handwriting	**10** minutes	📄

Content Background

Students will conclude a series of lessons centered around the article "The Life of a Butterfly" from the magazine *K12 World: Invaluable Insects*. In this lesson, they will learn how to sequence events and how to use reflexive pronouns.

Reading **Sequence** is another word for *order*. To sequence steps, you can number them or use **order words**, also called *signal words*, such as *first* and *next*. Sequencing is one way that authors organize information in a text.

Writing Skills A **pronoun** is a word that takes the place of one or more nouns in a sentence. A **reflexive pronoun** ends in *–self* or *–selves* and refers back to another noun or pronoun in the sentence.

Point of View	Singular Pronoun	Plural Pronoun
first person	myself	ourselves
second person	yourself	yourselves
third person	himself, herself, itself	themselves

Advance Preparation

Gather students' cutouts from the Spelling List 9 activity page from "The Life of a Butterfly" (A). They will use the cutouts during Try It: Apply: Spelling List 9.

If students have removed My Speed Sort Times from the activity book, have them gather this activity page. They will use this activity page in Try It: Apply: Spelling List 9.

Lesson Goals

- Define and create compound words.
- Review new vocabulary.
- Learn how to sequence events.
- Use reflexive pronouns.
- Identify reasons for when and how to use certain spelling patterns.
- Read aloud to practice fluency.
- Develop letter formation fluency.

MATERIALS

Supplied
- *K12 World: Invaluable Insects*
  - "The Life of a Butterfly"
- *English Language Arts 2 Activity Book 1*
  - Use a Reflective Pronoun
  - Apply: Spelling List 9
  - My Speed Sort Times
- handwriting workbook

Also Needed
- Spelling List 9 activity page cutouts from "The Life of a Butterfly" (A)

KEYWORDS

order word – words that connect ideas, a series of steps, or create a sequence Examples: *first, next, later, finally*

reflexive pronoun – a pronoun that refers back to another noun or pronoun in a sentence Examples: *myself, yourselves*

sequence – the order in which things happen

GET READY

Introduction: "The Life of a Butterfly" (C)

Students will get a glimpse of what they will learn about in the lesson.

More Compound Words

Students will create compound words by combining two smaller words. They will also spell compound words.

Words to Know: "The Life of a Butterfly" (C)

Students will answer questions about the vocabulary words from the reading selection as a review.

LEARN   Sequence of Events

Students will learn what a sequence of events is and why it is important to do things in a particular order. They will learn to sequence events by numbering the steps or using order or signal words. They will learn that authors use sequencing to organize the information in the text.

TRY IT   Life Cycle of a Butterfly

Students will put the events in the life cycle of a butterfly into the correct order.

LEARN   Reflexive Pronouns

Through guided exploration of sentences from "The Life of a Butterfly," students will learn how to use reflexive pronouns.

SUPPORT   Guide students to notice that reflexive pronouns that end in *–self* are singular and reflexive pronouns that end in *–selves* are plural.

TRY IT   Use a Reflexive Pronoun

Students will complete Use a Reflexive Pronoun in *English Language Arts 2 Activity Book 1*.

TIP   Have students explain their answers aloud: "I knew to use *themselves* because...."

LEARNING COACH CHECK-IN   Discuss the meaning of the pronoun *yourselves*, a reflexive pronoun used when speaking to two or more people, before students answer Question 7.

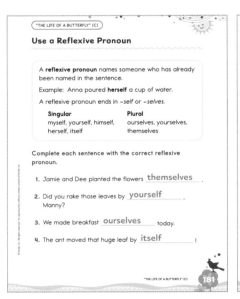

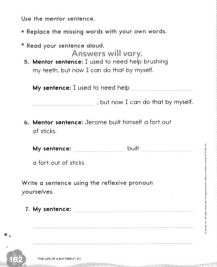

TRY IT   Apply: Spelling List 9

Students will apply what they have learned about the spelling patterns for Spelling List 9.

- In an online activity, students will complete a word sort and answer reflection questions.

- In *English Language Arts 2 Activity Book 1*, students will complete the Apply: Spelling List 9.

NOTE   Students will need their cutouts from the Spelling List 9 activity page to complete Apply: Spelling List 9.

TIP   Have students record their speed sort times on the My Speed Sort Times activity page, which is located at the back of the activity book. It can be motivating for students to see their progress as their ability to complete speed sorts should improve over time.

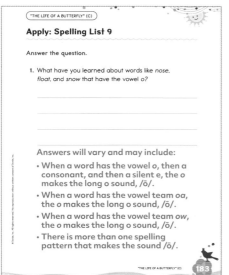

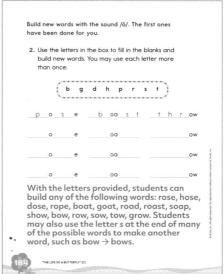

WRAP-UP

Questions About "The Life of a Butterfly" (C)

Students will answer questions to show that they understand the reading, writing, and spelling skills they learned in this lesson.

Read and Record

Good readers read quickly, smoothly, and with expression. This is called *fluency*. Students will record themselves reading aloud. They will listen to their recording and think about how quick, smooth, and expressive they sound.

TIP   Encourage students to rerecord as needed.

Handwriting

Students should gather their handwriting materials and begin where they left off. Remind students to form letters carefully and correctly.

TIP   Set a timer to help students stay focused during handwriting practice.

Praying Mantis (A)

Lesson Overview

ACTIVITY	ACTIVITY TITLE	TIME	ONLINE/OFFLINE
GET READY	Introduction: *Praying Mantis* (A)	**1** minute	🖥️
	Think About Reading: *Praying Mantis* (A)	**5** minutes	📄
	Words to Know: *Praying Mantis* (A)	**8** minutes	🖥️
READ	*Praying Mantis* (A)	**17** minutes	🖥️
	Reflect: *Praying Mantis* (A)	**5** minutes	📄
LEARN AND TRY IT	Answering Questions	**10** minutes	🖥️
	I Know That!	**5** minutes	🖥️
ALL ABOUT ME	Brain Break	**1** minute	🖥️ or 📄
LEARN AND TRY IT	Can We Agree?	**10** minutes	🖥️
	Make the Subject and Verb Agree **LEARNING COACH CHECK-IN**	**15** minutes	📄
ALL ABOUT ME	Brain Break	**1** minute	🖥️ or 📄
TRY IT	More Practice: Spelling List 9	**20** minutes	🖥️ and 📄
WRAP-UP	Questions About *Praying Mantis* (A)	**2** minutes	🖥️
	Handwriting	**10** minutes	📄
	Go Read!	**10** minutes	🖥️ or 📄

Content Background

Students will begin a series of lessons centered around the book *Praying Mantis* by Tamra B. Orr. In this lesson, they will answer questions about the text, use synonyms and antonyms, and explore subject-verb agreement.

Vocabulary   Students will explore these words from the book: *predator*, *prey*, *capture*, *escape*, *usual*, and *unusual*. These are the definitions of the words as used in *Praying Mantis*:

- **predator** (noun) – an animal that hunts and kills other animals

- **prey** (noun) – anything that is hunted

- **capture** (verb) – to catch someone or something

- **escape** (verb) – to get away or run off

- **usual** (adjective) – normal or typical

- **unusual** (adjective) – different or special

Antonyms are words with opposite meanings. The word pairs *predator* and *prey*, *capture* and *escape*, and *usual* and *unusual* are antonyms. **Synonyms** are words with similar meanings. For example, *catch* and *capture* are synonyms.

Reading   Answering questions that begin with the words *what*, *where*, *when*, *why*, and *how* supports reading comprehension.

Writing Skills   A subject and verb must **agree**. A singular subject agrees with a singular verb. A plural subject agrees with a plural verb.

Examples: A raindrop falls from the sky.

Raindrops fall from the sky.

The pronouns *I* and *you* agree with plural verbs.

Example: You say the most thoughtful things!

Other words in the sentence don't affect subject-verb agreement. In this example, the plural subject *birds* agrees with the plural verb *sing*.

Example: The birds in that nest sing very loudly!

Note that there are other rules related to subject-verb agreement that will not be covered in this course.

Advance Preparation

Gather students' cutouts from the Spelling List 9 activity page from "The Life of a Butterfly" (A). They will use the cutouts during Try It: More Practice: Spelling List 9.

If students have removed My Speed Sort Times from the activity book, have them gather this activity page. They will use this activity page in Try It: More Practice: Spelling List 9.

During the Go Read! activity, students will have the option of using the digital library. Allow extra time for students to make their reading selection, or have students make a selection before beginning the lesson.

Supplied
- *Praying Mantis* by Tamra B. Orr (in digital library; link is in online lesson)
- *English Language Arts 2 Activity Book 1*
  - Think About Reading: *Praying Mantis* (A)
  - Reflect: *Praying Mantis* (A)
  - Make the Subject and Verb Agree
  - More Practice: Spelling List 9
  - My Speed Sort Times
- handwriting workbook

Also Needed
- crayons or markers (optional)
- Spelling List 9 activity page cutouts from "The Life of a Butterfly" (A)
- reading material for Go Read!

KEYWORDS

antonym – a word that means the opposite of another word

subject-verb agreement – the way a subject and verb match when both are singular or both are plural Examples: The hawk glides, and the eagles soar.

synonym – a word that means the same, or almost the same, as another word

Praying Mantis Synopsis

The book *Praying Mantis* explains why the praying mantis is such an unusual creature. The insect's front legs are bent as if it is praying. The legs have spikes that allow the mantis to hold its prey so it cannot escape. A mantis is the color of leaves and grass so that it can hide from predators and sneak up on prey. A mantis can cover its victims with a foul-smelling liquid that immobilizes and kills them. Females lay up to 400 eggs on twigs or stem. They cover their eggs with an ootheca, which protects the eggs from enemies and cold weather.

Lesson Goals

- Learn new vocabulary, and explore synonyms and antonyms.
- Read *Praying Mantis*.
- Answer questions that ask *what*, *where*, *when*, *why*, and *how*.
- Use subject-verb agreement.
- Identify and write spelling patterns that stand for sounds within words.
- Develop letter formation fluency.
- Read independently to develop fluency.

GET READY

Introduction: *Praying Mantis* (A)
Students will get a glimpse of what they will learn about in the lesson.

Think About Reading: *Praying Mantis* (A)
Students will complete Think About Reading: *Praying Mantis* (A) in *English Language Arts 2 Activity Book 1*.

NOTE   Students may wish to use crayons or markers to draw their picture.

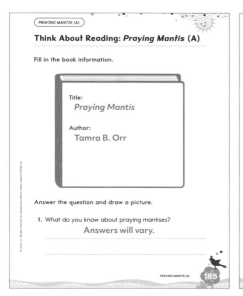

Words to Know: *Praying Mantis* (A)

Students will preview and answer questions about six vocabulary words from the reading selection. They also will explore synonyms and antonyms of the words.

READ

Praying Mantis (A)

Students will read *Praying Mantis* by Tamra B. Orr.

NOTE   The reading selection for this activity is located in the digital library, which is linked in the online lesson.

Reflect: *Praying Mantis* (A)

Students will complete Reflect: *Praying Mantis* (A) in *English Language Arts 2 Activity Book 1*.

TIP   Students may require help in making an inference. An inference is something that is implied but not actually stated in the text. Guide them through the concept of *reading between the lines*.

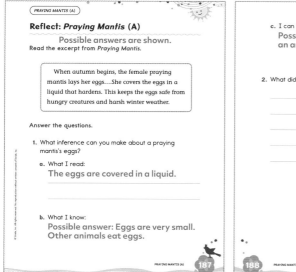

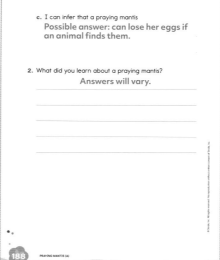

LEARN AND TRY IT

LEARN Answering Questions

Students will learn to use details from *Praying Mantis* to answer questions that ask *what*, *where*, *when*, *why*, and *how*. They will use the text and the pictures to help them answer reading comprehension questions.

TRY IT I Know That!

Students will answer questions that ask *what*, *why*, and *how*.

LEARN Can We Agree?

Through guided exploration of sentences from *Praying Mantis*, students will explore subject-verb agreement.

TIP Discuss the meaning of the word *agree*. How is the everyday meaning like the meaning we use to talk about subjects and verbs?

NOTE This activity uses regular verbs in the simple present tense only.

TRY IT Make the Subject and Verb Agree

Students will complete Make the Subject and Verb Agree in *English Language Arts 2 Activity Book 1*.

LEARNING COACH CHECK-IN It may be helpful for students to answer Questions 5 and 6 aloud before writing their responses.

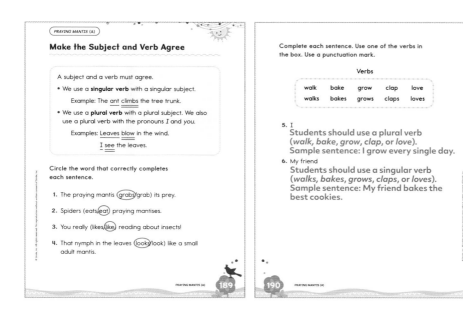

TRY IT   More Practice: Spelling List 9

Students will continue to practice the spelling patterns for Spelling List 9 to increase automatic recognition of the patterns.

- In an online activity, students will practice the spelling words and patterns.

- In *English Language Arts 2 Activity Book 1*, students will complete More Practice: Spelling List 9.

NOTE   Students will need their cutouts from the Spelling List 9 activity page to complete More Practice: Spelling List 9.

TIP   Have students record their speed sort times on the My Speed Sort Times activity page, which is located at the back of the activity book. It can be motivating for students to see their progress as their ability to complete speed sorts should improve over time.

Questions About *Praying Mantis* (A)

Students will answer questions to show that they understand the reading and writing skills they learned in this lesson.

Handwriting

Students should gather their handwriting materials and begin where they left off. Remind students to form letters carefully and correctly.

TIP   Set a timer to help students stay focused during handwriting practice.

Go Read!

Students will read for pleasure. They should choose a book or a magazine that interests them, or they may choose a selection from the digital library, linked in the online lesson.

- Have students read aloud a few paragraphs of their selection.

- Then have students read silently for the rest of the time.

SUPPORT   Students should make no more than five errors in decoding when they read aloud a few paragraphs of their Go Read! selection. If students struggle or make more than five errors, they need to select a different (and easier) text for the Go Read! activity.

TIP   Have students select something to read ahead of time to help them stay focused.

Praying Mantis (B)

Lesson Overview

ACTIVITY	ACTIVITY TITLE	TIME	ONLINE/OFFLINE
GET READY	Introduction: *Praying Mantis* (B)	**1** minute	🖥️
	Homonyms	**10** minutes	🖥️
	Words to Know: *Praying Mantis* (B)	**5** minutes	🖥️
READ	*Praying Mantis* (B)	**15** minutes	🖥️
ALL ABOUT ME	Brain Break	**1** minute	🖥️ or 📄
LEARN AND **TRY IT**	Asking Questions	**20** minutes	🖥️
	Any Questions?	**10** minutes	📄
	Write and Rearrange Sentences	**10** minutes	🖥️
WRAP-UP	Questions About *Praying Mantis* (B)	**2** minutes	🖥️
ALL ABOUT ME	Brain Break	**1** minute	🖥️ or 📄
QUIZ	Spelling List 9	**25** minutes	🖥️
WRAP-UP	Read and Record	**10** minutes	🖥️
	Handwriting	**10** minutes	📄

Content Background

Students will conclude a series of lessons centered around the book *Praying Mantis* by Tamra B. Orr. In this lesson, they will learn how to ask questions about the text, identify homonyms, and write and rearrange sentences based on mentor sentences.

Reading   Asking questions about a text is an important comprehension skill that requires practice. There are many types of relevant questions; this lesson focuses on questions intended to clarify meaning.

MATERIALS

Supplied
- *Praying Mantis* by Tamra B. Orr (in digital library; link is in online lesson)
- *English Language Arts 2 Activity Book 1*
  - Any Questions?
- handwriting workbook

Lesson Goals

- Identify and use homonyms.
- Use new vocabulary.
- Reread *Praying Mantis.*
- Ask questions about a text.
- Rearrange and write sentences.
- Take a spelling quiz.
- Read aloud to practice fluency.
- Develop letter formation fluency.

GET READY

Introduction: *Praying Mantis* (B)

Students will get a glimpse of what they will learn about in the lesson.

Homonyms

Student will identify and use homonyms, including homophones and homographs.

Words to Know: *Praying Mantis* (B)

Students will review and answer questions about vocabulary words from the reading selection.

READ

Praying Mantis (B)

Students will reread *Praying Mantis* by Tamra B. Orr.

NOTE The reading selection for this activity is located in the digital library, which is linked in the online lesson.

LEARN AND TRY IT

LEARN   Asking Questions

Students will learn the importance of asking relevant questions about the text as they read. They will learn to distinguish between asking important questions and asking irrelevant questions. Students will demonstrate that they can ask questions to clarify the meaning of the text.

TRY IT   Any Questions?

Students will complete Any Questions? in *English Language Arts 2 Activity Book 1*.

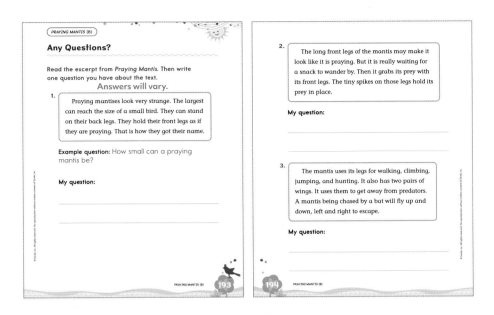

TRY IT   Write and Rearrange Sentences

Students will practice writing and rearranging simple and compound sentences.

WRAP-UP

Questions About *Praying Mantis* (B)

Students will answer questions to show that they understand the reading and writing skills they learned in this lesson.

QUIZ

Spelling List 9

Students will take the Spelling List 9 quiz.

Read and Record

Good readers read quickly, smoothly, and with expression. This is called *fluency*. Students will record themselves reading aloud. They will listen to their recording and think about how quick, smooth, and expressive they sound.

TIP Encourage students to rerecord as needed.

Handwriting

Students should gather their handwriting materials and begin where they left off. Remind students to form letters carefully and correctly.

TIP Set a timer to help students stay focused during handwriting practice.

"Honey from the Hive" (A)

Lesson Overview

ACTIVITY	ACTIVITY TITLE	TIME	ONLINE/OFFLINE
GET READY	Introduction: "Honey from the Hive" (A)	**1** minute	🖥️
READ	Think About Reading: "Honey from the Hive" (A)	**5** minutes	📄
	"Honey from the Hive" (A)	**14** minutes	🖥️ or 📄
	Check-In: "Honey from the Hive" (A)	**5** minutes	🖥️
	Reflect: "Honey from the Hive" (A)	**5** minutes	📄
LEARN	Follow the Steps	**15** minutes	🖥️
ALL ABOUT ME	Brain Break	**1** minute	🖥️ or 📄
LEARN AND TRY IT	Spoken Directions	**8** minutes	🖥️
	Draw a Cartoon Bee **LEARNING COACH CHECK-IN**	**18** minutes	🖥️ and 📄
ALL ABOUT ME	Brain Break	**1** minute	🖥️ or 📄
LEARN	Spelling List 10	**25** minutes	🖥️ and 📄
WRAP-UP	Questions About "Honey from the Hive" (A)	**2** minutes	🖥️
	Handwriting	**10** minutes	📄
	Go Read!	**10** minutes	🖥️ or 📄

Content Background

Students will begin a series of lessons centered around the article "Honey from the Hive" from the magazine *K12 Word: Invaluable Insects*. In this lesson, they will learn how to identify the steps in a sequence; how to use order words; and how to give, restate, and follow oral directions.

Reading It is important to complete steps in a sequence; thus, authors use order words such as *first*, *next*, and *last* to connect steps in writing. By recognizing order words, students can better comprehend and follow sequences.

Speaking and Listening   Clear spoken directions share many of the same qualities as clear written directions. The speaker says the steps in order, uses order words, and gives enough detail about each step. Restating, or repeating back directions in one's own words, is an active listening strategy that students can use to make sure they understand oral directions.

Spelling   In this lesson, students will learn the following symbols and spelling patterns for the sound long double o. It is called long double o because it is the sound that two o's make together, like in the word *moon*:

- The vowel u-consonant-silent e (uCe) pattern ends with a silent e, as in the word *tube*. The silent e signals that the letter *u* makes a long sound, the sound /$\overline{oo}$/.

- The vowel team *ew* has two letters that make one vowel sound, the sound /$\overline{oo}$/, like in the word *flew*.

- The vowel team *ue* has two letters that make one vowel sound, the sound /$\overline{oo}$/, like in the word *blue*.

- The vowel team *oo* has two letters that make one vowel sound, the sound /$\overline{oo}$/, like in the word *moon*.

Students will sort words into groups. For a word to fit into a group, it must match **both** the target sound and the spelling pattern.

- Words with the sound of long double o and the uCe pattern will go under the heading **uCe *tube***.

- Words with the vowel team *ew* go under the heading **ew *flew***.

- Words with the vowel team *ue* go under the heading **ue *blue***.

- Words with the vowel team *oo* go under the heading **oo *moon***.

Advance Preparation

During the Go Read! activity, students will have the option of using the digital library. Allow extra time for students to make their reading selection, or have students make a selection before beginning the lesson.

Supplied
- *K12 World: Invaluable Insects*
  - "Honey from the Hive"
- *English Language Arts 2 Activity Book 1*
  - Think About Reading: "Honey from the Hive" (A)
  - Draw a Cartoon Bee
  - Spelling List 10
- handwriting workbook

Also Needed
- crayons or markers
- scissors
- envelope or baggie to store spelling cutouts
- reading material for Go Read!

"Honey from the Hive" Synopsis

This article explains how honeybees make honey. First, the worker bees gather the nectar. Next, the house bees take the nectar and chew it before putting it into cells in the hive. The next step is for the bees to remove the water from the nectar. In the final step, the bees produce wax that seals the cells that hold the honey. Bees eat the stored honey all winter. Beekeepers then collect the honey from the hives and send it to stores and markets.

Lesson Goals

- Read "Honey from the Hive."
- Identify steps in a written sequence, use order words to connect steps, and follow the steps.
- Give, restate, and follow spoken directions.
- Sort words by sound and spelling pattern.
- Develop letter formation fluency.
- Read independently to develop fluency.

GET READY

Introduction: "Honey from the Hive" (A)

Students will get a glimpse of what they will learn about in the lesson.

READ

Think About Reading: "Honey from the Hive" (A)

Students will complete Question 1 on Think About Reading: "Honey from the Hive" (A) in *English Language Arts 2 Activity Book 1*.

NOTE In this activity, students will predict how bees make honey. They will come back to the activity page to compare and contrast their prediction with what they learned in the article.

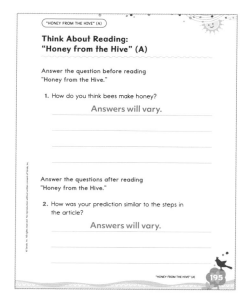
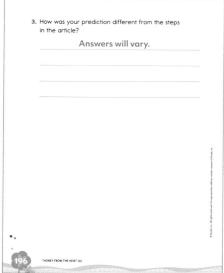

"Honey from the Hive" (A)

Students will read "Honey from the Hive" in *K12 World: Invaluable Insects*. Encourage them to reread their favorite passages.

Check-In: "Honey from the Hive" (A)

Students will answer several questions to demonstrate their comprehension of "Honey from the Hive."

Reflect: "Honey from the Hive" (A)

Students will compare and contrast the prediction they made about how bees make honey with what they learned from the article "Honey from the Hive." They will complete Questions 2 and 3 on Think About Reading: "Honey from the Hive" (A) in *English Language Arts 2 Activity Book 1*.

LEARN AND TRY IT

LEARN   Follow the Steps

Students will learn how to follow written instructions in the correct order. They will learn how to use order words to connect steps.

LEARN   Spoken Directions

Through guided exploration of oral directions, students will analyze what makes directions clear.

TRY IT   Draw a Cartoon Bee

Students will complete Draw a Cartoon Bee in *English Language Arts 2 Activity Book 1*.

NOTE   Students will need to follow oral directions located in the online activity to complete this activity page. Ensure they have access to a device.

NOTE   Students will need crayons or markers to complete this activity page.

LEARNING COACH CHECK-IN   Question 3 asks students to give someone oral directions. Provide students with feedback about their directions. For example, "When you used the word *next*, that helped me know you were saying a new step." And, "When you said, 'Color the wings blue,' I didn't know if you meant all of the wings. Can you give more detail?'"

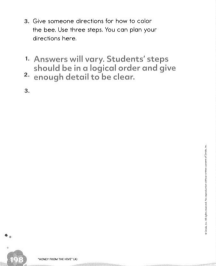

LEARN   Spelling List 10

Students will learn and sort words with spelling patterns for the sound of long double o.

- In an online activity, students will learn about the spelling patterns and the sounds they represent. They will learn how to sort words according to those sounds and patterns. They will also complete a word sort.

- In *English Language Arts 2 Activity Book 1*, students will complete Spelling List 10.

NOTE   Students will need scissors to cut out the spelling words on the activity page. Have students store their cutouts in a safe place, such as an envelope.

This is the complete list of words students will work with to learn the spelling patterns for the sound of long double o.

uCe *tube*	ew *flew*	ue *blue*	oo *moon*
June	dew	clue	boot
rule	knew	due	pool
tune	new	glue	
		true	

WRAP-UP

Questions About "Honey from the Hive" (A)

Students will answer questions to show that they understand the reading and spelling skills they learned in this lesson.

Handwriting

Students should gather their handwriting materials and begin where they left off. Remind students to form letters carefully and correctly.

TIP Set a timer to help students stay focused during handwriting practice.

Go Read!

Students will read for pleasure. They should choose a book or a magazine that interests them, or they may choose a selection from the digital library, linked in the online lesson.

- Have students read aloud a few paragraphs of their selection.

- Then have students read silently for the rest of the time.

SUPPORT   Students should make no more than five errors in decoding when they read aloud a few paragraphs of their Go Read! selection. If students struggle or make more than five errors, they need to select a different (and easier) text for the Go Read! activity.

TIP   Have students select something to read ahead of time to help them stay focused.

"Honey from the Hive" (B)

Lesson Overview

ACTIVITY	ACTIVITY TITLE	TIME	ONLINE/OFFLINE
GET READY	Introduction: "Honey from the Hive" (B)	**1** minute	🖥️
	Words with More Than One Meaning	**15** minutes	🖥️
READ	"Honey from the Hive" (B)	**10** minutes	🖥️ or 📄
LEARN AND **TRY IT**	How to Follow Directions	**20** minutes	🖥️
	How to Play a Game	**15** minutes	🖥️
ALL ABOUT ME	Brain Break	**1** minute	🖥️ or 📄
TRY IT	Choose a Topic for Your How-To **LEARNING COACH CHECK-IN**	**15** minutes	📄
ALL ABOUT ME	Brain Break	**1** minute	🖥️ or 📄
TRY IT	Practice: Spelling List 10	**20** minutes	🖥️ and 📄
WRAP-UP	Questions About "Honey from the Hive" (B)	**2** minutes	🖥️
	Read and Record	**10** minutes	🖥️
	Handwriting	**10** minutes	📄

Content Background

Students will conclude a series of lessons centered around the article "Honey from the Hive" from the magazine *K12 World: Invaluable Insects*. In this lesson, they will learn how to follow written directions, use order words, and choose a topic for their own how-to.

Reading   A recipe is a type of sequential writing—it contains steps that need to be followed in a **logical order** (the steps can be reordered). By studying recipes, students can learn about reading for signal words and for important details.

Writing Skills   A **how-to paper**, also called a procedural essay, process piece, or simply a how-to, explains a process.

Students will begin working on a how-to paragraph about a process they know well. They will complete this assignment over the course of several lessons by following a modified version of the writing process. (Students will not revise, proofread, or publish their how-to in this course.)

Writing Process

1 Prewriting	2 Drafting	3 Revising	4 Proofreading	5 Publishing

Students will complete the first part of prewriting in this lesson—choosing a topic.

Advance Preparation

Gather a folder that students can use to keep all activity pages related to their how-to.

Gather students' cutouts from the Spelling List 10 activity page from "Honey from the Hive" (A). They will use the cutouts during Try It: Practice: Spelling List 10.

Lesson Goals

- Use a dictionary to define words with more than one meaning.
- Read a recipe with multistep directions.
- Choose a topic for your own how-to.
- Identify and write spelling patterns that stand for sounds within words.
- Read aloud to practice fluency.
- Develop letter formation fluency.

MATERIALS

Supplied
- *K12 World: Invaluable Insects*
  - "Honey from the Hive"
- *English Language Arts 2 Activity Book 1*
  - Model How-To
  - Choose a Topic for Your How-To
  - Practice: Spelling List 9
- handwriting workbook

Also Needed
- folder for organizing how-to assignment pages
- Spelling List 10 activity page cutouts from "Honey from the Hive" (A)
- crayons or markers (optional)

KEYWORDS

how-to paper – a paragraph or essay that explains how to do or make something

logical order – a way to organize that groups details in a way that makes sense

GET READY

Introduction: "Honey from the Hive" (B)
Students will get a glimpse of what they will learn about in the lesson.

Words with More Than One Meaning
Students will use dictionary entries to help define words with more than one meaning.

"Honey from the Hive" (B)

Students will read the recipe in "Honey from the Hive" in *K12 World: Invaluable Insects.*

LEARN   How to Follow Directions

Students will learn that recipes are written in a logical order. They will also learn about using signal words to keep steps in order.

TIP   Students will read the recipe and answer questions about it. If appropriate, they could actually make the drink or follow a similar, simple recipe with adult supervision. Alternatively, students could also create a simple craft or drawing to reinforce the idea of following steps in order.

TRY IT   How to Play a Game

Students will answer questions about a simple board game, putting the directions in a logical order.

TIP   Talk about the steps in students' favorite board game (or a board game of their own creation). How to play a board game could be a great topic for students' how-to paragraph, which is introduced in the next activity.

TRY IT   Choose a Topic for Your How-To

Students will complete Choose a Topic for Your How-To in *English Language Arts 2 Activity Book 1.*

LEARNING COACH CHECK-IN   Make sure the topic that students choose (Question 2) is something that they are excited to write about and that they can write about without doing research.

TIP   Read the Model How-To together to ensure that students understand the assignment before they choose a topic.

NOTE   Have students put the Model How-To and their completed Choose a Topic for Your How-To activity page into a folder for safe keeping.

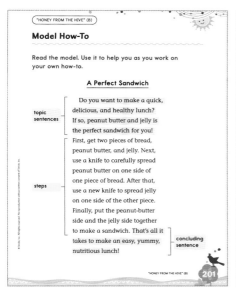

Model How-To

Read the model. Use it to help you as you work on your own how-to.

A Perfect Sandwich

topic sentences

Do you want to make a quick, delicious, and healthy lunch? If so, peanut butter and jelly is the perfect sandwich for you!

steps

First, get two pieces of bread, peanut butter, and jelly. Next, use a knife to carefully spread peanut butter on one side of one piece of bread. After that, use a new knife to spread jelly on one side of the other piece. Finally, put the peanut-butter side and the jelly side together to make a sandwich. That's all it takes to make an easy, yummy, nutritious lunch!

concluding sentence

201

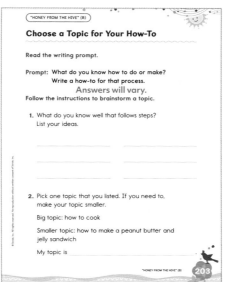

Choose a Topic for Your How-To

Read the writing prompt.

Prompt: What do you know how to do or make?
Write a how-to for that process.

Answers will vary.

Follow the instructions to brainstorm a topic.

1. What do you know well that follows steps? List your ideas.

_____

_____

_____

2. Pick one topic that you listed. If you need to, make your topic smaller.

Big topic: how to cook

Smaller topic: how to make a peanut butter and jelly sandwich

My topic is _____

203

TRY IT   Practice: Spelling List 10

Students will practice the spelling patterns for Spelling List 10.

- In *English Language Arts 2 Activity Book 1*, students will complete Practice: Spelling List 10.

- Online, students will answer questions that require them to reflect on the spelling patterns.

NOTE   Students will need their cutouts from the Spelling List 10 activity page to complete Practice: Spelling List 10.

NOTE   Students may wish to use crayons or markers to draw their pictures or comic strip.

Practice: Spelling List 10

Get your spelling cutouts. Set up the headings, and sort the spelling words again.

Look at your sort, and write down each spelling word under the correct heading on the chart.

uCe *tube*	ew *flew*	ue *blue*	oo *moon*
June	dew	clue	boot
rule	knew	due	pool
tune	new	glue	
		true	

205

Do one of the following activities to practice your spelling words:

Draw and label.

Choose four of your spelling words. Draw a picture for each word. Then write the word under the picture.

Create a comic strip.

Create four panels of a comic strip. Draw pictures and write text with four or more of your spelling words.

206

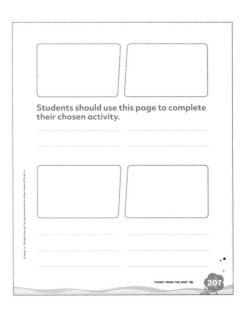

Students should use this page to complete their chosen activity.

207

Questions About "Honey from the Hive" (B)

Students will answer questions to show that they understand the reading and spelling skills they learned in this lesson.

Read and Record

Good readers read quickly, smoothly, and with expression. This is called *fluency*. Students will record themselves reading aloud. They will listen to their recording and think about how quick, smooth, and expressive they sound.

TIP Encourage students to rerecord as needed.

Handwriting

Students should gather their handwriting materials and begin where they left off. Remind students to form letters carefully and correctly.

TIP Set a timer to help students stay focused during handwriting practice.

"I See a Honeybee" (A)

Lesson Overview

ACTIVITY	ACTIVITY TITLE	TIME	ONLINE/OFFLINE
GET READY	Introduction: "I See a Honeybee" (A)	**1** minute	🖥️
	Words to Know: "I See a Honeybee" (A)	**10** minutes	🖥️
READ	Think About Reading: "I See a Honeybee" (A)	**5** minutes	📄
	"I See a Honeybee" (A)	**15** minutes	🖥️ or 📄
	Check-In: "I See a Honeybee" (A)	**5** minutes	🖥️
	Reflect: "I See a Honeybee" (A)	**5** minutes	📄
ALL ABOUT ME	Brain Break	**1** minute	🖥️ or 📄
LEARN AND **TRY IT**	Description	**10** minutes	🖥️
	What's the Structure?	**5** minutes	🖥️
ALL ABOUT ME	Brain Break	**1** minute	🖥️ or 📄
TRY IT	Plan Your How-To LEARNING COACH CHECK-IN	**20** minutes	📄
	Apply: Spelling List 10	**20** minutes	🖥️ and 📄
WRAP-UP	Questions About "I See a Honeybee" (A)	**2** minutes	🖥️
	Handwriting	**10** minutes	📄
	Go Read!	**10** minutes	🖥️ or 📄

Content Background

Students will begin a series of lessons centered around the article "I See a Honeybee" from the magazine *K12 Word: Invaluable Insects*. In this lesson, they will learn about description as a text structure and plan their how-to.

Vocabulary   Students will explore these words from the article: *hive*, *cell*, and *colony*. These are the definitions for how the words are used in "I See a Honeybee":

- **hive** (noun) – the nest where bees live

- **cell** (noun) – a section of a hive used for storage or for raising young bees

- **colony** (noun) – a group of the same kind of animal living in one place

Reading   *Description* is one way to organize a nonfiction text. The author of "I See a Honeybee" uses description to share information about the many bees in a hive. Good readers ask themselves, "What is being described?" as they read.

Writing Skills   Students will continue working on their **how-to** paragraph about a process they know well. They will complete this assignment over the course of several lessons by following a modified version of the writing process. (Students will not revise, proofread, or publish their how-to in this course.)

Writing Process

| 1 Prewriting | 2 Drafting | 3 Revising | 4 Proofreading | 5 Publishing |

Students will finish prewriting. They will plan their topic sentence, steps, and concluding sentence by filling out a graphic organizer.

Advance Preparation

Gather the folder that students are using to keep all activity pages related to their how-to.

- Model How-To from "Honey from the Hive" (B)

- Students' completed Choose a Topic for Your How-To activity page from "Honey from the Hive" (B)

Gather students' cutouts from the Spelling List 10 activity page from "Honey from the Hive" (A). They will use the cutouts during Try It: Apply: Spelling List 10.

If students have removed My Speed Sort Times from the activity book, have them gather this activity page. They will use this activity page in the Try It: Apply: Spelling List 10.

During the Go Read! activity, students will have the option of using the digital library. Allow extra time for students to make their reading selection, or have students make a selection before beginning the lesson.

MATERIALS

Supplied
- *K12 World: Invaluable Insects*
  - "I See a Honeybee"
- *English Language Arts 2 Activity Book 1*
  - Think About Reading: "I See a Honeybee" (A)
  - Plan Your How-To
  - Apply: Spelling List 10
  - My Speed Sort Times
- handwriting workbook

Also Needed
- crayons or markers (optional)
- folder in which students are storing how-to assignment pages
- Spelling List 10 activity page cutouts from "Honey from the Hive" (A)
- reading material for Go Read!

"I See a Honeybee" Synopsis

Honeybees live in hives with thousands of other bees. The female worker bees and male drones live with the queen bee. The queen bee lays eggs. The worker bees build the hive, take care of the young bees, spread pollen, and gather nectar. Scout bees search for nectar. They do a waggle dance at the hive to show the other bees where to find the nectar. Honeybees help fruit, vegetables, and flowers grow.

Lesson Goals

- Learn new vocabulary.
- Read "I See a Honeybee."
- Ask and answer questions about description as a text structure.
- Plan your how-to.
- Identify reasons for when and how to use certain spelling patterns.
- Develop letter formation fluency.
- Read independently to develop fluency.

GET READY

Introduction: "I See a Honeybee" (A)

Students will get a glimpse of what they will learn about in the lesson.

Words to Know: "I See a Honeybee" (A)

Students will preview and answer questions about three vocabulary words from the reading selection.

READ

Think About Reading: "I See a Honeybee" (A)

Students will complete Questions 1 and 2 on Think About Reading: "I See a Honeybee" (A) in *English Language Arts 2 Activity Book 1*.

In this activity, students will describe what they know about honeybees. Students will come back to the activity page to describe what they learned about honeybees after they read the article "I See a Honeybee."

Students may wish to use crayons or markers to draw their picture.

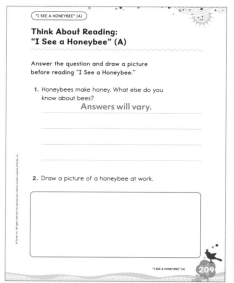

"I See a Honeybee"

Students will read "I See a Honeybee" in *K12 World: Invaluable Insects*. Encourage them to reread their favorite passages.

Check-In: "I See a Honeybee" (A)

Students will answer several questions to demonstrate their comprehension of "I See a Honeybee."

Reflect: "I See a Honeybee" (A)

Students will describe what they learned about honeybees by completing Question 3 on Think About Reading: "I See a Honeybee" (A) in *English Language Arts 2 Activity Book 1*.

LEARN AND TRY IT

LEARN   Description

Students will learn about description as a way to structure an informational text. They will ask and answer questions about what is being described. They will look for details that provide descriptive information.

TRY IT   What's the Structure?

Students will identify the structure of paragraphs as *description*, *sequence*, or *compare and contrast*.

TRY IT   Plan Your How-To

Students will complete Plan Your How-To in *English Language Arts 2 Activity Book 1*. Make sure students have their completed Choose a Topic for Your How-To activity page and Model How-To to refer to as they work.

LEARNING COACH CHECK-IN   Have students give their directions orally if they are stuck. Encourage them to try drawing their steps as an alternative to writing notes in the graphic organizer.

NOTE   Have students add their completed Plan Your How-To activity page to the folder they are using to store their how-to assignment pages.

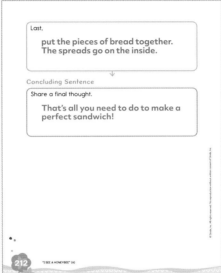

TRY IT   Apply: Spelling List 10

Students will apply what they have learned about the spelling patterns for Spelling List 10.

• In an online activity, students will complete a word sort and answer reflection questions.

• In *English Language Arts 2 Activity Book 1*, students will complete the Apply: Spelling List 10.

NOTE   Students will need their cutouts from the Spelling List 10 activity page to complete Apply: Spelling List 10.

TIP   Have students record their speed sort times on the My Speed Sort Times activity page, which is located at the back of the activity book. It can be motivating for students to see their progress as their ability to complete speed sorts should improve over time.

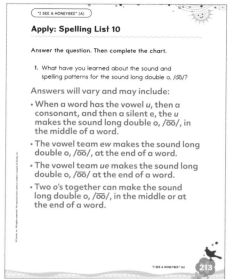

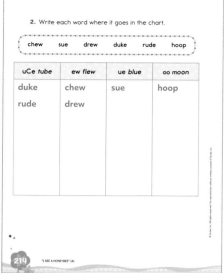

The worksheet pages (213 and 214) show:

"I SEE A HONEYBEE" (A)

Apply: Spelling List 10

Answer the question. Then complete the chart.

1. What have you learned about the sound and spelling patterns for the sound long double o. /o͞o/?

Answers will vary and may include:

- When a word has the vowel *u*, then a consonant, and then a silent e, the *u* makes the sound long double o, /o͞o/, in the middle of a word.
- The vowel team *ew* makes the sound long double o, /o͞o/, at the end of a word.
- The vowel team *ue* makes the sound long double o, /o͞o/ at the end of a word.
- Two *o*'s together can make the sound long double o, /o͞o/, in the middle or at the end of a word.

2. Write each word where it goes in the chart.

chew   sue   drew   duke   rude   hoop

uCe tube	ew flew	ue blue	oo moon
duke	chew	sue	hoop
rude	drew		

WRAP-UP

Questions About "I See a Honeybee" (A)

Students will answer questions to show that they understand the reading and spelling skills they learned in this lesson.

Handwriting

Students should gather their handwriting materials and begin where they left off. Remind students to form letters carefully and correctly.

TIP Set a timer to help students stay focused during handwriting practice.

Go Read!

Students will read for pleasure. They should choose a book or a magazine that interests them, or they may choose a selection from the digital library, linked in the online lesson.

- Have students read aloud a few paragraphs of their selection.

- Then have students read silently for the rest of the time.

SUPPORT Students should make no more than five errors in decoding when they read aloud a few paragraphs of their Go Read! selection. If students struggle or make more than five errors, they need to select a different (and easier) text for the Go Read! activity.

TIP Have students select something to read ahead of time to help them stay focused.

"I See a Honeybee" (B)

Lesson Overview

ACTIVITY	ACTIVITY TITLE	TIME	ONLINE/OFFLINE
GET READY	Introduction: "I See a Honeybee" (B)	**1** minute	🖥️
	Synonyms, Antonyms, and Homonyms	**15** minutes	🖥️
LEARN AND **TRY IT**	Compare and Contrast	**15** minutes	🖥️
	Same or Different?	**15** minutes	🖥️
ALL ABOUT ME	Brain Break	**1** minute	🖥️ or 📄
TRY IT	Write Your How-To **LEARNING COACH CHECK-IN**	**30** minutes	📄
ALL ABOUT ME	Brain Break	**1** minute	🖥️ or 📄
TRY IT	More Practice: Spelling List 10	**20** minutes	🖥️ and 📄
WRAP-UP	Questions About "I See a Honeybee" (B)	**2** minutes	🖥️
	Read and Record	**10** minutes	🖥️
	More Language Arts Practice	**10** minutes	🖥️

Content Background

Students will conclude a series of lessons centered around the article "I See a Honeybee" from the magazine *K12 World: Invaluable Insects*. They will compare this article to the article "Honey from the Hive." Students will also write their how-to.

Reading   **Comparing** means looking for similarities. **Contrasting** means looking for differences. Comparing and contrasting texts builds reading comprehension.

Writing Skills   Students will write their **how-to** paragraph about a process they know well. Students will not revise, proofread, or publish their how-to in this course.

Writing Process

1 Prewriting	2 Drafting	3 Revising	4 Proofreading	5 Publishing

Advance Preparation

Gather the folder that students are using to keep all activity pages related to their how-to.

- Model How-To from "Honey from the Hive" (B)

- Students' completed Choose a Topic for Your How-To activity page from "Honey from the Hive" (B)

- Students' completed Plan Your How-To activity page from "I See a Honeybee" (A)

Gather students' cutouts from the Spelling List 10 activity page from "Honey from the Hive" (A). They will use the cutouts during Try It: More Practice: Spelling List 10.

If students have removed My Speed Sort Times from the activity book, have them gather this activity page. They will use this activity page in the Try It: More Practice: Spelling List 10.

Lesson Goals

- Identify synonyms, antonyms, and homonyms, and use dictionary entries to help determine the meaning of words.

- Compare and contrast two informational texts.

- Write your how-to.

- Identify and write spelling patterns that stand for sounds within words.

- Read aloud to practice fluency.

MATERIALS

Supplied
- *K12 World: Invaluable Insects*
  - "I See a Honeybee"
  - "Honey from the Hive"
- *English Language Arts 2 Activity Book 1*
  - Write Your How-To
  - More Practice: Spelling List 10
  - My Speed Sort Times
- Writing Paper (printout)

Also Needed
- folder in which students are storing how-to assignment pages
- Spelling List 10 activity page cutouts from "Honey from the Hive" (A)

KEYWORDS

compare – to explain how two or more things are alike

contrast – to explain how two or more things are different

GET READY

Introduction: "I See a Honeybee" (B)
Students will get a glimpse of what they will learn about in the lesson.

Synonyms, Antonyms, and Homonyms
Students will learn about synonyms, antonyms, and homonyms. They will use dictionary entries to help find the exact definition of words with more than one meaning.

LEARN AND TRY IT

LEARN   Compare and Contrast

Students will compare and contrast "I See a Honeybee" with "Honey from the Hive."

TRY IT   Same or Different?

Students will identify details that are in "Honey from the Hive," "I See a Honeybee," or both articles.

TRY IT   Write Your How-To

Students will complete Write Your How-To in *English Language Arts 2 Activity Book 1*. Make sure students have their completed Plan Your How-To activity page and Model How-To to refer to as they work.

LEARNING COACH CHECK-IN   Ensure students are using their completed graphic organizer to help them write their how-to from beginning to end. Provide students feedback on their completed how-to, focusing on their writing growth.

NOTE   Additional sheets of Writing Paper are available online.

NOTE   Students will not turn in this assignment for grading.

TRY IT   More Practice: Spelling List 10

Students will continue to practice the spelling patterns for Spelling List 10 to increase automatic recognition of the patterns.

- In an online activity, students will practice the spelling words and patterns.

- In *English Language Arts 2 Activity Book 1*, students will complete More Practice: Spelling List 10.

TIP Have students record their speed sort times on the My Speed Sort Times activity page, which is located at the back of the activity book. It can be motivating for students to see their progress as their ability to complete speed sorts should improve over time.

Questions About "I See a Honeybee" (B)

Students will answer questions to show that they understand the reading skills they learned in this lesson.

Read and Record

Good readers read quickly, smoothly, and with expression. This is called *fluency*. Students will record themselves reading aloud. They will listen to their recording and think about how quick, smooth, and expressive they sound.

TIP Encourage students to rerecord as needed.

More Language Arts Practice

Students will practice skills according to their individual needs.

"The Bee's Knees: Insects Are Awesome!" (A)

Lesson Overview

ACTIVITY	ACTIVITY TITLE	TIME	ONLINE/OFFLINE
GET READY	Introduction: "The Bee's Knees" (A)	**1** minute	🖥️
	Words to Know: "The Bee's Knees" (A)	**10** minutes	🖥️
READ	Think About Reading: "The Bee's Knees" (A)	**5** minutes	📄
	"The Bee's Knees" (A)	**15** minutes	🖥️ or 📄
	Reflect: "The Bee's Knees" (A)	**5** minutes	📄
	Check-In: "The Bee's Knees" (A)	**5** minutes	🖥️
ALL ABOUT ME	Brain Break	**1** minute	🖥️ or 📄
LEARN AND **TRY IT**	Fact and Opinion	**10** minutes	🖥️
	The Spotted Lanternfly	**10** minutes	🖥️
	Write an Opinion Statement **LEARNING COACH CHECK-IN**	**10** minutes	📄
WRAP-UP	Questions About "The Bee's Knees" (A)	**2** minutes	🖥️
ALL ABOUT ME	Brain Break	**1** minute	🖥️ or 📄
QUIZ	Spelling List 10	**25** minutes	🖥️
WRAP-UP	Handwriting	**10** minutes	📄
	Go Read!	**10** minutes	🖥️ or 📄

Content Background

Students will begin a series lessons centered around the article "The Bee's Knees: Insects Are Awesome!" from the magazine *K12 World: Invaluable Insects*. In this lesson, they will learn how to distinguish facts from opinions and write an opinion statement about insects.

Vocabulary   Students will explore these words from the article: *pollinator*, *honor*, and *the bee's knees*. These are the definitions for how the words are used in "The Bee's Knees: Insects Are Awesome!":

- **pollinator** (noun) – an insect that carries pollen from one flower or plant to another

- **honor** (verb) – to treat with respect

- **the bee's knees** – an expression saying that someone is the best

Reading   **Facts** can be proven to be true. **Opinions** are beliefs or feelings that cannot be proven to be true. Distinguishing between a fact and an opinion is an important reading comprehension skill.

Writing Skills   People often share opinions by writing about them. This type of writing is called *opinion writing*. An *opinion statement* is simply a statement that gives an opinion.

Advance Preparation

During the Go Read! activity, students will have the option of using the digital library. Allow extra time for students to make their reading selection, or have students make a selection before beginning the lesson.

"The Bee's Knees: Insects Are Awesome!" Synopsis

"The Bee's Knees" expresses the opinion that insects are awesome. Insects do important jobs like helping plants and crops grow. They spread pollen and eat harmful insects that hurt plants. Insects make things that people use, such as honey, beeswax, and silk. Some insect pollinators are in danger. People should help pollinators survive because insects help us in many ways.

Lesson Goals

- Learn new vocabulary.

- Read "The Bee's Knees: Insects Are Awesome!"

- Identify and distinguish between facts and opinions.

- Write an opinion statement.

- Take a spelling quiz.

- Develop letter formation fluency.

- Read independently to develop fluency.

MATERIALS

Supplied
- *K12 World: Invaluable Insects*
  - "The Bee's Knees: Insects Are Awesome!"
- *English Language Arts 2 Activity Book 1*
  - Think About Reading: "The Bee's Knees" (A)
  - Write an Opinion Statement
- handwriting workbook

Also Needed
- reading material for Go Read!

KEYWORDS

fact – something that can be proven true

opinion – something that a person thinks or believes, but which cannot be proven to be true

Introduction: "The Bee's Knees" (A)

Students will get a glimpse of what they will learn about in the lesson.

Words to Know: "The Bee's Knees" (A)

Students will preview and answer questions about two vocabulary words and an expression from the reading selection.

READ

Think About Reading: "The Bee's Knees" (A)

Students will complete Question 1 on Think About Reading: "The Bee's Knees" (A) in *English Language Arts 2 Activity Book 1.*

NOTE In this activity, students will describe what they know about how insects help people. They will come back to the activity page to make an inference after they read the article "The Bee's Knees: Insects are Awesome!"

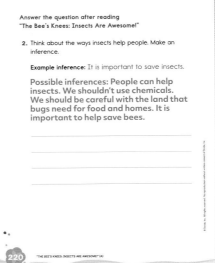

"The Bee's Knees" (A)

Students will read "The Bee's Knees: Insects Are Awesome!" in *K12 World: Invaluable Insects.* Encourage them to reread their favorite passages.

Reflect: "The Bee's Knees" (A)

Students will complete Question 2 on Think About Reading: "The Bee's Knees" (A) in *English Language Arts 2 Activity Book 1.* They will make an inference about how insects help people.

Check-In: "The Bee's Knees" (A)

Students will answer several questions to demonstrate their comprehension of "The Bee's Knees: Insects Are Awesome!"

LEARN AND TRY IT

LEARN   Fact and Opinion

Students will identify facts and opinions from "The Bee's Knees: Insects Are Awesome!" They will learn to distinguish between a fact and an opinion by examining excerpts from the text.

SUPPORT   If students are having difficulty distinguishing facts and opinions, you can offer additional practice using everyday items. For example, you can say, "This milk is cold and white. It is delicious." Then ask students to identify the facts and opinion in those sentences. Have students take turns coming up with their own examples.

LEARN   The Spotted Lanternfly

Students will explore an opinion expressed in a video about an invasive insect, the spotted lanternfly. They will learn words that signal that someone is giving an opinion.

TRY IT   Write an Opinion Statement

Students will complete Write an Opinion Statement in *English Language Arts 2 Activity Book 1*.

LEARNING COACH CHECK-IN   If students have difficulty forming their opinion statement, prompt them with "I believe that _____ " or "I feel that _____." When they actually write their opinion, have students omit those words.

NOTE   Have students keep their completed activity page in a safe place so they can refer to it later.

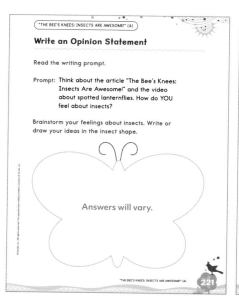

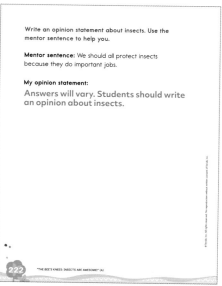

WRAP-UP

Questions About "The Bee's Knees" (A)

Students will answer questions to show that they understand the reading and writing skills they learned in this lesson.

QUIZ

Spelling List 10

Students will take the Spelling List 10 quiz.

WRAP-UP

Handwriting

Students should gather their handwriting materials and begin where they left off. Remind students to form letters carefully and correctly.

TIP Set a timer to help students stay focused during handwriting practice.

Go Read!

Students will read for pleasure. They should choose a book or a magazine that interests them, or they may choose a selection from the digital library, linked in the online lesson.

- Have students read aloud a few paragraphs of their selection.

- Then have students read silently for the rest of the time.

SUPPORT Students should make no more than five errors in decoding when they read aloud a few paragraphs of their Go Read! selection. If students struggle or make more than five errors, they need to select a different (and easier) text for the Go Read! activity.

TIP Have students select something to read ahead of time to help them stay focused.

"The Bee's Knees: Insects Are Awesome!" (B)

Lesson Overview

ACTIVITY	ACTIVITY TITLE	TIME	ONLINE/OFFLINE
GET READY	Introduction: "The Bee's Knees" (B)	**1** minute	🖥
	Words to Know: "The Bee's Knees" (B)	**15** minutes	🖥
	Building Background: Opinions	**10** minutes	🖥
READ	"The Bee's Knees" (B)	**20** minutes	🖥 or 📄
ALL ABOUT ME	Brain Break	**1** minute	🖥 or 📄
TRY IT	Support an Opinion	**25** minutes	📄
ALL ABOUT ME	Brain Break	**1** minute	🖥 or 📄
LEARN	Spelling List 11	**25** minutes	🖥 and 📄
WRAP-UP	Questions About "The Bee's Knees" (B)	**2** minutes	🖥
	Handwriting	**10** minutes	📄
	Read and Record	**10** minutes	🖥

Content Background

Students will conclude a series of lessons centered around the article "The Bee's Knees: Insects Are Awesome!" from the magazine *K12 World: Invaluable Insects*. In this lesson, they will identify the facts and details that support an author's point and write reasons to support an opinion.

Reading   In effective opinion writing, an opinion is supported with **reasons**. These reasons are directly related to the opinion, stated clearly, and based in fact.

Writing Skills   Writers use words like *too*, *also*, *and*, and *another* to connect an opinion and reasons.

Spelling   In this lesson, students will learn the following symbols and spelling patterns:

- The vowel a-consonant-silent e (aCe) pattern comes at the end of a word, as in the word *cake*. The silent e signals that the letter *a* has its long a sound, /ā/.

- The vowel team *ai* has two letters that make one vowel sound, /ā/, like in the word *rain*.

- The vowel team *ay* has two letters that make one vowel sound, /ā/, like in the word *day*.

Students will sort words into groups. For a word to fit into a group, it must match **both** the target sound and the spelling pattern.

- Words in which the vowel a-consonant-silent e (aCe) pattern represents the sound /ā/ will go under the head **aCe *cake***.

- Words in which the vowel team *ai* represents the sound /ā/ will go under the heading **ai *rain***.

- Words in which the vowel team *ay* represents the sound /ā/ will go under the heading **ay *day***.

- The word *said* has the vowel team *ai* but does not have the sound /ā/. So, the word *said* will go under the heading **oddball**.

Advance Preparation

Gather students' completed Write an Opinion activity page from "The Bee's Knees: Insects Are Awesome!" (A). Students will refer to this page during Try It: Support an Opinion.

Lesson Goals

- Learn new vocabulary.
- Identify facts and details that support an author's opinion.
- Reread "The Bee's Knees: Insects Are Awesome!"
- Write reasons to support your opinion.
- Sort words by sound and spelling pattern.
- Develop letter formation fluency.
- Read aloud to practice fluency.

MATERIALS

Supplied

- *K12 World: Invaluable Insects*
  - "The Bee's Knees: Insects Are Awesome!"
- *English Language Arts 2 Activity Book 1*
  - Support an Opinion
  - Spelling List 11
- handwriting workbook

Also Needed

- Write an Opinion Statement activity page from "The Bee's Knees: Insects Are Awesome!" (A)
- scissors
- envelope or baggie to store spelling cutouts

KEYWORDS

reason – a statement that explains why something is or why it should be

GET READY

Introduction: "The Bee's Knees" (B)
Students will get a glimpse of what they will learn about in the lesson.

Words to Know: "The Bee's Knees" (B)
Students will answer questions about six vocabulary words they have already learned.

Building Background: Opinions
Students will learn that authors express their opinion in their writing. They will learn that opinions need to be backed up by facts and reasons. They will look for facts that support opinions.

"The Bee's Knees" (B)

Students will reread "The Bee's Knees: Insects Are Awesome!" in *K12 World: Invaluable Insects*.

LEARN AND TRY IT

TRY IT   Support an Opinion

Students will complete Support an Opinion in *English Language Arts 2 Activity Book 1*. Make sure students have their completed Write an Opinion Statement activity page to refer to as they work.

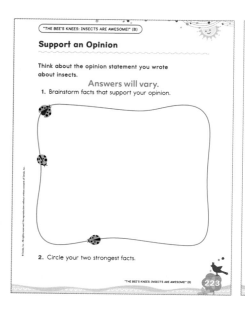
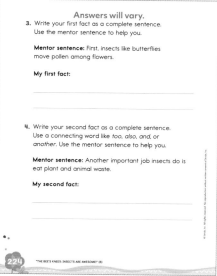

LEARN   Spelling List 11

Students will learn and sort words with the sound and spelling patterns for long a.

- In an online activity, students will learn about the spelling patterns and the sounds they represent. They will learn how to sort words according to those sounds and patterns. They will also complete a word sort.

- In *English Language Arts 2 Activity Book 1*, students will complete Spelling List 11.

- **NOTE**   Students will need scissors to cut out the spelling words on the activity page. Have students store their cutouts in a safe place, such as an envelope.

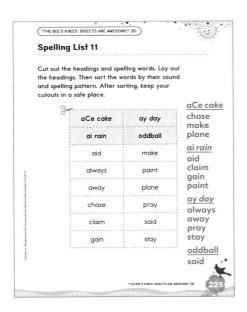

This is the complete list of words students will work with to learn the spelling patterns for the sound of long a.

aCe *cake*	ai *rain*	ay *day*	oddball
chase	aid	always	said
make	claim	away	
plane	gain	pray	
	paint	stay	

Questions About "The Bee's Knees" (B)

Students will answer questions to show that they understand the writing and spelling skills they learned in this lesson.

Handwriting

Students should gather their handwriting materials and begin where they left off. Remind students to form letters carefully and correctly.

TIP Set a timer to help students stay focused during handwriting practice.

Read and Record

Good readers read quickly, smoothly, and with expression. This is called *fluency*. Students will record themselves reading aloud. They will listen to their recording and think about how quick, smooth, and expressive they sound.

TIP Encourage students to rerecord as needed.

Insect Poetry (A)

Lesson Overview

ACTIVITY	ACTIVITY TITLE	TIME	ONLINE/OFFLINE
GET READY	Introduction: Insect Poetry (A)	**1** minute	🖥️
	Words to Know: Insect Poetry (A)	**10** minutes	🖥️
READ	Insect Poetry (A)	**15** minutes	🖥️ or 📄
ALL ABOUT ME	Brain Break	**1** minute	🖥️ or 📄
LEARN AND TRY IT	Picturing Poems	**20** minutes	🖥️
	Write a Shape Poem	**30** minutes	📄
ALL ABOUT ME	Brain Break	**1** minute	🖥️ or 📄
TRY IT	Practice: Spelling List 11	**20** minutes	🖥️ and 📄
WRAP-UP	Questions About Insect Poetry (A)	**2** minutes	🖥️
	Handwriting	**10** minutes	📄
	Go Read!	**10** minutes	🖥️ or 📄

Content Background

Students will continue to learn about poetry. In this lesson, they will learn some elements of poetry, including repetition and sensory language. Students will also learn about concrete (shape) poetry, and they will write their own shape poem.

Vocabulary   Students will explore these words from the poems: *compound eye* and *compost*. These are the definitions for how the words are used in the poems "Insect" and "Housefly":

- **compound eye** (noun) – an eye made up of many simple eyes

- **compost** (noun) – a pile of decaying and rotting leaves, food, and manure

Reading   **Concrete poems**, or *shape poems*, are poems that are written in the shape of the poem's topic or main idea. The poem "Insect" is a shape poem because its words form the shape of an insect. Shape poetry has poetic elements such as repetition and sensory language.

MATERIALS

Supplied
- *English Language Arts 2 Activity Book 1*
  - Read: Insect Poetry (A)
  - Write a Shape Poem
  - Practice: Spelling List 11
- handwriting workbook

Also Needed
- Spelling List 11 activity page cutouts from "The Bee's Knees: Insects Are Awesome!" (B)
- reading material for Go Read!

Poetry uses repeated words and phrases to create a rhythm. In some poems, a single phrase is repeated; in others, several words or phrases are repeated. **Repetition** may occur once, a few times, or throughout a poem.

Sensory language evokes the senses of hearing, smell, sight, taste, and touch. Poets use sensory language to help readers create mental images of and make connections to the words being shared.

KEYWORDS

concrete poem – a poem whose words are written in a shape that relates to what the poem is about; also called a "shape poem"

repetition – the use of a word or phrase more than once

sensory language – language that appeals to the five senses

Advance Preparation

Gather students' cutouts from the Spelling List 11 activity page from "The Bee's Knees" (B). They will use the cutouts during Try It: Practice: Spelling List 11.

During the Go Read! activity, students will have the option of using the digital library. Allow extra time for students to make their reading selection, or have students make a selection before beginning the lesson.

Lesson Goals

- Learn new vocabulary.
- Read "Insects," "How Many?," and "Housefly."
- Learn about shape poetry, repetition, and sensory language.
- Write a shape poem.
- Identify and write spelling patterns that stand for sounds within words.
- Develop letter formation fluency.
- Read independently to develop fluency.

GET READY

Introduction: Insect Poetry (A)
Students will get a glimpse of what they will learn about in the lesson.

Words to Know: Insect Poetry (A)
Students will preview and answer questions about two vocabulary words from the poems.

Insect Poetry (A)

Students will read "Insects," "How Many?," and "Housefly" in *English Language Arts 2 Activity Book 1*. Encourage them to reread their favorite poem.

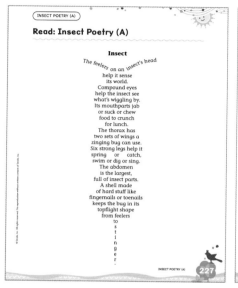

LEARN AND TRY IT

LEARN   Picturing Poems

Students will learn about these elements of poetry: shape, repeated lines, and sensory language.

TRY IT   Write a Shape Poem

Students will complete Write a Shape Poem in *English Language Arts 2 Activity Book 1*.

TRY IT   Practice: Spelling List 11

Students will practice the spelling patterns for Spelling List 11.

- In *English Language Arts 2 Activity Book 1*, students will complete Spelling List 11.

- Online, students will answer questions that require them to reflect on the spelling patterns.

NOTE   Students will need their cutouts from the Spelling List 11 activity page to complete Practice: Spelling List 11.

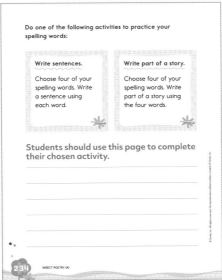

Questions About Insect Poetry (A)

Students will answer questions to show that they understand the reading and spelling skills they learned in this lesson.

Handwriting

Students should gather their handwriting materials and begin where they left off. Remind students to form letters carefully and correctly.

TIP   Set a timer to help students stay focused during handwriting practice.

Go Read!

Students will read for pleasure. They should choose a book or a magazine that interests them, or they may choose a selection from the digital library, linked in the online lesson.

- Have students read aloud a few paragraphs of their selection.

- Then have students read silently for the rest of the time.

SUPPORT   Students should make no more than five errors in decoding when they read aloud a few paragraphs of their Go Read! selection. If students struggle or make more than five errors, they need to select a different (and easier) text for the Go Read! activity.

TIP   Have students select something to read ahead of time to help them stay focused.

Insect Poetry (B)

Lesson Overview

ACTIVITY	ACTIVITY TITLE	TIME	ONLINE/OFFLINE
GET READY	Introduction: Insect Poetry (B)	**1** minute	🖥️
	VCe Syllables	**10** minutes	🖥️
READ	Insect Poetry (B)	**15** minutes	🖥️ or 📄
ALL ABOUT ME	Brain Break	**1** minute	🖥️ or 📄
LEARN	Meaning and Rhythm	**15** minutes	🖥️
ALL ABOUT ME	Brain Break	**1** minute	🖥️ or 📄
LEARN AND **TRY IT**	Record a Poem	**10** minutes	🖥️
	Record Your Poem	**25** minutes	🖥️ and 📄
	Apply: Spelling List 11	**20** minutes	🖥️ and 📄
WRAP-UP	Questions About Insect Poetry (B)	**2** minutes	🖥️
	Read and Record	**10** minutes	🖥️
	Handwriting	**10** minutes	📄

Content Background

Students will continue to learn about poetry. In this lesson, they will learn how words and phrases can affect the meaning and rhythm of a poem. Students will also learn about and try reading a poem aloud.

Reading   Poets use words and phrases to affect the meaning of a poem. They use descriptive language that conveys the message, emotion, and feelings they want to convey.

In addition, poets use words and phrases to create a rhythm in a poem. **Alliteration** is when a group of words or phrases all begin with the same sound. Poets use alliteration to help create a rhythm. Alliteration can emphasize particular words, which in turn creates meaning.

MATERIALS

Supplied
- *English Language Arts 2 Activity Book 1*
  - Read: Insect Poetry (B)
  - Apply: Spelling List 11
  - My Speed Sort Times
- handwriting workbook

Also Needed
- Spelling List 11 activity page cutouts from "The Bee's Knees: Insects Are Awesome!" (B)

Speaking and Listening Students will record themselves reading a poem aloud. When reading a poem aloud, it's important to pay attention to punctuation and line breaks. Punctuation and line breaks dictate when readers should pause, stop, and use intonation.

Advance Preparation

Gather students' cutouts from the Spelling List 11 activity page from "The Bee's Knees: Insects Are Awesome!" (B). They will use the cutouts during Try It: Apply: Spelling List 11.

If students have removed My Speed Sort Times from the activity book, have them gather this activity page. They will use this activity page in Try It: Apply: Spelling List 11.

Lesson Goals

- Identify the vowel-consonant-silent e (VCe) patterns in the syllables of words.
- Read "A Caterpillar's Job" and "Pesky Pests."
- Learn about how poets use language to create meaning and rhythm.
- Read and record a poem.
- Identify reasons for when and how to use certain spelling patterns.
- Read aloud to practice fluency.
- Develop letter formation fluency.

GET READY

Introduction: Insect Poetry (B)

Students will get a glimpse of what they will learn about in the lesson.

VCe Syllables

Students will identify vowel-consonant-silent e patterns when breaking words into syllables.

Insect Poetry (B)

Students will read "A Caterpillar's Job" and "Pesky Pests" in *English Language Arts 2 Activity Book 1*. Encourage them to reread their favorite poem.

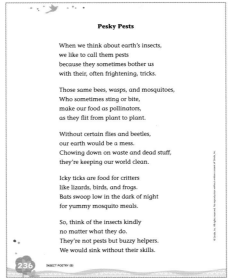

LEARN   Meaning and Rhythm

Students will learn how words and phrases affect the meaning and rhythm of a poem.

LEARN   Record a Poem

Students will learn about special considerations for reading a poem aloud.

TRY IT   Record Your Poem

Students will use a recording tool to record themselves reading a poem aloud.

TIP   Encourage students to listen to themselves and rerecord as needed.

TRY IT   Apply: Spelling List 11

Students will apply what they have learned about the spelling patterns for Spelling List 11.

- In an online activity, students will complete a word sort and answer reflection questions.

- In *English Language Arts 2 Activity Book 1*, students will complete Apply: Spelling List 11.

Students will need their cutouts from the Spelling List 11 activity page to complete the word sort.

TIP Have students record their speed sort times on the My Speed Sort Times activity page, which is located at the back of the activity book. It can be motivating for students to see their progress as their ability to complete speed sorts should improve over time.

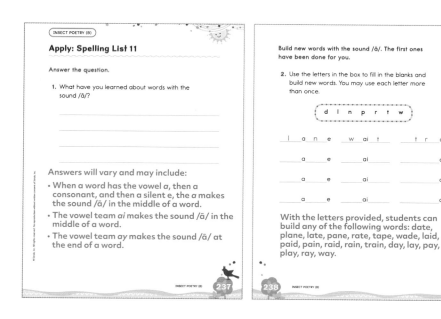

Questions About Insect Poetry (B)

Students will answer questions to show that they understand the reading and spelling skills they learned in this lesson.

Read and Record

Good readers read quickly, smoothly, and with expression. This is called *fluency*. Students will record themselves reading aloud. They will listen to their recording and think about how quick, smooth, and expressive they sound.

TIP Encourage students to rerecord as needed.

Handwriting

Students should gather their handwriting materials and begin where they left off. Remind students to form letters carefully and correctly.

TIP Set a timer to help students stay focused during handwriting practice.

Insects Wrap-Up (A)

Lesson Overview

ACTIVITY	ACTIVITY TITLE	TIME	ONLINE/OFFLINE
GET READY	Introduction: Insects Wrap-Up (A)	**1** minute	🖥
QUIZ	Spelling List 11	**25** minutes	🖥
ALL ABOUT ME	Brain Break	**1** minute	🖥 or 📄
GET READY	VCe Syllables	**5** minutes	🖥
REVIEW	Insects	**25** minutes	🖥
ALL ABOUT ME	Brain Break	**1** minute	🖥 or 📄
WRAP-UP	Theme Time: Insects LEARNING COACH CHECK-IN	**42** minutes	📄
	Your Choice Time	**20** minutes	🖥 or 📄

Advance Preparation

During the Your Choice Time activity, students will be given the option to read something of their choice. If students are using the digital library, allow extra time for them to make their reading selection, or have them make a selection before beginning the lesson.

Lesson Goals

- Take a spelling quiz.
- Decode words with VCe spelling patterns.
- Review writing, vocabulary, and reading skills from the unit.
- Make connections among the texts in the unit.

MATERIALS

Supplied

- *English Language Arts 2 Activity Book 1*
  - Theme Time: Insects

Also Needed

- reading material for Your Choice Time (optional)

Introduction: Insects Wrap-Up (A)

Students will get a glimpse of what they will do in the lesson.

Spelling List 11

Students will complete the Spelling List 11 quiz.

VCe Syllables

Students will use vowel-consonant-silent e spelling patterns to decode words with one or two syllables.

Insects

Students will answer questions to review the vocabulary, writing, and reading skills they learned in the unit.

Theme Time: Insects

Students will complete Theme Time: Insects in *English Language Arts 2 Activity Book 1*.

NOTE This activity page includes an optional ungraded project. Students may need additional materials to complete the project.

LEARNING COACH CHECK-IN Discuss students' responses to the questions. If they complete the project, ask them to demonstrate how the different types of bees work together.

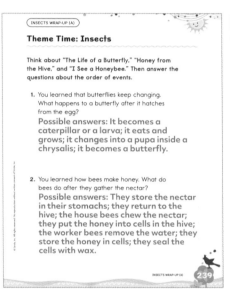

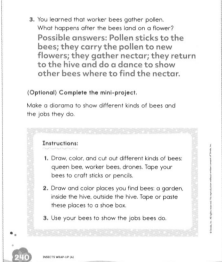

Your Choice Time

Students will choose among the following activities:

- Independent reading

- Independent writing

- Completing the optional project from the Theme Time: Insects activity page

Insects Wrap-Up (B)

Lesson Overview

ACTIVITY	ACTIVITY TITLE	TIME	ONLINE/OFFLINE
GET READY	Introduction: Insects Wrap-Up (B)	**1** minute	🖥️
QUIZ	Insects	**33** minutes	🖥️
ALL ABOUT ME	Brain Break	**1** minute	🖥️ or 📄
REFLECTION	Go Write! and Set a Goal **LEARNING COACH CHECK-IN**	**30** minutes	📄
WRAP-UP	Celebrate: Insects	**20** minutes	📄
	Discussion: What Would You Do? **LEARNING COACH CHECK-IN**	**15** minutes	🖥️
	More Language Arts Practice	**10** minutes	🖥️
	Your Choice Time	**10** minutes	🖥️ or 📄

Advance Preparation

If students have removed the My Reading Log and My Badge Book activity pages from the activity book, have them gather these pages. They will use these activity pages in the Celebrate: Insects activity.

During the Your Choice Time activity, students will be given the option to read something of their choice. If students are using the digital library, allow extra time for them to make their reading selection, or have them make a selection before beginning the lesson.

Lesson Goals

- Take a quiz on the writing, vocabulary, and reading skills from the unit.
- Freewrite to develop fluency and reflect on learning.
- Set a goal for future learning.
- Celebrate accomplishments from the unit.
- Participate in a discussion.

GET READY

Introduction: Insects Wrap-Up (B)

Students will get a glimpse of what they will do in the lesson.

QUIZ

Insects

Students will complete the Insects quiz.

REFLECTION

Go Write! and Set a Goal

Students will complete Go Write! and Set a Goal in *English Language Arts 2 Activity Book 1*.

NOTE   The Go Write! activity is intended to build writing fluency. Students should write for 10 minutes.

LEARNING COACH CHECK-IN   Discuss students' goal, including any steps they can take as well as support you can provide in helping them meet it.

A goal is something that you want to do.

You are getting ready to start a new unit. Choose one goal for yourself as a reader or writer. Or, write your own goal.

My GOAL!

- ☐ Read each book twice.
- ☐ Read for 10 minutes a day.
- ☐ Read to someone in my family.
- ☐ Write a paragraph on my own.
- ☐ _____

Write one thing you can do to help reach your goal.

I will _____

243

244 INSECTS WRAP-UP (B)

WRAP-UP

Celebrate: Insects

Students will celebrate accomplishments from the unit.

- They will record what they read this unit in their reading log.

- They will color the badge for this unit in their badge book. They may also color a badge to celebrate reading accomplishments.

    NOTE My Reading Log and My Badge Book are located at the back of the activity book.

    NOTE Students will need crayons or markers to color in their badges.

Discussion: What Would You Do?

Students will respond to a discussion prompt.

LEARNING COACH CHECK-IN Students should discuss the question shown on-screen with an adult. In some cases, teachers may facilitate a group discussion.

More Language Arts Practice

Students will practice skills according to their individual needs.

Your Choice Time

Students will choose among the following activities:

- Independent reading

- Independent writing

- Completing the optional project from the Theme Time: Insects activity page

Interesting People

A Weed is a Flower (A)

Lesson Overview

ACTIVITY	ACTIVITY TITLE	TIME	ONLINE/OFFLINE
GET READY	Introduction: *A Weed is a Flower* (A)	**1** minute	🖥️
	Building Background: Important Topics	**7** minutes	🖥️
	Words to Know: *A Weed is a Flower* (A)	**5** minutes	🖥️
READ	Think About Reading: *A Weed is a Flower* (A)	**5** minutes	📄
	A Weed is a Flower (A)	**15** minutes	🖥️ and 📄
	Check-In: *A Weed is a Flower* (A)	**5** minutes	🖥️
ALL ABOUT ME	Brain Break	**1** minute	🖥️ or 📄
LEARN AND TRY IT	Book Reviews	**8** minutes	🖥️
	Choose a Topic for a Book Review	**5** minutes	🖥️
	Choose a Topic for Your Book Review	**20** minutes	📄
ALL ABOUT ME	Brain Break	**1** minute	🖥️ or 📄
LEARN	Spelling List 12	**25** minutes	🖥️ and 📄
WRAP-UP	Questions About *A Weed is a Flower* (A)	**2** minutes	🖥️
	Handwriting	**10** minutes	📄
	Go Read!	**10** minutes	🖥️ or 📄

Content Background

Students will begin a series of lessons centered around the book *A Weed is a Flower* by Aliki. In this lesson, they will build background and make connections to the book and learn about book reviews.

Vocabulary Students will explore these words from the story: *despair*, *devote*, *professor*, and *yearn*. These are the definitions for how the words are used in *A Weed is a Flower*:

• **despair** (noun) – feeling like there is no hope

• **devote** (verb) – to give all your time to doing something

- **professor** (noun) – a type of teacher

- **yearn** (verb) – to want something very badly

Writing Skills Students will begin working on a **book review**, which is a type of opinion writing. They will complete this assignment over the course of several lessons by following the writing process.

Writing Process

1 Prewriting	2 Drafting	3 Revising	4 Proofreading	5 Publishing

Students will complete the first part of prewriting, choosing a topic. They will use the prewriting technique of making idea webs. To make an idea web, students will record a topic—in this case, a book—in a central circle. They will connect details to the central idea, free-associating their thoughts and visually representing them.

Spelling Students will learn about words that begin with consonant blends that have the letter *l*. Students will sort words under these headings: **bl–**, **cl–**, **fl–**, **pl–**.

Students will learn that words can begin with the sound of two consonants that blend, or mix, together. When they say these words aloud, they will hear the sound of both consonants. The sorting depends on the consonant blend at the beginning of each word.

- Words that go under the heading **bl–** begin with the consonant blend *bl–*.

- Words that go under the heading **cl–** begin with the consonant blend *cl–*.

- Words that go under the heading **fl–** begin with the consonant blend *fl–*.

- Words that go under the heading **pl–** begin with the consonant blend *pl–*.

Advance Preparation

Gather a folder that students can use to keep all activity pages related to their book review.

During the Go Read! activity, students will have the option of using the digital library. Allow extra time for students to make their reading selection, or have students make a selection before beginning the lesson.

MATERIALS

Supplied
- *A Weed is a Flower* by Aliki
- *English Language Arts 2 Activity Book 1*
  - Think About Reading: *A Weed is a Flower* (A)
  - Model Book Review
  - Choose a Topic for Your Book Review
  - Spelling List 12
- handwriting workbook

Also Needed
- crayons or markers (optional)
- map of the United States
- folder for organizing book review assignment pages
- scissors
- envelope or baggie to store spelling cutouts
- reading material for Go Read!

KEYWORDS

biography – the story of a person's life written by another person

book review – a piece of writing that gives an opinion about a book and tells about it

A Weed is a Flower Synopsis

This book is a biography of George Washington Carver, a man born into enslavement who became a leading expert on agriculture and taught people during his tenure as a professor at the Tuskegee Institute for African Americans. The first part of the story is about Carver's early life. The next part of the story details Carver's struggle to earn money and find schools that would teach African Americans. Carver succeeds as a professor and an inventor, earning himself a place in American history.

NOTE   The story discusses enslavement and describes the abduction of the infant Carver and his mother, which led to her disappearance.

Lesson Goals

- Learn new vocabulary.
- Read *A Weed is a Flower*.
- Choose a topic for a book review.
- Sort words by sound and spelling pattern.
- Develop letter formation fluency.
- Read independently to develop fluency.

GET READY

Introduction: *A Weed is a Flower* (A)
Students will get a glimpse of what they will learn about in the lesson.

Building Background: Important Topics
Students will learn about important topics that will prepare them for the reading selection. These topics include biographies, growing peanuts, and enslavement.

Words to Know: *A Weed is a Flower* (A)
Students will preview and answer questions about four vocabulary words from the reading selection.

Think About Reading: *A Weed is a Flower* (A)

Students will complete Think About Reading: *A Weed is a Flower* (A) in *English Language Arts 2 Activity Book 1*.

NOTE Encourage students to preview the reading selection by completing a book walk on their own.

NOTE Students may wish to use crayons or markers to draw their picture.

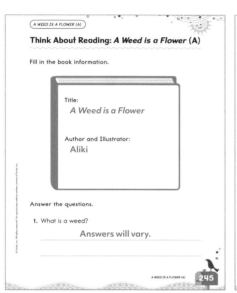
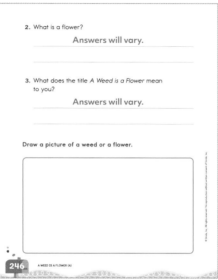

A Weed is a Flower (A)

Students will listen to and follow along with a read-aloud of *A Weed is a Flower* by Aliki. They may choose to read the story on their own. Encourage students to reread their favorite passages.

TIP Show students a map of the United States. Point out the states mentioned in the book.

Check-In: *A Weed is a Flower* (A)

Students will answer several questions to demonstrate their comprehension of *A Weed is a Flower*.

LEARN Book Reviews

Students will explore a model book review in preparation for writing their own book review.

LEARN Choose a Topic for a Book Review

Students will learn how to choose a topic by making idea webs.

TRY IT Choose a Topic for Your Book Review

Students will complete Choose a Topic for Your Book Review in *English Language Arts 2 Activity Book 1*.

SUPPORT Before students begin the activity page, talk with them about the books they have read recently (including books in the course and books they have read for pleasure). Discuss which books they liked and disliked. Discuss which books they would tell their friends or family members to read.

TIP Read the Model Book Review together to ensure that students understand the assignment before they choose a topic.

NOTE Have students put the Model Book Review and their completed Choose a Topic for Your Book Review activity page into a folder for safe keeping.

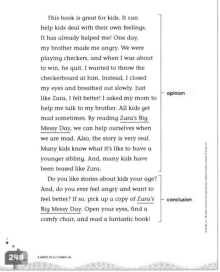

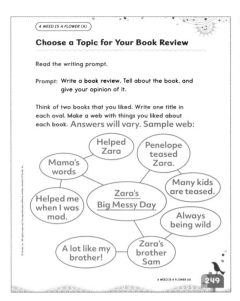

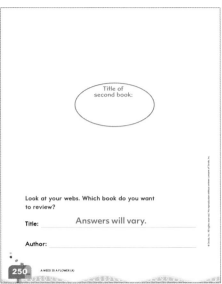

LEARN   Spelling List 12

Students will learn and sort words with spelling patterns with consonant blends that have the letter *l*.

- In an online activity, students will learn about the spelling patterns and the sounds they represent. They will learn how to sort words according to those sounds and patterns. They will also complete a word sort.

- In *English Language Arts 2 Activity Book 1*, students will complete Spelling List 12.

NOTE   Students will need scissors to cut out the spelling words on the activity page. Have students store their cutouts in a safe place, such as an envelope.

This is the complete list of words students will work with to learn the spelling patterns.

bl–	cl–	fl–	pl–
black	clay	flat	plain
bloom	click	flood	plant
blow	clothes	flower	play

WRAP-UP

Questions About *A Weed is a Flower* (A)

Students will answer questions to show that they understand the reading, writing, and spelling skills they learned in this lesson.

Handwriting

Students should gather their handwriting materials and begin where they left off. Remind students to form letters carefully and correctly.

TIP Set a timer to help students stay focused during handwriting practice.

Go Read!

Students will read for pleasure. They should choose a book or a magazine that interests them, or they may choose a selection from the digital library, linked in the online lesson.

- Have students read aloud a few paragraphs of their selection.

- Then have students read silently for the rest of the time.

SUPPORT Students should make no more than five errors in decoding when they read aloud a few paragraphs of their Go Read! selection. If students struggle or make more than five errors, they need to select a different (and easier) text for the Go Read! activity.

TIP Have students select something to read ahead of time to help them stay focused.

A Weed is a Flower (B)

Lesson Overview

ACTIVITY	ACTIVITY TITLE	TIME	ONLINE/OFFLINE
GET READY	Introduction: *A Weed is a Flower* (B)	**1** minute	📶
	To, Two, Too Much!	**5** minutes	📶
	Words to Know: *A Weed is a Flower* (B)	**10** minutes	📶
LEARN	What Did I Read?	**25** minutes	📶
ALL ABOUT ME	Brain Break	**1** minute	📶 or 📄
LEARN AND TRY IT	Plan a Summary	**10** minutes	📶
	Plan Your Summary	**25** minutes	📄
ALL ABOUT ME	Brain Break	**1** minute	📶 or 📄
TRY IT	Practice: Spelling List 12	**20** minutes	📶 and 📄
WRAP-UP	Questions About *A Weed is a Flower* (B)	**2** minutes	📶
	Handwriting	**10** minutes	📄
	Go Read!	**10** minutes	📶 or 📄

Content Background

Students will continue a series of lessons centered around the book *A Weed is a Flower* by Aliki. In this lesson, they will learn how to identify the main idea and details and how to plan the summary of their book review.

Reading Foundations Homophones are words that sound the same but have different meanings and are spelled differently. Examples of homophones are *to*, *two*, and *too*.

Vocabulary Students will explore these words from the story: *band*, *snatch*, and *livelihood*. These are the definitions for how the words are used in *A Weed is a Flower*:

- **band** (noun) – a group

- **snatch** (verb) – to take or grab, usually without permission

- **livelihood** (noun) – a person's job or way of making a living

Reading Readers can check if they understand what they are reading by identifying the **main idea** and key **details** of a paragraph. The main idea is what the paragraph is mostly about. The details support and add information about the main idea.

Writing Skills Students will continue working on their **book review**. They will complete this assignment over the course of several lessons by following the writing process.

Writing Process

1 Prewriting	2 Drafting	3 Revising	4 Proofreading	5 Publishing

Good opinion writing begins by giving readers enough background information to understand the writer's opinion. In a book review, writers provide background information about the book in a **summary**. The summary includes the book's title; author; main characters; setting; and key details about the beginning, middle, and end. Students will use a graphic organizer to plan the summary part of their book review.

Advance Preparation

Gather the folder that students are using to keep all activity pages related to their book review.

• Model Book Review from *A Weed is a Flower* (A)

• Students' completed Choose a Topic for Your Book Review activity page from *A Weed is a Flower* (A)

Gather students' cutouts from the Spelling List 12 activity page from *A Weed is a Flower* (A). They will use the cutouts during Try It: Practice: Spelling List 12.

During the Go Read! activity, students will have the option of using the digital library. Allow extra time for students to make their reading selection, or have students make a selection before beginning the lesson.

Lesson Goals

- Learn about homophones.
- Learn new vocabulary.
- Identify main ideas and key details.
- Plan the summary part of a book review.
- Identify and write spelling patterns that stand for sounds within words.
- Develop letter formation fluency.
- Read independently to develop fluency.

GET READY

Introduction: *A Weed is a Flower* (B)

Students will get a glimpse of what they will learn about in the lesson.

To, Two, Too Much!

Students will learn about homophones.

Words to Know: *A Weed is a Flower* (B)

Students will preview and answer questions about three vocabulary words from the reading selection.

LEARN AND TRY IT

LEARN   What Did I Read?

Students will learn to check their understanding of what they've read by identifying the main idea and key details of a paragraph.

LEARN   Plan a Summary

Students will learn why including background information is important in opinion writing. They will learn how to plan a summary of their book to include in their book review.

TRY IT Plan Your Summary

Students will complete Plan Your Summary in *English Language Arts 2 Activity Book 1*.

TIP Read the summary (Paragraph 1) in the Model Book Review together. Discuss why certain details from the book being reviewed are included and others are not included. Emphasize that the purpose of the summary is to provide enough information about the book being reviewed so that the writer's opinion about the book makes sense.

NOTE Have students put their completed Plan Your Summary activity page into the folder they are using to store their book review assignment pages.

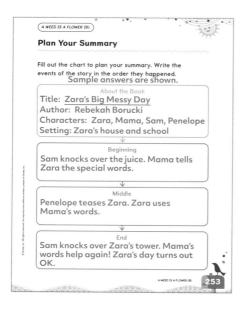

TRY IT Practice: Spelling List 12

Students will practice the spelling patterns for Spelling List 12.

- In *English Language Arts 2 Activity Book 1*, students will complete Practice: Spelling List 12.

- Online, students will answer questions that require them to reflect on the spelling patterns.

NOTE Students will need their cutouts from the Spelling List 12 activity page to complete Practice: Spelling List 12.

NOTE Students may wish to use crayons or markers to draw their pictures or comic strip.

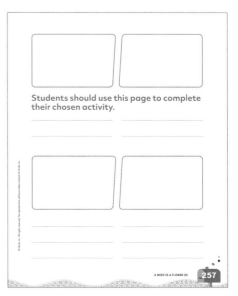

WRAP-UP

Questions About *A Weed is a Flower* (B)

Students will answer questions to show that they understand the reading, writing, and spelling skills they learned in this lesson.

Handwriting

Students should gather their handwriting materials and begin where they left off. Remind students to form letters carefully and correctly.

TIP Set a timer to help students stay focused during handwriting practice.

Go Read!

Students will read for pleasure. They should choose a book or a magazine that interests them, or they may choose a selection from the digital library, linked in the online lesson.

- Have students read aloud a few paragraphs of their selection.

- Then have students read silently for the rest of the time.

SUPPORT Students should make no more than five errors in decoding when they read aloud a few paragraphs of their Go Read! selection. If students struggle or make more than five errors, they need to select a different (and easier) text for the Go Read! activity.

TIP Have students select something to read ahead of time to help them stay focused.

A Weed is a Flower (C)

Lesson Overview

ACTIVITY	ACTIVITY TITLE	TIME	ONLINE/OFFLINE
GET READY	Introduction: *A Weed is a Flower* (C)	**1** minute	🖥️
	Sorting Syllable Types	**15** minutes	📶
READ	*A Weed is a Flower* (C)	**25** minutes	🖥️ and 📄
ALL ABOUT ME	Brain Break	**1** minute	🖥️ or 📄
LEARN AND TRY IT	Plan an Opinion Statement and Reasons	**10** minutes	📶
	Plan Your Opinion Statement and Reasons	**25** minutes	📄
ALL ABOUT ME	Brain Break	**1** minute	🖥️ or 📄
TRY IT	Apply: Spelling List 12	**20** minutes	🖥️ and 📄
WRAP-UP	Questions About *A Weed is a Flower* (C)	**2** minutes	🖥️
	Handwriting	**10** minutes	📄
	Go Read!	**10** minutes	🖥️ or 📄

Content Background

Students will continue a series of lessons centered around the book *A Weed is a Flower* by Aliki. In this lesson, they will plan the opinion statement and reasons for their book review.

Reading Foundations Students will review three types of syllables: open, closed, and vowel-consonant-silent e (VCe). An open syllable has either a vowel by itself or it ends with a vowel. The vowel makes a long sound. A closed syllable has a vowel followed by a consonant. The vowel makes a short sound. The third type of syllable has a vowel followed by a consonant and a silent e.

Writing Skills Students will continue working on their **book review**. They will complete this assignment over the course of several lessons by following the writing process.

Writing Process

| 1 Prewriting | 2 Drafting | 3 Revising | 4 Proofreading | 5 Publishing |

MATERIALS

Supplied
- *A Weed is a Flower* by Aliki
- *English Language Arts 2 Activity Book 1*
  - Plan Your Opinion Statement and Reasons
  - Apply: Spelling List 12
  - My Speed Sort Times
- handwriting workbook

Also Needed
- folder in which students are storing book review assignment pages
- Spelling List 12 activity page cutouts from *A Weed is a Flower* (A)
- reading material for Go Read!

Effective opinion writing includes reasons for an opinion. Weak reasons essentially restate an opinion. Strong reasons use facts, examples, and other details to support or explain the reason.

Opinion: This book is great for kids.

Weak reason: It is so good for children! It really is!

Strong reason: It helps kids deal with big feelings. It even helped me when I was mad at my little brother.

Students will use a graphic organizer to plan their opinion statement and reasons.

Advance Preparation

Gather the folder that students are using to keep all activity pages related to their book review.

- Model Book Review from *A Weed is a Flower* (A)

- Students' completed Choose a Topic for Your Book Review activity page from *A Weed is a Flower* (A)

- Students' completed Plan Your Summary activity page from *A Weed is a Flower* (B)

Gather students' cutouts from the Spelling List 12 activity page from *A Weed is a Flower* (A). They will use the cutouts during Try It: Apply: Spelling List 12.

If students have removed My Speed Sort Times from the activity book, have them gather this activity page. They will use this activity page in Try It: Apply: Spelling List 12.

During the Go Read! activity, students will have the option of using the digital library. Allow extra time for students to make their reading selection, or have students make a selection before beginning the lesson.

Lesson Goals

- Review three types of syllables.
- Plan an opinion statement and reasons.
- Identify reasons for when and how to use certain spelling patterns.
- Develop letter formation fluency.
- Read independently to develop fluency.

GET READY

Introduction: *A Weed is a Flower* (C)

Students will get a glimpse of what they will learn about in the lesson.

Sorting Syllable Types

Students will review what they have learned about three types of syllables.

SUPPORT   For students having difficulty recognizing these types of syllables, continue practicing with additional words.

READ

A Weed is a Flower (C)

Students will listen to and follow along with a read-aloud of *A Weed is a Flower* by Aliki again. They may choose to read the story on their own. Encourage students to reread their favorite passages.

LEARN AND TRY IT

LEARN   Plan an Opinion Statement and Reasons

Students will learn about writing effective reasons to support an opinion. They will learn how to plan an opinion statement and reasons for their book review.

TRY IT   Plan Your Opinion Statement and Reasons

Students will complete Plan Your Opinion Statement and Reasons in *English Language Arts 2 Activity Book 1*.

TIP   Read the opinion statement and reasons (Paragraph 2) in the Model Book Review together. Discuss how each reason supports the writer's opinion.

NOTE   Have students put their completed Plan Your Opinion Statement and Reasons activity page into the folder they are using to store their book review assignment pages.

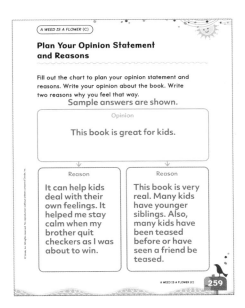

TRY IT Apply: Spelling List 12

Students will apply what they have learned about the spelling patterns for Spelling List 12.

- In an online activity, students will complete a word sort and answer reflection questions.

- In *English Language Arts 2 Activity Book 1*, students will complete Apply: Spelling List 12.

NOTE Students will need their cutouts from the Spelling List 12 activity page to complete the word sort.

TIP Have students record their speed sort times on the My Speed Sort Times activity page, which is located at the back of the activity book. It can be motivating for students to see their progress as their ability to complete speed sorts should improve over time.

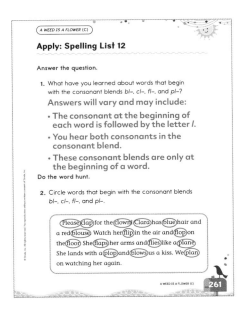

Questions About *A Weed is a Flower* (C)

Students will answer questions to show that they understand the reading, writing, and spelling skills they learned in this lesson.

Handwriting

Students should gather their handwriting materials and begin where they left off. Remind students to form letters carefully and correctly.

TIP Set a timer to help students stay focused during handwriting practice.

Go Read!

Students will read for pleasure. They should choose a book or a magazine that interests them, or they may choose a selection from the digital library, linked in the online lesson.

- Have students read aloud a few paragraphs of their selection.

- Then have students read silently for the rest of the time.

SUPPORT Students should make no more than five errors in decoding when they read aloud a few paragraphs of their Go Read! selection. If students struggle or make more than five errors, they need to select a different (and easier) text for the Go Read! activity.

TIP Have students select something to read ahead of time to help them stay focused.

A Weed is a Flower (D)

Lesson Overview

ACTIVITY	ACTIVITY TITLE	TIME	ONLINE/OFFLINE
GET READY	Introduction: *A Weed is a Flower* (D)	**1** minute	🖥️
	Word Relationships	**10** minutes	🖥️
LEARN	Growing in the Wrong Place	**15** minutes	🖥️
ALL ABOUT ME	Brain Break	**1** minute	🖥️ or 📄
LEARN AND **TRY IT**	Connect and Conclude a Book Review	**10** minutes	🖥️
	Start Drafting Your Book Review	**35** minutes	📄
WRAP-UP	Questions About *A Weed is a Flower* (D)	**2** minutes	🖥️
ALL ABOUT ME	Brain Break	**1** minute	🖥️ or 📄
QUIZ	Spelling List 12	**25** minutes	🖥️
WRAP-UP	Read and Record	**10** minutes	🖥️
	More Language Arts Practice	**10** minutes	🖥️

Content Background

Students will conclude a series of lessons centered around the book *A Weed is a Flower* by Aliki. In this lesson, they will examine the setting and events in the story and start drafting their book review.

Reading Foundations Students will learn about word relationships. The term *word relationships* may be unfamiliar, though students have been introduced to synonyms and antonyms.

Reading Students will reexamine *A Weed is a Flower* to analyze the effect of the time and place on George Washington Carver's life. It is an opportunity for students to make connections between the text and their own life.

Writing Skills Students will continue working on their **book review**. They will complete this assignment over the course of several lessons by following the writing process.

MATERIALS

Supplied
- *A Weed is a Flower* by Aliki
- *English Language Arts 2 Activity Book 1*
  - Draft Your Book Review
- Drafting Paper (printout)

Also Needed
- folder in which students are storing book review assignment pages

Writing Process

1 Prewriting	2 Drafting	3 Revising	4 Proofreading	5 Publishing

Transitions are words or phrases that connect ideas. Students at this level refer to transitions as *connecting words* or *signal words*. In opinion writing, transitions such as *also, and, another, too,* and *plus* can clarify how reasons relate to an opinion. In a summary, *order words* such as *first, next,* and *last* can clarify sequence.

The last paragraph of the book review is the **conclusion**. In opinion writing, an effective conclusion restates the opinion in a new way. It may also summarize the reasons and provide a final thought—something for readers to remember or "take away" from the piece.

Advance Preparation

Gather the folder that students are using to keep all activity pages related to their book review.

- Model Book Review from *A Weed is a Flower* (A)

- Students' completed Choose a Topic for Your Book Review activity page from *A Weed is a Flower* (A)

- Students' completed Plan Your Summary activity page from *A Weed is a Flower* (B)

- Students' completed Plan Your Opinion Statement and Reasons activity page from *A Weed is a Flower* (C)

Lesson Goals

- Learn about word relationships.

- Analyze how setting and events affect a person's life.

- Start drafting a book review.

- Take a spelling quiz.

- Read aloud to practice fluency.

Introduction: *A Weed is a Flower* (D)

Students will get a glimpse of what they will learn about in the lesson.

Word Relationships

Students will learn about word relationships: synonyms, antonyms, and shades of meaning.

LEARN AND TRY IT

LEARN   Growing in the Wrong Place

Students will take a closer look at the setting and time period of the story and analyze how both affected George Washington Carver's life. They will also think about the role unfairness played in Carver's life.

LEARN   Connect and Conclude a Book Review

Students will learn about using connecting words and writing the conclusion to a book review.

TRY IT   Start Drafting Your Book Review

Students will complete about half of their draft using Draft Your Book Review in *English Language Arts 2 Activity Book 1*. Make sure students have their completed Plan Your Summary, Plan Your Opinion Statement and Reasons, and Model Book Review to refer to as they work.

TIP   Read the conclusion (Paragraph 3) in the Model Book Review together. Identify the parts of the conclusion (restatement of opinion, restatement of reasons, final thought).

NOTE   Have students put their in-progress Draft Your Book Review activity pages into the folder they are using to store their book review assignment pages.

NOTE   Additional sheets of Drafting Paper are available online.

Draft Your Book Review

Write the first draft of your book review. Write only on the white rows. You will use the purple rows later.

Title: _____

start here ►

keep writing ►

263

264

keep writing ►

keep writing ►

265

266

keep writing ►

keep writing ►

267

268

WRAP-UP

Questions About *A Weed is a Flower* (D)

Students will answer questions to show that they understand the reading and writing skills they learned in this lesson.

QUIZ

Spelling List 12

Students will complete the Spelling List 12 quiz.

WRAP-UP

Read and Record

Good readers read quickly, smoothly, and with expression. This is called *fluency*. Students will record themselves reading aloud. They will listen to their recording and think about how quick, smooth, and expressive they sound.

TIP   Encourage students to rerecord as needed.

More Language Arts Practice

Students will practice skills according to their individual needs.

The Girl Who Thought in Pictures (A)

Lesson Overview

ACTIVITY	ACTIVITY TITLE	TIME	ONLINE/OFFLINE
GET READY	Introduction: *The Girl Who Thought in Pictures* (A)	**1** minute	🖥
	Words to Know: *The Girl Who Thought in Pictures* (A)	**5** minutes	🖥
	Before You Read: Fiction or Nonfiction?	**8** minutes	🖥
READ	Think About Reading: *The Girl Who Thought in Pictures* (A)	**5** minutes	📄
	The Girl Who Thought in Pictures (A)	**12** minutes	🖥 and 📄
	Check-In: *The Girl Who Thought in Pictures* (A)	**5** minutes	🖥
ALL ABOUT ME	Brain Break	**1** minute	🖥 or 📄
LEARN AND TRY IT	Use Your Best Words	**10** minutes	🖥
	Finish Drafting Your Book Review	**35** minutes	📄
ALL ABOUT ME	Brain Break	**1** minute	🖥 or 📄
LEARN	Spelling List 13	**25** minutes	🖥 and 📄
WRAP-UP	Questions About *The Girl Who Thought in Pictures* (A)	**2** minutes	🖥
	Go Read!	**10** minutes	🖥 or 📄

Content Background

Students will begin a series of lessons centered around the book *The Girl Who Thought in Pictures* by Julia Finley Mosca. In this lesson, they will learn about text structures and features, and they will finish drafting a book review.

Vocabulary Students will explore these words from the story: *unique*, *degree*, and *grand*. These are the definitions for how the words are used in *The Girl Who Thought in Pictures*:

- **unique** (adjective) – special or unusual

- **degree** (noun) – something you earn in school for finishing your studies

- **grand** (adjective) – great or wonderful

Build Background Students will learn about the differences between fiction and nonfiction. *The Girl Who Thought in Pictures* is about a real person, so it is nonfiction. The back of the book has text features—an interview and a time line—that are only found in nonfiction. But, the style of the book is more like fiction. It is actually one long poem, written in rhyme.

Writing Skills Students will continue working on their **book review**. They will complete this assignment over the course of several lessons by following the writing process.

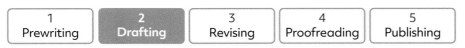

Writing Process

| 1 Prewriting | 2 Drafting | 3 Revising | 4 Proofreading | 5 Publishing |

Writers use precise language to express their ideas clearly.

>**Imprecise:** The weather is bad today. *Is it raining? Snowing? Scorching hot?*

>**Precise:** It 40 degrees and drizzling today.

Students will not be introduced to the term *precise*; instead, they will learn how to use their "best words."

Spelling Students will learn about three spelling patterns for words with the vowel *o* followed by two consonants. They will sort words under these headings: **ŏCC**, **ōCC –ost**, **ōCC –old**.

Students will learn that these words have the sound of short o, /ŏ/, or long o, /ō/. The sorting depends on the sound of the letter *o* and the spelling pattern in each word.

- Words that go under the heading **ŏCC** have the spelling pattern of the vowel *o*, a consonant, and another consonant. The *o* in this spelling pattern has its short sound, /ŏ/.

- Words that go under the heading **ōCC –ost** have the spelling pattern of the vowel *o* followed by the consonants *s-t*. The *o* in this spelling pattern has its long sound, /ō/.

- Words that go under the heading **ōCC –old** have the spelling pattern of the vowel *o* followed by the consonants *l-d*. The *o* in this spelling pattern has its long sound, /ō/.

MATERIALS

Supplied
- *The Girl Who Thought in Pictures* by Julia Finley Mosca
- *English Language Arts 2 Activity Book 1*
  - Think About Reading: *The Girl Who Thought in Pictures* (A)
  - Spelling List 13
- Drafting Paper (printout)

Also Needed
- folder in which students are storing book review assignment pages
- scissors
- envelope or baggie to store spelling cutouts
- reading material for Go Read!

Advance Preparation

Gather the folder that students are using to keep all activity pages related to their book review.

- Model Book Review from *A Weed is a Flower* (A)

- Students' completed Choose a Topic for Your Book Review activity page from *A Weed is a Flower* (A)

- Students' completed Plan Your Summary activity page from *A Weed is a Flower* (B)

- Students' completed Plan Your Opinion Statement and Reasons activity page from *A Weed is a Flower* (C)

- Students' in-progress Draft Your Book Review activity page from *A Weed is a Flower* (D)

During the Go Read! activity, students will have the option of using the digital library. Allow extra time for students to make their reading selection, or have students make a selection before beginning the lesson.

The Girl Who Thought in Pictures Synopsis

This book tells the story of Temple Grandin, a professor of animal science who cares about animals. Temple also has autism. She didn't learn to speak until she was nearly four years old. Temple thought in pictures instead of words. When she started school, the other children noticed that she was different. They made fun of her, and her mother had to remove her from the school. Temple's love of animals turned into a career as a professor and scientist. She earned a Ph.D. and the title of doctor. She conducts research on both animal science and autism. In addition to teaching, Temple Grandin has written a best-selling book, has had her story turned into a movie, and has earned respect and fame throughout the country.

Lesson Goals

- Learn new vocabulary.

- Compare fiction and nonfiction.

- Read *The Girl Who Thought in Pictures*.

- Learn how to use precise language in writing.

- Finish drafting a book review.

- Sort words by sound and spelling pattern.

- Read independently to develop fluency.

GET READY

Introduction: *The Girl Who Thought in Pictures* (A)

Students will get a glimpse of what they will learn about in the lesson.

Words to Know: *The Girl Who Thought in Pictures* (A)

Students will preview and answer questions about three vocabulary words from the reading selection.

Before You Read: Fiction or Nonfiction?

Students will learn about the differences between fiction and nonfiction.

READ

Think About Reading: *The Girl Who Thought in Pictures* (A)

Students will complete Think About Reading: *The Girl Who Thought in Pictures* (A) in *English Language Arts 2 Activity Book 1*.

NOTE Encourage students to preview the reading selection by completing a book walk on their own.

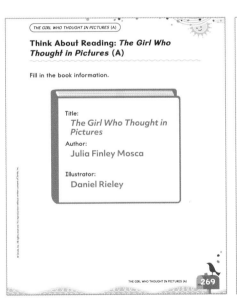

The Girl Who Thought in Pictures (A)

Students will listen to and follow along with a read-aloud of *The Girl Who Thought in Pictures* by Julia Finley Mosca. They may choose to read the story on their own. Encourage students to reread their favorite passages.

Remind students that Temple Grandin is a real person. She has persevered and had a successful career while living with autism. You might want to share photos of her with students.

Check-In: *The Girl Who Thought in Pictures* (A)

Students will answer several questions to demonstrate their comprehension of *The Girl Who Thought in Pictures*.

LEARN AND TRY IT

LEARN Use Your Best Words

Students will explore how using their "best words" (precise language) can strengthen their writing.

TRY IT Finish Drafting Your Book Review

Students will complete Draft Your Book Review in *English Language Arts 2 Activity Book 1*. In addition to their in-progress draft, make sure students have their completed Plan Your Summary, Plan Your Opinion Statement and Reasons, and Model Book Review to refer to as they work.

NOTE Have students put their completed Draft Your Book Review activity pages into the folder they are using to store their book review assignment pages.

NOTE Additional sheets of Drafting Paper are available online.

keep writing ▶
keep writing ▶

LEARN   Spelling List 13

Students will learn and sort words with three spelling patterns for the vowel o followed by two consonants.

- In an online activity, students will learn about the spelling patterns and the sounds they represent. They will learn how to sort words according to those sounds and patterns. They will also complete a word sort.

- In *English Language Arts 2 Activity Book 1*, students will complete Spelling List 13.

NOTE   Students will need scissors to cut out the spelling words on the activity page. Have students store their cutouts in a safe place, such as an envelope.

This is the complete list of words students will work with to learn the spelling patterns.

ŏCC	ōCC –ost	ōCC –old
cost	ghost	cold
lost	most	gold
moss	post	hold
odd		told
soft		

WRAP-UP

Questions About *The Girl Who Thought in Pictures* (A)

Students will answer questions to show that they understand the reading, writing, and spelling skills they learned in this lesson.

Go Read!

Students will read for pleasure. They should choose a book or a magazine that interests them, or they may choose a selection from the digital library, linked in the online lesson.

- Have students read aloud a few paragraphs of their selection.

- Then have students read silently for the rest of the time.

SUPPORT   Students should make no more than five errors in decoding when they read aloud a few paragraphs of their Go Read! selection. If students struggle or make more than five errors, they need to select a different (and easier) text for the Go Read! activity.

TIP   Have students select something to read ahead of time to help them stay focused.

The Girl Who Thought in Pictures (B)

Lesson Overview

ACTIVITY	ACTIVITY TITLE	TIME	ONLINE/OFFLINE
GET READY	Introduction: *The Girl Who Thought in Pictures* (B)	**1** minute	🖥
	Shades of Meaning	**8** minutes	🖥
	Words to Know: *The Girl Who Thought in Pictures* (B)	**5** minutes	🖥
READ	*The Girl Who Thought in Pictures* (B)	**12** minutes	🖥 and 📄
LEARN	Graphic Features: Time Line	**10** minutes	🖥
ALL ABOUT ME	Brain Break	**1** minute	🖥 or 📄
LEARN AND **TRY IT**	Give and Get Feedback	**10** minutes	🖥
	Revise Your Book Review **LEARNING COACH CHECK-IN**	**40** minutes	📄
ALL ABOUT ME	Brain Break	**1** minute	🖥 or 📄
TRY IT	Practice: Spelling List 13	**20** minutes	🖥 and 📄
WRAP-UP	Questions About *The Girl Who Thought in Pictures* (B)	**2** minutes	🖥
	Go Read!	**10** minutes	🖥 or 📄

Content Background

Students will continue a series of lessons centered around the book *The Girl Who Thought in Pictures* by Julia Finley Mosca. In this lesson, they will read the backmatter of the book and learn how to read a time line. They will also revise their book review.

Reading Foundations Similar verbs and adjectives can have slightly different meanings, or shades of meaning. These are words that are very similar but their meanings are not exactly the same, such as the difference between the verbs *say* and *shout* or the adjectives *big* and *huge*.

Vocabulary Students will explore these words from the story: *proclaim*, *taunt*, and *soar*. These are the definitions for how the words are used in *The Girl Who Thought in Pictures*:

- **proclaim** (verb) – to announce with confidence

- **taunt** (verb) – to insult or put down

- **soar** (verb) – to fly high into the air

Reading The backmatter of *The Girl Who Thought in Pictures* includes a **time line**. The time line lists events in chronological order. It includes dates or years and a description of the events that took place.

Writing Skills Students will continue working on their **book review**. They will complete this assignment over the course of several lessons by following the writing process.

Writing Process

1 Prewriting	2 Drafting	3 Revising	4 Proofreading	5 Publishing

During the revising step of the writing process, writers often ask others for feedback on their drafts. Effective feedback is specific.

Not specific: That paragraph confused me.

Specific: Using order words in that paragraph would help me follow along.

Feedback to writers should always be respectful. Even constructive feedback should be delivered with sensitivity.

Not respectful: That paragraph is so boring.

Respectful: You give a lot of details. One or two might be enough.

Advance Preparation

Gather the folder that students are using to keep all activity pages related to their book review.

- Model Book Review from *A Weed is a Flower* (A)

- Students' completed Choose a Topic for Your Book Review activity page from *A Weed is a Flower* (A)

- Students' completed Plan Your Summary activity page from *A Weed is a Flower* (B)

- Students' completed Plan Your Opinion Statement and Reasons activity page from *A Weed is a Flower* (C)

MATERIALS

Supplied
- *The Girl Who Thought in Pictures* by Julia Finley Mosca
- *English Language Arts 2 Activity Book 1*
  - Revise Your Book Review
  - Practice: Spelling List 13
- Book Review: Feedback Sheet (printout)

Also Needed
- folder in which students are storing book review assignment pages
- Spelling List 13 activity page cutouts from *The Girl Who Thought in Pictures* (A)
- reading material for Go Read!

KEYWORDS

time line – a line showing dates and events in the order that they happened

- Students' completed Draft Your Book Review activity page from *The Girl Who Thought in Pictures* (A)

Prior to Try It: Revise Your Book Review, read students' draft and complete the revising part of Book Review: Feedback Sheet.

Gather students' cutouts from the Spelling List 13 activity page from *The Girl Who Thought in Pictures* (A). They will use the cutouts during Try It: Practice: Spelling List 13.

During the Go Read! activity, students will have the option of using the digital library. Allow extra time for students to make their reading selection, or have students make a selection before beginning the lesson.

Lesson Goals

- Learn about shades of meaning.
- Learn new vocabulary.
- Learn about a time line.
- Revise a book review.
- Identify and write spelling patterns that stand for sounds within words.
- Read independently to develop fluency.

GET READY

Introduction: *The Girl Who Thought in Pictures* (B)
Students will get a glimpse of what they will learn about in the lesson.

Shades of Meaning
Students will learn about verbs and adjectives with shades of meaning.

Words to Know: *The Girl Who Thought in Pictures* (B)
Students will review and answer questions about three vocabulary words from the reading selection.

READ

The Girl Who Thought in Pictures (B)
Students will read the backmatter of *The Girl Who Thought in Pictures*. They will examine the time line.

LEARN   Graphic Features: Time Line

Students will learn how to read and explore a time line. They will learn that the dates and events on the time line correspond to the events happening in the story. There are also pictures in the time line that help explain the major events of Temple Grandin's life.

TIP   Encourage students to think about what a time line of their own life might look like. Major dates would include when they were born; when they started school; when they were in kindergarten, first grade, and now in second grade.

LEARN   Give and Get Feedback

Students will learn how to give feedback effectively and respectfully to writers. They will also explore what to do with the feedback that they receive.

TRY IT   Revise Your Book Review

Students will revise their book review using Revise Your Book Review in *English Language Arts 2 Activity Book 1*. They will need their draft from *The Girl Who Thought in Pictures* (A).

LEARNING COACH CHECK-IN   Guide students through the revising process using the revising part of the Book Review: Feedback Sheet that you completed.

OPTIONAL   Have students exchange their draft with a peer and provide each other with feedback.

NOTE   Have students put their revised draft into the folder they are using to store their book review assignment pages.

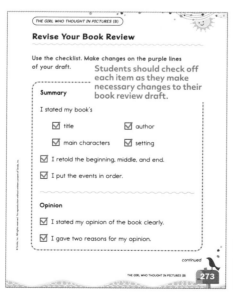
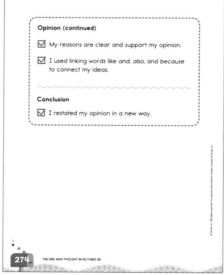

TRY IT Practice: Spelling List 13

Students will practice the spelling patterns for Spelling List 13.

- In *English Language Arts 2 Activity Book 1*, students will complete Practice: Spelling List 13.

- Online, students will answer questions that require them to reflect on the spelling patterns.

NOTE Students will need their cutouts from the Spelling List 13 activity page to complete Practice: Spelling List 13.

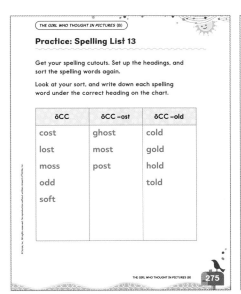

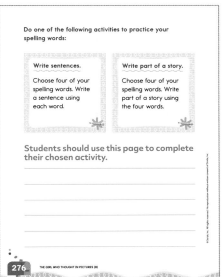

WRAP-UP

Questions About *The Girl Who Thought in Pictures* (B)

Students will answer questions to show that they understand the reading, writing, and spelling skills they learned in this lesson.

Go Read!

Students will read for pleasure. They should choose a book or a magazine that interests them, or they may choose a selection from the digital library, linked in the online lesson.

- Have students read aloud a few paragraphs of their selection.

- Then have students read silently for the rest of the time.

SUPPORT Students should make no more than five errors in decoding when they read aloud a few paragraphs of their Go Read! selection. If students struggle or make more than five errors, they need to select a different (and easier) text for the Go Read! activity.

TIP Have students select something to read ahead of time to help them stay focused.

The Girl Who Thought in Pictures (C)

Lesson Overview

ACTIVITY	ACTIVITY TITLE	TIME	ONLINE/OFFLINE
GET READY	Introduction: *The Girl Who Thought in Pictures* (C)	**1** minute	🖥️
	Nuances of Meaning	**15** minutes	🖥️
	Review Words to Know from *The Girl Who Thought in Pictures*	**10** minutes	🖥️
LEARN	OK to Be Different	**20** minutes	🖥️
ALL ABOUT ME	Brain Break	**1** minute	🖥️ or 📄
TRY IT	Proofread Your Book Review **LEARNING COACH CHECK-IN**	**30** minutes	📄
ALL ABOUT ME	Brain Break	**1** minute	🖥️ or 📄
TRY IT	Apply: Spelling List 13	**20** minutes	🖥️ and 📄
WRAP-UP	Questions About *The Girl Who Thought in Pictures* (C)	**2** minutes	🖥️
	More Language Arts Practice	**10** minutes	🖥️
	Go Read!	**10** minutes	🖥️ or 📄

Content Background

Students will continue a series of lessons centered around the book *The Girl Who Thought in Pictures* by Julia Finley Mosca. In this lesson, they will learn about what it means to be different, and they will proofread their book review.

Reading Foundations Some words are very similar, but their meanings are not exactly the same, such as the difference between a giggle and a laugh. A slight difference is sometimes called a *nuance*.

Writing Skills Students will continue working on their **book review**. They will complete this assignment over the course of several lessons by following the writing process.

Writing Process

1 Prewriting	2 Drafting	3 Revising	**4 Proofreading**	5 Publishing

Advance Preparation

Gather the folder that students are using to keep all activity pages related to their book review.

- Model Book Review from *A Weed is a Flower* (A)

- Students' completed Choose a Topic for Your Book Review activity page from *A Weed is a Flower* (A)

- Students' completed Plan Your Summary activity page from *A Weed is a Flower* (B)

- Students' completed Plan Your Opinion Statement and Reasons activity page from *A Weed is a Flower* (C)

- Students' revised Draft Your Book Review activity page from *The Girl Who Thought in Pictures* (B)

Prior to Try It: Proofread Your Book Review, read students' draft and complete the proofreading part of Book Review: Feedback Sheet.

Gather students' cutouts from the Spelling List 13 activity page from *The Girl Who Thought in Pictures* (A). They will use the cutouts during Try It: Apply: Spelling List 13.

If students have removed the My Speed Sort Times from the activity book, have them gather this activity page. They will use this activity page in Try It: Apply: Spelling List 13.

During the Go Read! activity, students will have the option of using the digital library. Allow extra time for students to make their reading selection, or have students make a selection before beginning the lesson.

MATERIALS

Supplied
- *The Girl Who Thought in Pictures* by Julia Finley Mosca
- *English Language Arts 2 Activity Book 1*
  - Proofread Your Book Review
  - Apply: Spelling List 13
  - My Speed Sort Times
- Book Review: Feedback Sheet (printout)

Also Needed
- folder in which students are storing book review assignment pages
- Spelling List 13 activity page cutouts from *The Girl Who Thought in Pictures* (A)
- reading material for Go Read!

Lesson Goals

- Learn about nuances of meaning.
- Review vocabulary.
- Learn that it is OK to be different.
- Proofread a book review.
- Identify reasons for when and how to use certain spelling patterns.
- Read independently to develop fluency.

Introduction: *The Girl Who Thought in Pictures* (C)

Students will get a glimpse of what they will learn about in the lesson.

Nuances of Meaning

Students will learn about nuances of meaning. They will explore similar words with slightly different meanings.

Review Words to Know from *The Girl Who Thought in Pictures*

Students will answer questions about the vocabulary words from the reading selection.

LEARN AND TRY IT

LEARN   OK to Be Different

Students will learn that everyone is not alike and that it is OK to be different. They will examine how being different didn't stop Temple Grandin from achieving her dream.

TIP   Have students share something that makes them different and how that difference makes them special.

TRY IT   Proofread Your Book Review

Students will proofread their book review using Proofread Your Book Review in *English Language Arts 2 Activity Book 1*. They will need their revised draft from *The Girl Who Thought in Pictures* (B).

LEARNING COACH CHECK-IN   Guide students through the proofreading process using the proofreading part of the Book Review: Feedback Sheet that you completed.

TIP   Students can use an online or printed learner's dictionary to check spelling during proofreading.

NOTE   Have students put their edited draft into the folder they are using to store their book review assignment pages.

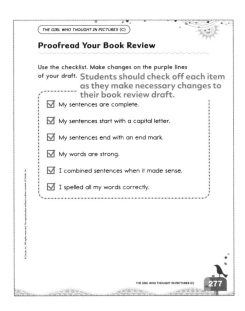

THE GIRL WHO THOUGHT IN PICTURES (C)

Proofread Your Book Review

Use the checklist. Make changes on the purple lines of your draft. Students should check off each item as they make necessary changes to their book review draft.

- ☑ My sentences are complete.
- ☑ My sentences start with a capital letter.
- ☑ My sentences end with an end mark.
- ☑ My words are strong.
- ☑ I combined sentences when it made sense.
- ☑ I spelled all my words correctly.

THE GIRL WHO THOUGHT IN PICTURES (C) **277**

TRY IT   Apply: Spelling List 13

Students will apply what they have learned about the spelling patterns for Spelling List 13.

- In an online activity, students will complete a word sort and answer reflection questions.

- In *English Language Arts 2 Activity Book 1*, students will complete the Apply: Spelling List 13.

NOTE   Students will need their cutouts from the Spelling List 13 activity page to complete the word sort.

TIP   Have students record their speed sort times on the My Speed Sort Times activity page, which is located at the back of the activity book. It can be motivating for students to see their progress as their ability to complete speed sorts should improve over time.

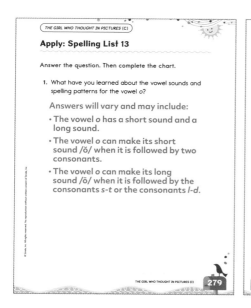

Apply: Spelling List 13

Answer the question. Then complete the chart.

1. What have you learned about the vowel sounds and spelling patterns for the vowel *o*?

   Answers will vary and may include:

   • The vowel *o* has a short sound and a long sound.

   • The vowel *o* can make its short sound /ŏ/ when it is followed by two consonants.

   • The vowel *o* can make its long sound /ō/ when it is followed by the consonants *s-t* or the consonants *l-d*.

279

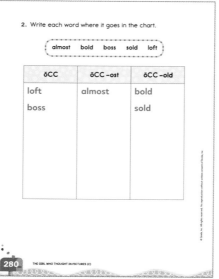

2. Write each word where it goes in the chart.

almost   bold   boss   sold   loft

ŏCC	ŏCC –ost	ŏCC –old
loft	almost	bold
boss		sold

280   THE GIRL WHO THOUGHT IN PICTURES (C)

WRAP-UP

Questions About *The Girl Who Thought in Pictures* (C)

Students will answer questions to show that they understand the reading, writing, and spelling skills they learned in this lesson.

More Language Arts Practice

Students will practice skills according to their individual needs.

Go Read!

Students will read for pleasure. They should choose a book or a magazine that interests them, or they may choose a selection from the digital library, linked in the online lesson.

• Have students read aloud a few paragraphs of their selection.

• Then have students read silently for the rest of the time.

SUPPORT   Students should make no more than five errors in decoding when they read aloud a few paragraphs of their Go Read! selection. If students struggle or make more than five errors, they need to select a different (and easier) text for the Go Read! activity.

TIP   Have students select something to read ahead of time to help them stay focused.

The Girl Who Thought in Pictures (D)

Lesson Overview

ACTIVITY	ACTIVITY TITLE	TIME	ONLINE/OFFLINE
GET READY	Introduction: *The Girl Who Thought in Pictures* (D)	**1** minute	🖥️
READ	*The Girl Who Thought in Pictures* (D)	**25** minutes	🖥️ or 📄
LEARN	Paint a Picture with Words	**25** minutes	🖥️
ALL ABOUT ME	Brain Break	**1** minute	🖥️ or 📄
TRY IT	Start Publishing Your Book Review **LEARNING COACH CHECK-IN**	**30** minutes	📄
WRAP-UP	Question About *The Girl Who Thought in Pictures* (D)	**2** minutes	🖥️
ALL ABOUT ME	Brain Break	**1** minute	🖥️ or 📄
QUIZ	Spelling List 13	**25** minutes	🖥️
WRAP-UP	Read and Record	**10** minutes	🖥️

Content Background

Students will conclude a series of lessons centered around the book *The Girl Who Thought in Pictures* by Julia Finley Mosca. In this lesson, they will examine how figurative language is used in the story and begin publishing their book review.

Reading Writers use colorful words and phrases to help readers visualize what they are reading and create **imagery**. **Figurative language** helps create that imagery by going beyond the actual literal meaning of a word. Often, words are used to compare two different things. For example, fluffy clouds might be described as looking like mashed potatoes. Figurative language includes figures of speech, such as **similes** and **personification**, and literary devices, such as **alliteration** and **onomatopoeia**.

Writing Skills Students will continue working on their **book review**. They will complete this assignment over the course of several lessons by following the writing process.

MATERIALS

Supplied
- *The Girl Who Thought in Pictures* by Julia Finley Mosca
- *English Language Arts 2 Activity Book 1*
  - Publish Your Book Review
- Writing Paper (printout)

Also Needed
- folder in which students are storing book review assignment pages

Writing Process

Advance Preparation

Gather the folder that students are using to keep all activity pages related to their book review.

- Model Book Review from *A Weed is a Flower* (A)

- Students' completed Choose a Topic for Your Book Review activity page from *A Weed is a Flower* (A)

- Students' completed Plan Your Summary activity page from *A Weed is a Flower* (B)

- Students' completed Plan Your Opinion Statement and Reasons activity page from *A Weed is a Flower* (C)

- Students' revised and edited Draft Your Book Review activity page from *The Girl Who Thought in Pictures* (C)

Lesson Goals

- Learn about figurative language.

- Begin publishing a book review.

- Take a spelling quiz.

- Read aloud to practice fluency.

GET READY

Introduction: *The Girl Who Thought in Pictures* (D)

Students will get a glimpse of what they will learn about in the lesson.

READ

The Girl Who Thought in Pictures (D)

Students will reread the book, paying close attention to the author's choice of words.

LEARN AND TRY IT

LEARN   Paint a Picture with Words

Students will learn about different kinds of figurative language. They will learn how colorful words and phrases paint a picture for readers.

TRY IT   Start Publishing Your Book Review

Students will begin Publish Your Book Review in *English Language Arts 2 Activity Book 1*. They should gather their draft and write a clean copy of their summary (Paragraph 1) that incorporates the changes they made during revising and proofreading.

LEARNING COACH CHECK-IN   Ensure that students are using their revised and edited draft to create their final copy. Otherwise, they should work independently.

NOTE   Have students put their in-progress clean copy into the folder they are using to store their book review assignment pages.

NOTE   Additional sheets of Writing Paper are available online.

WRAP-UP

Question About *The Girl Who Thought in Pictures* (D)

Students will answer a question to show that they understand the reading skills they learned in this lesson.

QUIZ

Spelling List 13

Students will complete the Spelling List 13 quiz.

WRAP-UP

Read and Record

Good readers read quickly, smoothly, and with expression. This is called *fluency*. Students will record themselves reading aloud. They will listen to their recording and think about how quick, smooth, and expressive they sound.

TIP   Encourage students to rerecord as needed.

The Fabled Life of Aesop (A)

Lesson Overview

ACTIVITY	ACTIVITY TITLE	TIME	ONLINE/OFFLINE
GET READY	Introduction: *The Fabled Life of Aesop* (A)	**1** minute	📶
	Book Walk: *The Fabled Life of Aesop* (A)	**20** minutes	📶
READ	Think About Reading: *The Fabled Life of Aesop* (A)	**10** minutes	📄
	The Fabled Life of Aesop (A)	**20** minutes	📶 and 📄
	Check-In: *The Fabled Life of Aesop* (A)	**5** minutes	📶
ALL ABOUT ME	Brain Break	**1** minute	📶 or 📄
TRY IT	Keep Publishing Your Book Review	**25** minutes	📄
ALL ABOUT ME	Brain Break	**1** minute	📶 or 📄
LEARN	Spelling List 14	**25** minutes	📶 and 📄
WRAP-UP	Questions About *The Fabled Life of Aesop* (A)	**2** minutes	📶
	Go Read!	**10** minutes	📶 or 📄

Content Background

Students will begin a series of lessons centered around the book *The Fabled Life of Aesop* by Ian Lendler. In this lesson, students will learn about Aesop and his fables, and they will continue publishing their book review.

Writing Skills Students will continue working on their **book review**. They will complete this assignment over the course of several lessons by following the writing process.

Writing Process

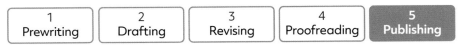

1 Prewriting	2 Drafting	3 Revising	4 Proofreading	5 Publishing

Spelling Students will learn about three r-controlled spelling patterns with the vowel *a*. Students will sort words under these headings: **ar *farm***, **are *care***, **air *chair***, **oddball**.

Students will learn that when a vowel is followed by the consonant *r*, the vowel's sound is affected. These spelling patterns are called r-controlled vowels because the *r* is in

charge. The *r* changes the vowel's sound. You don't hear a long or short vowel sound, but something different.

- Words that go under the heading **ar *farm*** have the r-controlled spelling pattern *ar*.

- Words that go under the heading **are *care*** have an r-controlled vowel sound and an *are* spelling pattern.

- Words that go under the heading **air *chair*** have an r-controlled vowel sound and an *air* spelling pattern.

- Words that go under the heading **oddball** have an r-controlled vowel sound, but their spelling patterns do not match the target patterns.

Advance Preparation

Gather the folder that students are using to keep all activity pages related to their book review.

- Model Book Review from *A Weed is a Flower* (A)

- Students' completed Choose a Topic for Your Book Review activity page from *A Weed is a Flower* (A)

- Students' completed Plan Your Summary activity page from *A Weed is a Flower* (B)

- Students' completed Plan Your Opinion Statement and Reasons activity page from *A Weed is a Flower* (C)

- Students' revised and edited Draft Your Book Review activity page from *The Girl Who Thought in Pictures* (C)

- Students' in-progress Publish Your Book Review activity page from *The Girl Who Thought in Pictures* (D)

During the Go Read! activity, students will have the option of using the digital library. Allow extra time for students to make their reading selection, or have students make a selection before beginning the lesson.

MATERIALS

Supplied
- *The Fabled Life of Aesop* by Ian Lendler
- *English Language Arts 2 Activity Book 1*
  - Think About Reading: *The Fabled Life of Aesop* (A)
  - Spelling List 14
- Writing Paper (printout)

Also Needed
- folder in which students are storing book review assignment pages
- scissors
- envelope or baggie to store spelling cutouts
- reading material for Go Read!

KEYWORDS

fable – a story that teaches a lesson and may contain animal characters

moral – the lesson of a story, particularly a fable

The Fabled Life of Aesop Synopsis

This illustrated book tells the story of Aesop, an enslaved person who became a famous storyteller. Aesop began telling stories as a way to speak in code so that his enslavers Xanthus and Jadon would not get angry with him. His stories told about animals and ended with a moral or lesson. The stories showed that Aesop was very clever. He was so clever that Jadon asked for his help. Jadon became very successful and well-respected with Aesop's help. Jadon was so thankful that he told Aesop he would grant him any wish. Aesop expressed his wish through a story—he wanted his freedom. Jadon kept his promise; Aesop was free. Aesop's stories were told and retold for generations. Centuries later, his stories were gathered into a book that became one of the most popular books ever. The author has included some of Aesop's fables in this book.

Lesson Goals

- Take a book walk through *The Fabled Life of Aesop*.
- Read *The Fabled Life of Aesop*.
- Keep publishing a book review.
- Sort words by sound and spelling pattern.
- Read independently to develop fluency.

GET READY

Introduction: *The Fabled Life of Aesop* (A)

Students will get a glimpse of what they will learn about in the lesson.

Book Walk: *The Fabled Life of Aesop* (A)

Students will preview the book, which includes the story of Aesop the storyteller and some of the fables he wrote.

TIP   Suggest that students study the illustrations as they look through the book and then later when they read it.

Think About Reading: *The Fabled Life of Aesop* (A)

Students will complete Think About Reading: *The Fabled Life of Aesop* (A) in *English Language Arts 2 Activity Book 1*.

NOTE Encourage students to talk about any fables they've read or know about.

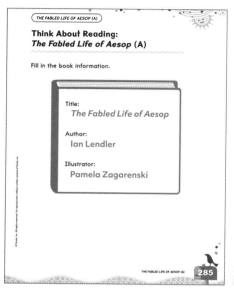

The Fabled Life of Aesop (A)

Students will listen to and follow along with a read-aloud of *The Fabled Life of Aesop* by Ian Lendler. The read-aloud is of the story of Aesop's life only, not of Aesop's fables. If students choose to read on their own instead of listening to the read-aloud, ensure they only read Aesop's life story (pages 4–16 and 46–58). Students will read some of the fables in later lessons.

TIP Remind students that Aesop never wrote his stories down: They were retold. There is no way to actually prove Aesop wrote all these stories as there is no real information about enslaved people from centuries ago. Aesop is credited with writing these fables even though it is possible some of them were written by other people.

Check-In: *The Fabled Life of Aesop* (A)

Students will answer several questions to demonstrate their comprehension of Aesop's life story from *The Fabled Life of Aesop*.

TRY IT   Keep Publishing Your Book Review

Students will continue working on Publish Your Book Review in *English Language Arts 2 Activity Book 1*. In addition to their in-progress clean copy, they will need their draft. Using their draft, they should write a clean copy of their opinion statement and reasons (Paragraph 2) that incorporates the changes they made during revising and proofreading.

NOTE   Have students put their in-progress clean copy into the folder they are using to store their book review assignment pages.

NOTE   Additional sheets of Writing Paper are available online.

THE GIRL WHO THOUGHT IN PICTURES (D)

Publish Your Book Review

Write a clean copy of your book review.
Include these parts:

☐ Title

☐ Summary

☐ Opinion

☐ Conclusion

Title: _____

LEARN Spelling List 14

Students will learn and sort words with three r-controlled spelling patterns with the vowel *a*.

- In an online activity, students will learn about the spelling patterns and the sounds they represent. They will learn how to sort words according to those sounds and patterns. They will also complete a word sort.

- In *English Language Arts 2 Activity Book 1*, students will complete Spelling List 14.

NOTE Students will need scissors to cut out the spelling words on the activity page. Have students store their cutouts in a safe place, such as an envelope.

This is the complete list of words students will work with to learn the spelling patterns.

ar *farm*	are *care*	air *chair*	oddball
argue	hare	fair	their
hard	scare	hair	where
starve	share	stair	
	stare		

Questions About *The Fabled Life of Aesop* (A)

Students will answer questions to show that they understand the reading and spelling skills they learned in this lesson.

Go Read!

Students will read for pleasure. They should choose a book or a magazine that interests them, or they may choose a selection from the digital library, linked in the online lesson.

- Have students read aloud a few paragraphs of their selection.

- Then have students read silently for the rest of the time.

SUPPORT   Students should make no more than five errors in decoding when they read aloud a few paragraphs of their Go Read! selection. If students struggle or make more than five errors, they need to select a different (and easier) text for the Go Read! activity.

TIP   Have students select something to read ahead of time to help them stay focused.

The Fabled Life of Aesop (B)

Lesson Overview

ACTIVITY	ACTIVITY TITLE	TIME	ONLINE/OFFLINE
GET READY	Introduction: *The Fabled Life of Aesop* (B)	**1** minute	📶
	More Shades of Meaning	**10** minutes	📶
	Words to Know: *The Fabled Life of Aesop* (B)	**10** minutes	📶
READ	*The Fabled Life of Aesop* (B)	**15** minutes	📶 and 📄
LEARN	Character	**15** minutes	📶
ALL ABOUT ME	Brain Break	**1** minute	📶 or 📄
TRY IT	Finish Publishing Your Book Review	**25** minutes	📄
ALL ABOUT ME	Brain Break	**1** minute	📶 or 📄
TRY IT	Practice: Spelling List 14	**20** minutes	📶 and 📄
WRAP-UP	Questions About *The Fabled Life of Aesop* (B)	**2** minutes	📶
	Go Read!	**20** minutes	📶 or 📄

Content Background

Students will continue a series of lessons centered around the book *The Fabled Life of Aesop* by Ian Lendler. In this lesson, they will learn about characters' traits, motivations, and feelings. They will also finish publishing their book review.

Vocabulary Students will explore these words from the story: *wise*, *cruel*, *successful*, *well-respected*, *generous*, and *popular*. These are the definitions for how the words are used in *The Fabled Life of Aesop*:

- **wise** (adjective) – showing good judgment

- **cruel** (adjective) – causing pain to others

- **successful** (adjective) – doing something well

- **well-respected** (adjective) – admired, trusted, or considered worthy

- **generous** (adjective) – sharing with others

- **popular** (adjective) – used or liked by many

MATERIALS

Supplied
- *The Fabled Life of Aesop* by Ian Lendler
- *English Language Arts 2 Activity Book 1*
  - Practice: Spelling List 14
- Writing Paper (printout)

Also Needed
- folder in which students are storing book review assignment pages
- Spelling List 14 activity page cutouts from *The Fabled Life of Aesop* (A)
- crayons or markers (optional)
- reading material for Go Read!

Reading Character **traits** are the positive and negative qualities that make characters who they are. They contribute to a character's personality. Readers can identify character traits from what characters say, think, and do. A character's motivation is the reason why a character acts in a certain way. For example, Aesop is clever but what motivates him to tell his stories is fear.

Writing Skills Students will finish their **book review**.

KEYWORDS

trait – a quality of a person or other object; what something is like

Writing Process

1 Prewriting	2 Drafting	3 Revising	4 Proofreading	5 Publishing

Advance Preparation

Gather the folder that students are using to keep all activity pages related to their book review.

- Model Book Review from *A Weed is a Flower* (A)

- Students' completed Choose a Topic for Your Book Review activity page from *A Weed is a Flower* (A)

- Students' completed Plan Your Summary activity page from *A Weed is a Flower* (B)

- Students' completed Plan Your Opinion Statement and Reasons activity page from *A Weed is a Flower* (C)

- Students' revised and edited Draft Your Book Review activity page from *The Girl Who Thought in Pictures* (C)

- Students' in-progress Publish Your Book Review activity page from *The Fabled Life of Aesop* (A)

Gather students' cutouts from the Spelling List 14 activity page from *The Fabled Life of Aesop* (A). They will use the cutouts during Try It: Practice: Spelling List 14.

During the Go Read! activity, students will have the option of using the digital library. Allow extra time for students to make their reading selection, or have students make a selection before beginning the lesson.

Lesson Goals

- Distinguish between the meanings of similar words.
- Learn new vocabulary.
- Learn about character traits and feelings.
- Finish publishing a book review.
- Identify and write spelling patterns that stand for sounds within words.
- Read independently to develop fluency.

.

GET READY

Introduction: *The Fabled Life of Aesop* (B)
Students will get a glimpse of what they will learn about in the lesson.

More Shades of Meaning
Students will learn about distinguishing shades of meaning using synonyms and antonyms.

Words to Know: *The Fabled Life of Aesop* (B)
Students will preview and answer questions about six vocabulary words from the reading selection.

READ

The Fabled Life of Aesop (B)
Students will reread pages 4–16 and 46–58 of *The Fabled Life of Aesop* by Ian Lendler. They will focus on Aesop's character traits and feelings.

LEARN AND TRY IT

LEARN Character
Students will learn about what characters think and feel. They will explore how text and pictures help us learn about characters.

SUPPORT Have students talk about some of their own character traits. Ask them to come up with one or two words that describe their own character or personality.

TRY IT   Finish Publishing Your Book Review

Students will complete Publish Your Book Review in *English Language Arts 2 Activity Book 1*. In addition to their in-progress clean copy, they will need their draft. Using their draft, they should write a clean copy of their conclusion (Paragraph 3) that incorporates the changes they made during revising and proofreading.

NOTE   Have students put their clean copy in the folder they are using to store their book review assignment pages. Students will turn in this assignment to their teacher in Interesting People Wrap-Up (A).

NOTE   Additional sheets of Writing Paper are available online.

TRY IT   Practice: Spelling List 14

Students will practice the spelling patterns for Spelling List 14.

- In *English Language Arts 2 Activity Book 1*, students will complete Practice: Spelling List 14.

- Online, students will answer questions that require them to reflect on the spelling patterns.

NOTE   Students will need their cutouts from the Spelling List 14 activity page to complete Practice: Spelling List 14. Students may wish to use crayons or markers to draw their pictures or comic strip.

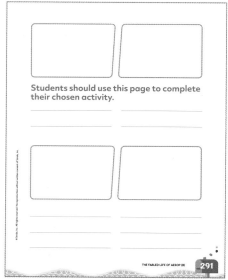

WRAP-UP

Questions About *The Fabled Life of Aesop* (B)

Students will answer questions to show that they understand the reading and spelling skills they learned in this lesson.

Go Read!

Students will read for pleasure. They should choose a book or a magazine that interests them, or they may choose a selection from the digital library, linked in the online lesson.

- Have students read aloud a few paragraphs of their selection.

- Then have students read silently for the rest of the time.

SUPPORT   Students should make no more than five errors in decoding when they read aloud a few paragraphs of their Go Read! selection. If students struggle or make more than five errors, they need to select a different (and easier) text for the Go Read! activity.

TIP   Have students select something to read ahead of time to help them stay focused.

The Fabled Life of Aesop (C)

Lesson Overview

ACTIVITY	ACTIVITY TITLE	TIME	ONLINE/OFFLINE
GET READY	Introduction: *The Fabled Life of Aesop* (C)	**1** minute	🖥️
	Syllables with r-Controlled Vowels	**10** minutes	🖥️
	Words to Know: *The Fabled Life of Aesop* (C)	**10** minutes	🖥️
READ	*The Fabled Life of Aesop* (C)	**10** minutes	🖥️ and 📄
LEARN	Plot	**15** minutes	🖥️
ALL ABOUT ME	Brain Break	**1** minute	🖥️ or 📄
LEARN AND TRY IT	Book Ads	**10** minutes	🖥️
	Plan Your Book Ad	**20** minutes	📄
ALL ABOUT ME	Brain Break	**1** minute	🖥️ or 📄
TRY IT	Apply: Spelling List 14	**20** minutes	🖥️ and 📄
WRAP-UP	Questions About *The Fabled Life of Aesop* (C)	**2** minutes	🖥️
	Handwriting	**10** minutes	📄
	Go Read!	**10** minutes	🖥️ or 📄

Content Background

Students will continue a series of lessons centered around the book *The Fabled Life of Aesop* by Ian Lendler. In this lesson, they will use the words and pictures to understand the events in the story, and they will plan a book ad.

Vocabulary Students will explore these words from the story: *survive*, *reward*, *service*, and *fame*. These are the definitions for how the words are used in *The Fabled Life of Aesop*:

- **survive** (verb) – to stay alive

- **reward** (noun) – a prize or an award

- **service** (noun) – help or work done for someone

- **fame** (noun) – being known or talked about by others

Writing Skills Writing is just one of many ways that people share ideas. Speech, music, visual art, and various uses of technology and multimedia can all be used to share ideas, including opinions.

Advertisements come in many forms and often incorporate both text and visual media. By creating an advertisement using elements of their book review, students will gain skills in expressing themselves effectively with various media and using that media purposefully.

Advance Preparation

Gather students' completed book review from *The Fabled Life of Aesop* (B). Students will refer to their book review during Try It: Plan Your Book Ad.

Gather students' cutouts from the Spelling List 14 activity page from *The Fabled Life of Aesop* (A). They will use the cutouts during Try It: Apply: Spelling List 14.

If students have removed My Speed Sort Times from the activity book, have them gather this activity page. They will use this activity page in Try It: Apply: Spelling List 14.

During the Go Read! activity, students will have the option of using the digital library. Allow extra time for students to make their reading selection, or have students make a selection before beginning the lesson.

MATERIALS

Supplied
- *The Fabled Life of Aesop* by Ian Lendler
- *English Language Arts 2 Activity Book 1*
  - Plan Your Book Ad
  - Apply: Spelling List 14
  - My Speed Sort Times
- Model Book Ad (PowerPoint file)
- handwriting workbook

Also Needed
- students' completed book review from *The Fabled Life of Aesop* (B)
- crayons or markers (optional)
- Spelling List 14 activity page cutouts from *The Fabled Life of Aesop* (A)
- reading material for Go Read!

Lesson Goals

- Learn about syllables with r-controlled vowels.
- Learn new vocabulary.
- Learn about the major events in *The Fabled Life of Aesop*.
- Plan a book ad.
- Identify reasons for when and how to use certain spelling patterns.
- Develop letter formation fluency.
- Read independently to develop fluency.

GET READY

Introduction: *The Fabled Life of Aesop* (C)
Students will get a glimpse of what they will learn about in the lesson.

Syllables with r-Controlled Vowels

Students will learn about syllables with r-controlled vowels. They will practice dividing words into syllables when at least one of the syllables has an r-controlled vowel.

SUPPORT   Remind students of the other types of syllables if they are having trouble identifying syllables with r-controlled vowels. Provide additional practice with other two-syllable words that have syllables with r-controlled vowels.

Words to Know: *The Fabled Life of Aesop* (C)

Students will preview and answer questions about four vocabulary words from the reading selection.

READ

The Fabled Life of Aesop (C)

Students will reread pages 4–16 and 46–58 of *The Fabled Life of Aesop* by Ian Lendler. They will explore the events that changed Aesop's life.

LEARN AND TRY IT

LEARN   Plot

Students will use the words and the pictures to explain the major events in the story. They will examine how characters in the story react to the events.

LEARN   Book Ads

By exploring a model book ad, students will learn how various media can be used and combined to express an opinion.

TRY IT   Plan Your Book Ad

Students will complete Plan Your Book Ad in *English Language Arts 2 Activity Book 1*. They will need to refer to their completed book review as they work.

TIP   Help students download and save the Model Book Ad, which is a PowerPoint file.

NOTE   Students may wish to use crayons or markers for their sketches.

NOTE   Have students store their Plan Your Book Ad activity page in a safe place.

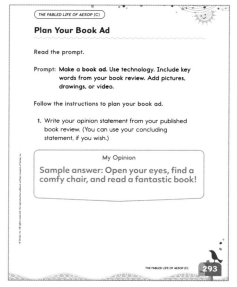

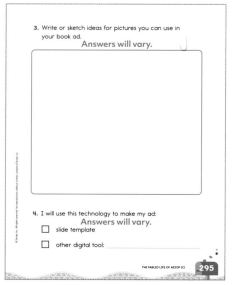

TRY IT   Apply: Spelling List 14

Students will apply what they have learned about the spelling patterns for Spelling List 14.

- In an online activity, students will complete a word sort and answer reflection questions.

- In *English Language Arts 2 Activity Book 1*, students will complete Apply: Spelling List 14.

NOTE   Students will need their cutouts from the Spelling List 14 activity page to complete the word sort.

TIP   Have students record their speed sort times on the My Speed Sort Times activity page, which is located at the back of the activity book. It can be motivating for students to see their progress as their ability to complete speed sorts should improve over time.

SUPPORT   For the offline task, students may benefit from having the letters they will use to build words written on small pieces of paper. It will allow them to physically move the letters into place and test where letters can be placed to make new words.

THE FABLED LIFE OF AESOP (C)

Apply: Spelling List 14

Answer the question.

1. What have you learned about words with the r-controlled vowel *a*?

   Answers will vary and may include:

   • The *r* controls the sound that the *a* makes.

   • The *a* does not make its short sound or long sound.

   • There are different spelling patterns: *ar*, *are*, and *air*.

THE FABLED LIFE OF AESOP (C)

297

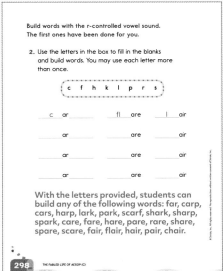

Build words with the r-controlled vowel sound. The first ones have been done for you.

2. Use the letters in the box to fill in the blanks and build words. You may use each letter more than once.

c   f   h   k   l   p   r   s

c ar	fl are	l air
___ ar	___ are	___ air
___ ar	___ are	___ air
___ ar	___ are	___ air

With the letters provided, students can build any of the following words: far, carp, cars, harp, lark, park, scarf, shark, sharp, spark, care, fare, hare, pare, rare, share, spare, scare, fair, flair, hair, pair, chair.

298 THE FABLED LIFE OF AESOP (C)

WRAP-UP

Questions About *The Fabled Life of Aesop* (C)

Students will answer questions to show that they understand the reading and spelling skills they learned in this lesson.

Handwriting

Students should gather their handwriting materials and begin where they left off. Remind students to form letters carefully and correctly.

TIP Set a timer to help students stay focused during handwriting practice.

Go Read!

Students will read for pleasure. They should choose a book or a magazine that interests them, or they may choose a selection from the digital library, linked in the online lesson.

• Have students read aloud a few paragraphs of their selection.

• Then have students read silently for the rest of the time.

SUPPORT Students should make no more than five errors in decoding when they read aloud a few paragraphs of their Go Read! selection. If students struggle or make more than five errors, they need to select a different (and easier) text for the Go Read! activity.

TIP Have students select something to read ahead of time to help them stay focused.

The Fabled Life of Aesop (D)

Lesson Overview

ACTIVITY	ACTIVITY TITLE	TIME	ONLINE/OFFLINE
GET READY	Introduction: *The Fabled Life of Aesop* (D)	**1** minute	🖥
	More r-Controlled Syllables	**5** minutes	🖥
READ	Think About Reading: *The Fabled Life of Aesop* (D)	**10** minutes	📄
LEARN	Speaking in Code	**10** minutes	🖥
ALL ABOUT ME	Brain Break	**1** minute	🖥 or 📄
TRY IT	Create Your Book Ad	**60** minutes	🖥
	More Practice: Spelling List 14	**20** minutes	🖥 and 📄
ALL ABOUT ME	Brain Break	**1** minute	🖥 or 📄
WRAP-UP	Question About *The Fabled Life of Aesop* (D)	**2** minutes	🖥
	Read and Record	**10** minutes	🖥

Content Background

Students will conclude a series of lessons centered around the book *The Fabled Life of Aesop* by Ian Lendler. In this lesson, they will learn about speaking in code, and they will create a book ad.

Reading The term *speaking in code* is used to explain how Aesop's fables hid the truth. Since Aesop feared what would happen to him if he told his master what he really thought, he disguised the truth by telling stories about animals that ended with morals.

Advance Preparation

Gather students' completed Plan Your Book Ad activity page from *The Fabled Life of Aesop* (C). Students will refer to this page during Try It: Create Your Book Ad.

If students have removed My Speed Sort Times from the activity book, have them gather this activity page. They will use this activity page in Try It: Apply: Spelling List 14.

Lesson Goals

- Learn about speaking in code.
- Create a book ad.
- Practice spelling patterns.
- Read aloud to practice fluency.

MATERIALS

Supplied

- *The Fabled Life of Aesop* by Ian Lendler
- *English Language Arts 2 Activity Book 1*
  - Think About Reading: *The Fabled Life of Aesop* (D)
  - More Practice: Spelling List 14
  - My Speed Sort Times
- Model Book Ad (PowerPoint file)
- Book Ad Template (PowerPoint file)

Also Needed

- students' completed book review from *The Fabled Life of Aesop* (C)
- Spelling List 14 activity page cutouts from *The Fabled Life of Aesop* (A)

GET READY

Introduction: *The Fabled Life of Aesop* (D)

Students will get a glimpse of what they will learn about in the lesson.

More r-Controlled Syllables

Students will review syllables with r-controlled vowels.

READ

Think About Reading: *The Fabled Life of Aesop* (D)

Students will complete Think About Reading: *The Fabled Life of Aesop* (D) in *English Language Arts 2 Activity Book 1.*

LEARN Speaking in Code

Students will learn what it meant for Aesop to speak in code. Aesop figured out a way to tell stories that hid what he was really saying. The moral of each fable always told his truth.

TRY IT Create Your Book Ad

Students will create their book ad following their plan on their completed Plan Your Book Ad activity page.

NOTE Students may use the Book Ad Template (PowerPoint file) or use different technology to create their book ad. Possible different approaches include creating a video, web page, or book trailer. Students may take their own unique approach as long as they (1) use some sort of technology; (2) include key words from their book review; and (3) add some sort of visual, such as a picture, drawing, or video.

TRY IT More Practice: Spelling List 14

Students will continue to practice the spelling patterns for Spelling List 14 to increase automatic recognition of the patterns.

• In an online activity, students will practice the spelling words and patterns.

• In *English Language Arts 2 Activity Book 1*, students will complete More Practice: Spelling List 14.

NOTE Students will need their cutouts from the Spelling List 14 activity page to complete More Practice: Spelling List 14.

TIP Have students record their speed sort times on the My Speed Sort Times activity page, which is located at the back of the activity book. It can be motivating for students to see their progress as their ability to complete speed sorts should improve over time.

Question About *The Fabled Life of Aesop* (D)

Students will answer a question to show that they understand the reading skills they learned in this lesson.

Read and Record

Good readers read quickly, smoothly, and with expression. This is called *fluency*. Students will record themselves reading aloud. They will listen to their recording and think about how quick, smooth, and expressive they sound.

TIP Encourage students to rerecord as needed.

Interesting People Wrap-Up (A)

Lesson Overview

ACTIVITY	ACTIVITY TITLE	TIME	ONLINE/OFFLINE
GET READY	Introduction: Interesting People Wrap-Up (A)	**1** minute	🖥️
QUIZ	Spelling List 14	**25** minutes	🖥️
ALL ABOUT ME	Brain Break	**1** minute	🖥️ or 📄
GET READY	Review Syllable Types	**5** minutes	🖥️
REVIEW	Interesting People	**25** minutes	🖥️
ALL ABOUT ME	Brain Break	**1** minute	🖥️ or 📄
WRAP-UP	Theme Time: Interesting People **LEARNING COACH CHECK-IN**	**20** minutes	📄
	Your Choice Time	**41** minutes	🖥️ or 📄
	Turn In Your Book Review	**1** minute	🖥️

Advance Preparation

During the Your Choice Time activity, students will be given the option to read something of their choice. If students are using the digital library, allow extra time for them to make their reading selection, or have them make a selection before beginning the lesson.

Gather students' completed Publish Your Book Review activity page from *The Fabled Life of Aesop* (B). Students will turn in this page during Wrap-Up: Turn In Your Book Review.

MATERIALS

Supplied
- *English Language Arts 2 Activity Book 1*
  - Theme Time: Interesting People

Also Needed
- reading material for Your Choice Time (optional)
- students' completed Publish Your Book Review activity page from *The Fabled Life of Aesop* (B)

Lesson Goals

- Take a spelling quiz.
- Review syllable types.
- Review vocabulary and reading skills from the unit.
- Make connections among the texts in the unit.
- Submit your book review.

GET READY

Introduction: Interesting People Wrap-Up (A)

Students will get a glimpse of what they will do in the lesson.

QUIZ

Spelling List 14

Students will complete the Spelling List 14 quiz.

GET READY

Review Syllable Types

Students will review four syllable types: open, closed, r-controlled, and vowel-consonant-silent e (VCe).

REVIEW

Interesting People

Students will answer questions to review the vocabulary and reading skills they learned in the unit.

WRAP-UP

Theme Time: Interesting People

Students will complete Theme Time: Interesting People in *English Language Arts 2 Activity Book 1*.

NOTE This activity page includes an optional ungraded project. Students may need additional materials to complete the project.

LEARNING COACH CHECK-IN Discuss students' responses to the questions. Have them share their time line, if they choose to complete the optional project.

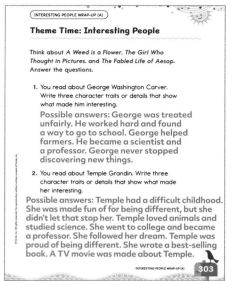

Theme Time: Interesting People

Think about *A Weed is a Flower*, *The Girl Who Thought in Pictures*, and *The Fabled Life of Aesop*. Answer the questions.

1. You read about George Washington Carver. Write three character traits or details that show what made him interesting.

   Possible answers: George was treated unfairly. He worked hard and found a way to go to school. George helped farmers. He became a scientist and a professor. George never stopped discovering new things.

2. You read about Temple Grandin. Write three character traits or details that show what made her interesting.

Possible answers: Temple had a difficult childhood. She was made fun of for being different, but she didn't let that stop her. Temple loved animals and studied science. She went to college and became a professor. She followed her dream. Temple was proud of being different. She wrote a best-selling book. A TV movie was made about Temple.

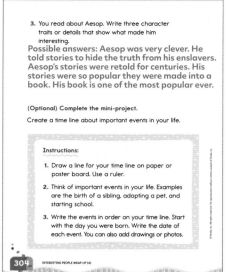

3. You read about Aesop. Write three character traits or details that show what made him interesting.

Possible answers: Aesop was very clever. He told stories to hide the truth from his enslavers. Aesop's stories were retold for centuries. His stories were so popular they were made into a book. His book is one of the most popular ever.

(Optional) Complete the mini-project.

Create a time line about important events in your life.

Instructions:

1. Draw a line for your time line on paper or poster board. Use a ruler.

2. Think of important events in your life. Examples are the birth of a sibling, adopting a pet, and starting school.

3. Write the events in order on your time line. Start with the day you were born. Write the date of each event. You can also add drawings or photos.

Your Choice Time

Students will choose among the following activities:

- Independent reading

- Independent writing

- Completing the optional project from the Theme Time: Interesting People activity page

- Completing their Publish Your Book Review activity page

- Completing their book ad using technology

Turn In Your Book Review

Students will submit their completed Publish Your Book Review activity page to their teacher.

NOTE Students will not submit their book ad for grading. They will, however, have an opportunity to share their book ad in Interesting People Wrap-Up (B).

Interesting People Wrap-Up (B)

Lesson Overview

ACTIVITY	ACTIVITY TITLE	TIME	ONLINE/OFFLINE
GET READY	Introduction: Interesting People Wrap-Up (B)	**1** minute	🖥️
QUIZ	Interesting People	**25** minutes	🖥️
ALL ABOUT ME	Brain Break	**1** minute	🖥️ or 📄
REFLECTION	Go Write! and Set a Goal **LEARNING COACH CHECK-IN**	**30** minutes	📄
WRAP-UP	Celebrate: Interesting People	**20** minutes	📄
	Discussion: Asking Questions **LEARNING COACH CHECK-IN**	**20** minutes	🖥️
	More Language Arts Practice	**10** minutes	🖥️
	Your Choice Time	**13** minutes	🖥️ or 📄

Advance Preparation

If students have removed the My Reading Log and My Badge Book activity pages from the activity book, have them gather these pages. They will use these activity pages in the Celebrate: Interesting People activity.

During the Your Choice Time activity, students will be given the option to read something of their choice. If students are using the digital library, allow extra time for them to make their reading selection, or have them make a selection before beginning the lesson.

Lesson Goals

- Take a quiz on the vocabulary and reading skills from the unit.
- Freewrite to develop fluency and reflect on learning.
- Set a goal for future learning.
- Celebrate accomplishments from the unit.
- Participate in a discussion.

> **MATERIALS**
>
> **Supplied**
> - *English Language Arts 2 Activity Book 1*
>   - Go Write! and Set a Goal
>   - My Reading Log
>   - My Badge Book
>
> **Also Needed**
> - crayons or markers
> - students' completed book ad
> - reading material for Your Choice Time (optional)

Introduction: Interesting People Wrap-Up (B)

Students will get a glimpse of what they will do in the lesson.

Interesting People

Students will complete the Interesting People quiz.

Go Write! and Set a Goal

Students will complete Go Write! and Set a Goal in *English Language Arts 2 Activity Book 1*.

NOTE The Go Write! activity is intended to build writing fluency. Students should write for 10 minutes.

LEARNING COACH CHECK-IN Discuss students' goal, including any steps they can take as well as support you can provide in helping them meet it.

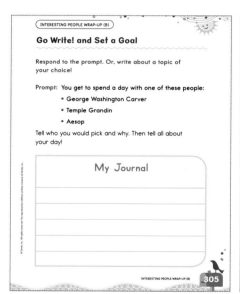

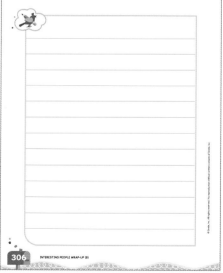

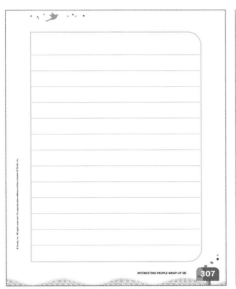

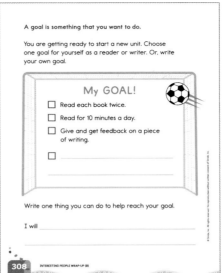

A goal is something that you want to do.

You are getting ready to start a new unit. Choose one goal for yourself as a reader or writer. Or, write your own goal.

My GOAL!

- ☐ Read each book twice.
- ☐ Read for 10 minutes a day.
- ☐ Give and get feedback on a piece of writing.
- ☐ _____

Write one thing you can do to help reach your goal.

I will _____

WRAP-UP

Celebrate: Interesting People

Students will celebrate accomplishments from the unit.

- They will record what they read this unit in their reading log.

- They will color the badge for this unit in their badge book. They may also color a badge to celebrate reading accomplishments.

NOTE   My Reading Log and My Badge Book are located at the back of the activity book.

NOTE   Students will need crayons or markers to color in their badges.

Discussion: Asking Questions

Students will respond to a discussion prompt. They will need their completed book ad that they created using technology.

LEARNING COACH CHECK-IN   Students should follow the steps shown on-screen with an adult. In some cases, teachers may facilitate a group discussion.

More Language Arts Practice

Students will practice skills according to their individual needs.

Your Choice Time

Students will choose among the following activities:

- Independent reading

- Independent writing

- Completing the optional project from the Theme Time: Interesting People activity page

Fables

Fables (A)

Lesson Overview

ACTIVITY	ACTIVITY TITLE	TIME	ONLINE/OFFLINE
GET READY	Introduction: Fables (A)	**1** minute	🖥️
	Book Walk: *Fables and Folktales*	**10** minutes	🖥️
	Before You Read: Fables (A)	**10** minutes	🖥️
	Words to Know: Fables (A)	**10** minutes	🖥️
READ	"The Ant and the Dove"	**10** minutes	🖥️ and 📄
LEARN	What Is the Moral?	**10** minutes	🖥️
ALL ABOUT ME	Brain Break	**1** minute	🖥️ or 📄
LEARN AND TRY IT	Adjectives	**10** minutes	🖥️
	Adjectives in Action	**10** minutes	📄
ALL ABOUT ME	Brain Break	**1** minute	🖥️ or 📄
LEARN	Spelling List 15	**25** minutes	🖥️ and 📄
WRAP-UP	Questions About Fables (A)	**2** minutes	🖥️
	Handwriting	**10** minutes	📄
	Go Read!	**10** minutes	🖥️ or 📄

Content Background

Students will begin a series of lessons about fables. In this lesson, they will read the fable "The Ant and the Dove" by Aesop, and they will learn about adjectives.

Vocabulary   Students will explore these words from the story: *pity*, *clung*, and *hurl*. These are the definitions for how the words are used in "The Ant and the Dove":

- **pity** (noun) – a feeling of sadness for someone or something

- **clung** (verb) – held on tightly to something

- **hurl** (verb) – to throw with force; to fling

Reading   A **fable** is a short story that teaches a lesson. The lesson in a fable is called a **moral**. The moral is usually stated at the end of the fable. Fables usually have animals as characters. Fables usually have a problem–solution structure. The story begins with a **problem**. The **solution** is shown through a series of actions. Then the moral is stated.

Writing Skills   An **adjective** is a word that describes a noun (or pronoun). Adjectives usually come before the noun they describe.

>   **Example:** The **old** dragon had **terrible**, **stinky** breath.

When an adjective comes after the noun it describes, a linking verb, such as *is*, *are*, or *was*, usually follows the noun.

>   **Example:** The broccoli was **green** and **raw**.

Spelling   Students will learn about three r-controlled spelling patterns with the vowel *e*. They will sort words under these headings: **er *her***, **ear *hear***, **eer *deer***, **oddball**.

Students will learn that when a vowel or a vowel team is followed by the consonant *r*, the vowel's sound is affected. These spelling patterns are called r-controlled vowels because the *r* is in charge. The *r* changes the vowel's sound. You don't hear a long or short vowel sound but something different.

Words that go under the heading **er *her*** have the r-controlled vowel sound and an *er* spelling pattern.

Words that go under the heading **ear *hear*** have an r-controlled vowel sound and an *ear* spelling pattern.

Words that go under the heading **eer *deer*** have an r-controlled vowel sound and an *eer* spelling pattern.

Words that go under the heading **oddball** have one of the spelling patterns. But, the sound of the spelling pattern is different from what we expect.

Advance Preparation

During the Go Read! activity, students will have the option of using the digital library. Allow extra time for students to make their reading selection, or have students make a selection before beginning the lesson.

> ### "The Ant and the Dove" Synopsis
>
> An Ant falls in a stream and cannot get to shore. A Dove helps the Ant by dropping a leaf in the water. The Ant uses the leaf to get to shore. Then the Ant sees a hunter who is about to throw a spear at the Dove. The Ant bites the man, giving the Dove time to fly away. Moral: One good turn deserves another.

MATERIALS

Supplied
- *Fables and Folktales*
  - "The Ant and the Dove"
- *English Language Arts 2 Activity Book 1*
  - Adjectives in Action
  - Spelling List 15
- handwriting workbook

Also Needed
- scissors
- envelope or baggie to store spelling cutouts
- reading material for Go Read!

KEYWORDS

adjective – a word that describes a noun or a pronoun
Examples: *purple*, *prickly*, *difficult*

fable – a story that teaches a lesson and may contain animal characters

moral – the lesson of a story, particularly a fable

problem – an issue a character must solve in a story

solution – how a character solves a problem in a story

Lesson Goals

- Learn about fables and morals.
- Learn new vocabulary.
- Listen to a read-aloud of "The Ant and the Dove."
- Explore the problem, solution, and moral of the fable.
- Learn about adjectives.
- Sort words by sound and spelling pattern.
- Develop letter formation fluency.
- Read independently to develop fluency.

GET READY

Introduction: Fables (A)

Students will get a glimpse of what they will learn about in the lesson.

Book Walk: *Fables and Folktales*

Students will preview the anthology *Fables and Folktales*, including the reading selections and the pictures.

> **TIP**   Have students follow along with the book walk using their own copy of the book.

Before You Read: Fables (A)

Students will learn about fables and morals in preparation for reading a fable.

> **TIP**   To help students understand what a moral is, use the words *message* or *lesson*. You can ask students for the lesson that the fable teaches.

Words to Know: Fables (A)

Students will review and answer questions about three vocabulary words from the reading selection.

READ

"The Ant and the Dove"

Students will listen to and read along with "The Ant and the Dove" by Aesop. They may choose to read the story on their own. Encourage students to reread their favorite parts.

> **NOTE**   Remind students that Aesop never wrote his stories down—they were retold. There is no way to actually prove Aesop wrote these stories. Aesop is credited with writing the fables even though it is possible some of them were written by other people.

LEARN AND TRY IT

LEARN   What Is the Moral?

Students will learn that the fable has a problem-and-solution organizational structure. The fable ends with a moral, or a central message that teaches a lesson.

LEARN   Adjectives

Through guided exploration of sentences from "The Ant and the Dove," students will learn about adjectives.

TRY IT   Adjectives in Action

Students will complete Adjectives in Action in *English Language Arts 2 Activity Book 1*.

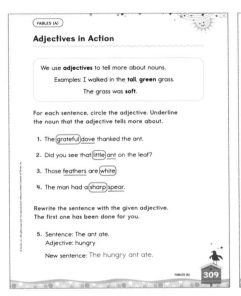

LEARN   Spelling List 15

Students will learn and sort words with three r-controlled spelling patterns with the vowel *e*.

- In an online activity, students will learn about the spelling patterns and the sounds they represent. They will learn how to sort words according to those sounds and patterns. They will also complete a word sort.

- In *English Language Arts 2 Activity Book 1*, students will complete Spelling List 15.

  NOTE   Students will need scissors to cut out the spelling words on the activity page. Have students store their cutouts in a safe place, such as an envelope.

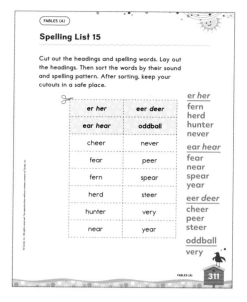

This is the complete list of words students will work with to learn the spelling patterns.

er *her*	ear *hear*	eer *deer*	oddball
fern	fear	cheer	very
herd	near	peer	
hunter	spear	steer	
never	year		

WRAP-UP

Questions About Fables (A)

Students will answer questions to show that they understand the reading, writing, and spelling skills they learned in this lesson.

Handwriting

Students should gather their handwriting materials and begin where they left off. Remind students to form letters carefully and correctly.

TIP Set a timer to help students stay focused during handwriting practice.

Go Read!

Students will read for pleasure. They should choose a book or a magazine that interests them, or they may choose a selection from the digital library, linked in the online lesson.

- Have students read aloud a few paragraphs of their selection.

- Then have students read silently for the rest of the time.

SUPPORT   Students should make no more than five errors in decoding when they read aloud a few paragraphs of their Go Read! selection. If students struggle or make more than five errors, they need to select a different (and easier) text for the Go Read! activity.

TIP   Have students select something to read ahead of time to help them stay focused.

Fables (B)

Lesson Overview

ACTIVITY	ACTIVITY TITLE	TIME	ONLINE/OFFLINE
GET READY	Introduction: Fables (B)	**1** minute	🖥️
	Vowel Team Syllables	**10** minutes	🖥️
	Words to Know: Fables (B)	**10** minutes	🖥️
READ	"The Tortoise and the Hare"	**15** minutes	🖥️ and 📄
LEARN AND **TRY IT**	Use Details to Find the Moral	**10** minutes	🖥️
	Choose Details to Support the Moral	**10** minutes	🖥️
ALL ABOUT ME	Brain Break	**1** minute	🖥️ or 📄
TRY IT	Add Adjectives	**20** minutes	📄
ALL ABOUT ME	Brain Break	**1** minute	🖥️ or 📄
TRY IT	Practice: Spelling List 15	**20** minutes	🖥️ and 📄
WRAP-UP	Questions About Fables (B)	**2** minutes	🖥️
	Handwriting	**10** minutes	📄
	Go Read!	**10** minutes	🖥️ or 📄

Content Background

Students will continue a series of lessons about fables. In this lesson, they will read the fable "The Tortoise and the Hare." They will learn how to use details to find the moral of a fable. Students will also practice using adjectives in writing.

Vocabulary   Students will explore these words from the story: *tortoise*, *hare*, *steady*, and *sprint*. These are the definitions for how the words are used in "The Tortoise and the Hare":

- **tortoise** (noun) – a kind of turtle that lives on land

- **hare** (noun) – an animal that is larger than a rabbit, with long ears, and runs quickly

- **steady** (adjective) – showing little change

- **sprint** (verb) – to run at top speed; to increase in speed

Advance Preparation

Gather students' cutouts from the Spelling List 15 activity page from Fables (A). They will use the cutouts during Try It: Practice: Spelling List 15.

During the Go Read! activity, students will have the option of using the digital library. Allow extra time for students to make their reading selection, or have students make a selection before beginning the lesson.

"The Tortoise and the Hare" Synopsis

A tortoise challenges a hare to race. The hare shoots ahead and decides to take a nap at the halfway point. The tortoise walks slowly and steadily, never stopping. When he passes the hare, the other animals cheer, waking up the hare. The hare sprints toward the finish line, but the tortoise is too far ahead and wins the race. Moral: Slow and steady wins the race.

Lesson Goals

- Learn about vowel team syllables.
- Learn new vocabulary.
- Listen to a read-aloud of "The Tortoise and the Hare."
- Learn about using details to find the moral.
- Use adjectives in writing.
- Identify and write spelling patterns that stand for sounds within words.
- Develop letter formation fluency.
- Read independently to develop fluency.

GET READY

Introduction: Fables (B)

Students will get a glimpse of what they will learn about in the lesson.

Vowel Team Syllables

Students will learn about vowel team syllables.

Words to Know: Fables (B)

Students will review and answer questions about four vocabulary words from the reading selection.

MATERIALS

Supplied
- *The Fabled Life of Aesop* by Ian Lendler
  - "The Tortoise and the Hare"
- *English Language Arts 2 Activity Book 1*
  - Add Adjectives
  - Practice: Spelling List 15
- handwriting workbook

Also Needed
- Spelling List 15 activity page cutouts from Fables (A)
- reading material for Go Read!

KEYWORDS

vowel team syllable – a syllable that contains a vowel sound spelled with two or more letters

"The Tortoise and the Hare"

Students will listen to and read along with "The Tortoise and the Hare" by Aesop. They may choose to read the story on their own. Encourage students to reread their favorite parts.

LEARN AND TRY IT

LEARN   Use Details to Find the Moral

Students will learn about examining details to figure out the moral of the fable.

TRY IT   Choose Details to Support the Moral

Students will identify details that support the moral of the fable.

TRY IT   Add Adjectives

Students will complete Add Adjectives in *English Language Arts 2 Activity Book 1*.

NOTE   This activity page includes practice with using adjectives as well as a question about the moral of "The Tortoise and the Hare."

FABLES (B)

Add Adjectives

Revise the beginning of "The Tortoise and the Hare."
Fill in each blank with an adjective. Use the adjectives in the box, or use other adjectives.
Make the fable funny, if you wish!

Adjectives

| long | short | quick | clever | shiny | important |
| old | large | green | goofy | tired | mean |

Answers will vary.

Once a _____ hare was making

fun of a _____ tortoise for being

slow. "It's true, I am slow," said the tortoise, "but I can still

beat you in a _____ race."

As soon as the _____ race

started, the hare shot out of sight. At the halfway point,

313

---

he was so far ahead that he decided to lie down and

take a _____ nap.

Meanwhile, the _____ tortoise

kept walking, slowly and steadily, never stopping.

Answer the questions.

1. How did the adjectives you added change the beginning of "The Tortoise and the Hare"? Explain.
   Answers will vary. Students may reflect on specific details that they added (e.g., the adjective *long* helps readers understand what type of race the tortoise is talking about).

314   FABLES (B)

---

2. What does the moral of this fable mean to you? Explain with an example.

Moral: Slow and steady wins the race.

Answers will vary. Success takes time and patience. It is better to take small actions for a long time than to take a single, quick action. Possible example: I can't sit down and write a long story all at once. I need to work on it a little bit each day.

FABLES (B)   315

TRY IT   Practice: Spelling List 15

Students will practice the spelling patterns for Spelling List 15.

- In *English Language Arts 2 Activity Book 1*, students will complete Practice: Spelling List 15.

- Online, students will answer questions that require them to reflect on the spelling patterns.

Students will need their cutouts from the Spelling List 15 activity page to complete Practice: Spelling List 15.

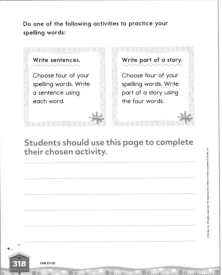

WRAP-UP

Questions About Fables (B)

Students will answer questions to show that they understand the reading, writing, and spelling skills they learned in this lesson.

Handwriting

Students should gather their handwriting materials and begin where they left off. Remind students to form letters carefully and correctly.

TIP Set a timer to help students stay focused during handwriting practice.

Go Read!

Students will read for pleasure. They should choose a book or a magazine that interests them, or they may choose a selection from the digital library, linked in the online lesson.

- Have students read aloud a few paragraphs of their selection.

- Then have students read silently for the rest of the time.

SUPPORT Students should make no more than five errors in decoding when they read aloud a few paragraphs of their Go Read! selection. If students struggle or make more than five errors, they need to select a different (and easier) text for the Go Read! activity.

TIP Have students select something to read ahead of time to help them stay focused.

Fables (C)

Lesson Overview

ACTIVITY	ACTIVITY TITLE	TIME	ONLINE/OFFLINE
GET READY	Introduction: Fables (C)	**1** minute	🖥
	More Vowel Team Syllables	**5** minutes	🖥
	Words to Know: Fables (C)	**15** minutes	🖥
READ	"The Boy Who Cried Wolf"	**10** minutes	🖥 and 📄
LEARN AND TRY IT	Plot and Moral	**10** minutes	🖥
	Explain the Plot and Moral	**10** minutes	🖥
ALL ABOUT ME	Brain Break	**1** minute	🖥 or 📄
LEARN AND TRY IT	Picture the Plot	**10** minutes	🖥
	Connect Pictures and Plot	**15** minutes	📄
ALL ABOUT ME	Brain Break	**1** minute	🖥 or 📄
TRY IT	Apply: Spelling List 15	**20** minutes	🖥 and 📄
WRAP-UP	Questions About Fables (C)	**2** minutes	🖥
	Handwriting	**10** minutes	📄
	Go Read!	**10** minutes	🖥 or 📄

Content Background

Students will continue a series of lessons about fables. In this lesson, they will read the fable "The Boy Who Cried Wolf." They will learn about the plot and moral and how the pictures illustrate the plot.

Vocabulary   Students will review these words from the story: *tending, realize, grumbling,* and *entire.* These are the definitions for how the words are used in "The Boy Who Cried Wolf":

- **tending** (verb) – taking care of; paying attention to

- **realize** (verb) – to become aware of; to understand

- **grumbling** (verb) – complaining in a quiet voice

- **entire** (adjective) – whole; total

Reading   Along with the words in a story, pictures show the story's **plot**, or sequence of events. Readers can use pictures to better understand what is happening in a story.

Advance Preparation

Gather students' cutouts from the Spelling List 15 activity page from Fables (A). They will use the cutouts during Try It: Apply: Spelling List 15.

If students have removed My Speed Sort Times from the activity book, have them gather this activity page. They will use this activity page in Try It: Apply: Spelling List 15.

During the Go Read! activity, students will have the option of using the digital library. Allow extra time for students to make their reading selection, or have students make a selection before beginning the lesson.

"The Boy Who Cried Wolf" Synopsis

A shepherd boy wants to have some fun, so he cries, "Wolf! Wolf!" and the villagers coming running out to help him. The boy laughs at them. He does the same thing the following day. This time, the villagers are annoyed at being tricked twice. On the third day, a real wolf appears. The boy cries, "Wolf! Wolf!" but this time no one comes to help him. The wolf eats the sheep and the boy. Moral: No one believes a liar, even when they tell the truth.

Lesson Goals

- Learn about vowel team syllables.

- Learn new vocabulary.

- Listen to a read-aloud of "The Boy Who Cried Wolf."

- Learn about the plot and the moral of the fable.

- Learn how the pictures help tell the plot.

- Identify reasons for when and how to use certain spelling patterns.

- Develop letter formation fluency.

- Read independently to develop fluency.

Introduction: Fables (C)

Students will get a glimpse of what they will learn about in the lesson.

More Vowel Team Syllables

Students will practice identifying vowel team syllables.

Words to Know: Fables (C)

Students will review and answer questions about four vocabulary words from the previous two lessons.

READ

"The Boy Who Cried Wolf"

Students will listen to and read along with "The Boy Who Cried Wolf" by Aesop. They may choose to read the story on their own. Encourage students to reread their favorite parts.

LEARN AND TRY IT

LEARN   Plot and Moral

Students will explore how the plot of the fable supports the fable's moral.

TRY IT   Explain the Plot and Moral

Students will answer questions about the plot and moral of the fable.

LEARN   Picture the Plot

Students will revisit the plot by looking at the pictures. They will examine how the pictures help them visualize the setting and the plot, as well as provide additional information.

TRY IT   Connect Pictures and Plot

Students will complete Connect Pictures and Plot in *English Language Arts 2 Activity Book 1*.

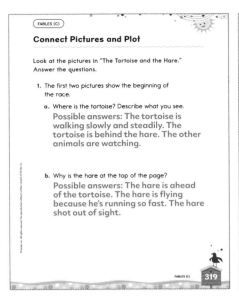

TRY IT   Apply: Spelling List 15

Students will apply what they have learned about the spelling patterns for Spelling List 15.

- In an online activity, students will complete a word sort and answer reflection questions.

- In *English Language Arts 2 Activity Book 1*, students will complete Apply: Spelling List 15.

NOTE   Students will need their cutouts from the Spelling List 15 activity page to complete the word sort.

TIP   Have students record their speed sort times on the My Speed Sort Times activity page, which is located at the back of the activity book. It can be motivating for students to see their progress as their ability to complete speed sorts should improve over time.

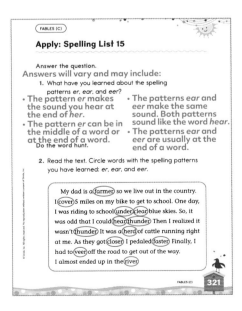

Questions About Fables (C)

Students will answer questions to show that they understand the reading and spelling skills they learned in this lesson.

Handwriting

Students should gather their handwriting materials and begin where they left off. Remind students to form letters carefully and correctly.

TIP Set a timer to help students stay focused during handwriting practice.

Go Read!

Students will read for pleasure. They should choose a book or a magazine that interests them, or they may choose a selection from the digital library, linked in the online lesson.

- Have students read aloud a few paragraphs of their selection.

- Then have students read silently for the rest of the time.

SUPPORT Students should make no more than five errors in decoding when they read aloud a few paragraphs of their Go Read! selection. If students struggle or make more than five errors, they need to select a different (and easier) text for the Go Read! activity.

TIP Have students select something to read ahead of time to help them stay focused.

Fables (D)

Lesson Overview

ACTIVITY	ACTIVITY TITLE	TIME	ONLINE/OFFLINE
GET READY	Introduction: Fables (D)	**1** minute	🖥
	Syllable Review	**10** minutes	🖥
	Words to Know: Fables (D)	**10** minutes	🖥
READ	"The Fox and the Grapes"	**10** minutes	🖥 and 📄
LEARN AND **TRY IT**	Connect the Plot and Moral	**10** minutes	🖥
	Make Connections from Plot to Moral	**10** minutes	🖥
ALL ABOUT ME	Brain Break	**1** minute	🖥 or 📄
LEARN AND **TRY IT**	Adverbs That Tell How	**10** minutes	🖥
	Use Adverbs That Tell How	**15** minutes	📄
ALL ABOUT ME	Brain Break	**1** minute	🖥 or 📄
TRY IT	More Practice: Spelling List 15	**20** minutes	🖥 and 📄
WRAP-UP	Questions About Fables (D)	**2** minutes	🖥
	Handwriting	**10** minutes	📄
	Go Read!	**10** minutes	🖥 or 📄

Content Background

Students will continue a series of lessons about fables. In this lesson, students will read the fable "The Fox and the Grapes." They will learn about the plot and moral. They will also learn about adverbs.

Vocabulary   Students will review these words and this phrase from the story: *scornfully*, *contempt*, and *make your mouth water*. These are the definitions for how the words and phrase are used in "The Fox and the Grapes":

- **scornfully** (adverb) – with anger or disgust

- **contempt** (noun) – lack of respect; disapproval

- **make your mouth water** (verb) – make you feel hungry

Writing Skills An **adverb** is a word that describes a verb, an adjective, or another adverb. An adverb can tell *how* something happens. These types of adverbs are sometimes called *adverbs of manner*.

> **Examples:** The dog barked **loudly** in response to the doorbell.
>
> I **quickly** ran to the door.

NOTE In this course, students will focus on identifying and using adverbs that tell about the manner or time of a verb. In future courses, students will learn more about other functions of adverbs.

Advance Preparation

Gather students' cutouts from the Spelling List 15 activity page from Fables (A). They will use the cutouts during Try It: More Practice: Spelling List 15.

If students have removed My Speed Sort Times from the activity book, have them gather this activity page. They will use this activity page in Try It: More Practice: Spelling List 15.

During the Go Read! activity, students will have the option of using the digital library. Allow extra time for students to make their reading selection, or have students make a selection before beginning the lesson.

"The Fox and the Grapes" Synopsis

A hungry fox tries to reach some grapes that are above his head. He jumps up and misses several times. Finally, he looks at the grapes scornfully and says he didn't really want the grapes anyway because they were probably sour. He walks away with contempt. Moral: It is easy to pretend to dislike what you cannot have.

Lesson Goals

- Review syllables.
- Learn new vocabulary.
- Listen to a read-aloud of "The Fox and the Grapes."
- Learn about the plot and the moral of the fable.
- Learn about adverbs that tell how something happens.
- Identify and write spelling patterns that stand for sounds within words.
- Develop letter formation fluency.
- Read independently to develop fluency.

Introduction: Fables (D)

Students will get a glimpse of what they will learn about in the lesson.

Syllable Review

Students will practice identifying different kinds of syllables.

Words to Know: Fables (D)

Students will review and answer questions about vocabulary from the reading selection.

READ

"The Fox and the Grapes"

Students will listen to and read along with "The Fox and the Grapes" by Aesop. They may choose to read the story on their own. Encourage students to reread their favorite parts.

LEARN AND TRY IT

LEARN   Connect the Plot and Moral

Students will learn to make connections between details in the plot and the moral of the fable.

TRY IT   Make Connections from Plot to Moral

Students will answer questions about the plot and the moral.

LEARN   Adverbs That Tell How

Through guided exploration of sentences about "The Fox and the Grapes," students will learn about adverbs of manner.

NOTE   Many adverbs end in *–ly*, but some do not (e.g., the adverb *fast*). Additionally, many words that are not adverbs *do* end in *–ly* (e.g., the adjectives *friendly* and *lonely*). Students should focus on how a word functions in a sentence—not whether it ends in *–ly*—to determine whether it is an adverb.

TRY IT   Use Adverbs That Tell How

Students will complete Use Adverbs That Tell How in *English Language Arts 2 Activity Book 1*.

Use Adverbs That Tell How

We use **adverbs** to tell more about verbs. Adverbs can show *how* something happens.

Example: I walked **happily** in the tall, green grass.

For each sentence, circle the adverb. Underline the verb that the adverb tells more about.

1. The fox jumped (high)

2. He looked at the grapes (greedily)

3. The fox (angrily) spoke about the grapes.

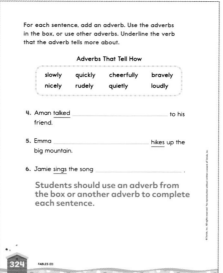

For each sentence, add an adverb. Use the adverbs in the box, or use other adverbs. Underline the verb that the adverb tells more about.

Adverbs That Tell How

slowly	quickly	cheerfully	bravely
nicely	rudely	quietly	loudly

4. Aman talked _____ to his friend.

5. Emma _____ hikes up the big mountain.

6. Jamie sings the song _____.

Students should use an adverb from the box or another adverb to complete each sentence.

TRY IT   More Practice: Spelling List 15

Students will continue to practice the spelling patterns for Spelling List 15 to increase automatic recognition of the patterns.

• In an online activity, students will practice the spelling words and patterns.

• In *English Language Arts 2 Activity Book 1*, students will complete More Practice: Spelling List 15.

NOTE   Students will need their cutouts from the Spelling List 15 activity page to complete More Practice: Spelling List 15.

TIP   Have students record their speed sort times on the My Speed Sort Times activity page, which is located at the back of the activity book. It can be motivating for students to see their progress as their ability to complete speed sorts should improve over time.

More Practice: Spelling List 15

Get your spelling cutouts. Do not use the heading cutouts.

Pile the cutouts face down. Turn over one cutout at a time, and then write the spelling word under the correct heading.

er her	ear hear	eer deer	oddball
fern	fear	cheer	very
herd	near	peer	
hunter	spear	steer	
never	year		

Questions About Fables (D)

Students will answer questions to show that they understand the reading and writing skills they learned in this lesson.

Handwriting

Students should gather their handwriting materials and begin where they left off. Remind students to form letters carefully and correctly.

TIP Set a timer to help students stay focused during handwriting practice.

Go Read!

Students will read for pleasure. They should choose a book or a magazine that interests them, or they may choose a selection from the digital library, linked in the online lesson.

- Have students read aloud a few paragraphs of their selection.

- Then have students read silently for the rest of the time.

SUPPORT Students should make no more than five errors in decoding when they read aloud a few paragraphs of their Go Read! selection. If students struggle or make more than five errors, they need to select a different (and easier) text for the Go Read! activity.

TIP Have students select something to read ahead of time to help them stay focused.

Fables (E)

Lesson Overview

ACTIVITY	ACTIVITY TITLE	TIME	ONLINE/OFFLINE
GET READY	Introduction: Fables (E)	**1** minute	🖥️
READ	"The Goose and the Golden Egg"	**10** minutes	🖥️ and 📄
LEARN AND TRY IT	The Plot and the Moral	**15** minutes	🖥️
	Connect the Plot and the Moral	**10** minutes	🖥️
ALL ABOUT ME	Brain Break	**1** minute	🖥️ or 📄
LEARN AND TRY IT	Adverbs That Tell When	**10** minutes	🖥️
	Use Adverbs That Tell When	**25** minutes	📄
WRAP-UP	Questions About Fables (E)	**2** minutes	🖥️
ALL ABOUT ME	Brain Break	**1** minute	🖥️ or 📄
QUIZ	Spelling List 15	**25** minutes	🖥️
WRAP-UP	Handwriting	**10** minutes	📄
	Go Read!	**10** minutes	🖥️ or 📄

Content Background

Students will continue a series of lessons about fables. In this lesson, they will read the fable "The Goose and the Golden Egg." They will learn about the plot and moral. Students will also learn about adverbs of time and degree.

Writing Skills   An adverb can tell *when* or *how frequently* something happens. These adverbs are sometimes called *adverbs of time* and *adverbs of degree*.

Examples: I will finish the book **soon**.

I **often** read before bedtime.

> ### MATERIALS
>
> **Supplied**
> - *The Fabled Life of Aesop* by Ian Lendler
>   - "The Goose and the Golden Egg"
> - *English Language Arts 2 Activity Book 1*
>   - Use Adverbs That Tell When
> - handwriting workbook
>
> **Also Needed**
> - reading material for Go Read!

Advance Preparation

During the Go Read! activity, students will have the option of using the digital library. Allow extra time for students to make their reading selection, or have students make a selection before beginning the lesson.

"The Goose and the Golden Egg" Synopsis

A farmer and his wife discover that their goose lays golden eggs. They become rich from selling the golden eggs. They want to get richer quickly, but the goose only lays one golden egg a day. They decide to kill the goose and collect all the golden eggs at one time. But when the goose is gone, they discover there are no golden eggs inside the goose. Without the goose and her golden eggs, the farmer and his wife cannot become richer. Moral: If you always want more, you'll lose what you have.

Lesson Goals

- Listen to a read-aloud of "The Goose and the Golden Egg."
- Learn about the plot and the moral of the fable.
- Learn about adverbs that tell when something happens.
- Take a spelling quiz.
- Develop letter formation fluency.
- Read independently to develop fluency.

GET READY

Introduction: Fables (E)

Students will get a glimpse of what they will learn about in the lesson.

READ

"The Goose and the Golden Egg"

Students will listen to and read along with "The Goose and the Golden Egg" by Aesop. They may choose to read the story on their own. Encourage students to reread their favorite parts.

LEARN   The Plot and the Moral

Students will explore the connection between the plot and the moral of the fable.

TRY IT   Connect the Plot and the Moral

Students will answer questions about the plot and the moral.

LEARN   Adverbs That Tell When

Through guided exploration of sentences about "The Goose and the Golden Egg," students will learn about adverbs of time and degree.

TIP   Many transition words that students encounter regularly in reading (e.g., *first*, *finally*) are adverbs of time.

NOTE   Many adverbs of time and degree do not end in *–ly* (e.g., *soon*, *today*, *always*, *never*).

TRY IT   Use Adverbs That Tell When

Students will complete Use Adverbs That Tell When in *English Language Arts 2 Activity Book 1*.

NOTE   This activity page includes practice with using adverbs as well as a question about the moral of "The Goose and the Golden Egg."

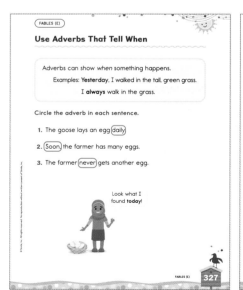

Answer the question.

4. What does the moral of the fable "The Goose and the Golden Egg" mean to you? Explain with an example.

    Moral: If you always want more, you'll lose what you have.

    Answers will vary. Possible answer: We need to stop and be thankful for what we have. We will never really see what we have if we always want more. Sample example: I wanted to watch two videos, but my mom said I could only watch one. I complained for ten minutes. Then I didn't even have time to watch one!

WRAP-UP

Questions About Fables (E)

Students will answer questions to show that they understand the reading and writing skills they learned in this lesson.

QUIZ

Spelling List 15

Students will complete the Spelling List 15 quiz.

WRAP-UP

Handwriting

Students should gather their handwriting materials and begin where they left off. Remind students to form letters carefully and correctly.

TIP Set a timer to help students stay focused during handwriting practice.

Go Read!

Students will read for pleasure. They should choose a book or a magazine that interests them, or they may choose a selection from the digital library, linked in the online lesson.

- Have students read aloud a few paragraphs of their selection.

- Then have students read silently for the rest of the time.

SUPPORT Students should make no more than five errors in decoding when they read aloud a few paragraphs of their Go Read! selection. If students struggle or make more than five errors, they need to select a different (and easier) text for the Go Read! activity.

TIP Have students select something to read ahead of time to help them stay focused.

Fables (F)

Lesson Overview

ACTIVITY	ACTIVITY TITLE	TIME	ONLINE/OFFLINE
GET READY	Introduction: Fables (F)	**1** minute	📶
	Book Walk: Drama	**10** minutes	📶
READ	*The Grasshopper and the Ant*	**15** minutes	📶 and 📄
LEARN AND **TRY IT**	Plot and Moral in Drama	**15** minutes	📶
	Explain Plot and Moral in Drama	**15** minutes	📶
ALL ABOUT ME	Brain Break	**1** minute	📶 or 📄
LEARN AND **TRY IT**	Adjective or Adverb?	**5** minutes	📶
	Choose Between Adjectives and Adverbs	**10** minutes	📶
ALL ABOUT ME	Brain Break	**1** minute	📶 or 📄
LEARN	Spelling List 16	**25** minutes	📶 and 📄
WRAP-UP	Questions About Fables (F)	**2** minutes	📶
	Handwriting	**10** minutes	📄
	Go Read!	**10** minutes	📶 or 📄

Content Backgrounds

Students will continue a series of lessons about fables. In this lesson, they will read *The Grasshopper and the Ant*, a fable in the format of a drama. They will also learn how to choose between using an adjective or an adverb in a sentence.

Reading   A **drama** is a play, or a story that is meant to be read or acted out on a stage. A drama is written in **scenes** (as opposed to chapters). Each scene might have a different setting or time. Note that longer dramas may be divided into *acts* as well as scenes.

Scenes include **dialogue** and **stage directions**. *Dialogue* refers to the words that the actors in a drama say. *Stage directions* include who is entering or leaving the scene, details on what characters are doing, and descriptions of characters or settings.

Writing Skills   Adjectives and adverbs are often misused in writing and speech.

Incorrect: She walked **slow** toward the door. (The adjective *slow* cannot describe the verb *walked*.)

Correct: She walked **slowly** toward the door. (The adverb *slowly* correctly describes the verb *walked*.)

If students are unsure whether to use an adjective or an adverb in a sentence, they are taught to follow this process: (1) identify the word they are describing; (2) use an adjective to describe a noun and an adverb to describe a verb.

Spelling   Students will learn about two r-controlled spelling patterns with the vowel *i*. They will also learn about words that begin with consonant-r blends. Students will sort words under these headings: **ire *fire*, ir *bird*, Cr blends**.

Students will learn that when a vowel or a vowel team is followed by the consonant *r*, the vowel's sound is affected. These spelling patterns are called r-controlled vowels because the *r* is in charge. The *r* changes the vowel's sound. You don't hear a long or short vowel sound but something different. Students will also learn that a consonant blend is when two consonants are together and make the sound of both consonants.

Words that go under the heading **ire *fire*** have the r-controlled vowel sound and an *ire* spelling pattern.

Words that go under the heading **ir *bird*** have an r-controlled vowel sound and an *ir* spelling pattern.

Words that go under the heading **Cr blends** begin with a consonant followed directly by *r*.

Advance Preparation

During the Go Read! activity, students will have the option of using the digital library. Allow extra time for students to make their reading selection, or have students make a selection before beginning the lesson.

The Grasshopper and the Ant Synopsis

In Scene 1, it is summer, and we meet Grasshopper who likes to sing and play and Ant who is busy working. Ant is storing food for the winter. Grasshopper makes fun of him. He prefers to be lazy and sit around all day. Ant prefers to plan ahead and prepare for winter. In Scene 2, it is now winter. Ant is now inside his house, having fun, with plenty of food to eat. Outside, we see a thin, hungry Grasshopper. He begs Ant for food. Ant gives him a grain to eat. Grasshopper is now sorry he didn't do any work during the summer. Moral: Work hard today so you're ready for tomorrow.

MATERIALS

Supplied
- *Fables and Folktales*
  - *The Grasshopper and the Ant*
- *English Language Arts 2 Activity Book 1*
  - Spelling List 16
- handwriting workbook

Also Needed
- scissors
- envelope or baggie to store spelling cutouts
- reading material for Go Read!

KEYWORDS

dialogue – the words that characters say in a written work

drama – another word for *play*

scene – a part of an act of a play that happens at a fixed time and place

stage directions – instructions in a play that tell the actors what to do

Lesson Goals

- Learn about the elements of drama.

- Listen to a read-aloud of *The Grasshopper and the Ant*.

- Learn about the plot and moral of the play.

- Determine whether to use an adjective or an adverb in a sentence.

- Sort words by sound and spelling pattern.

- Develop letter formation fluency.

- Read independently to develop fluency.

GET READY

Introduction: Fables (F)

Students will get a glimpse of what they will learn about in the lesson.

Book Walk: Drama

Students will preview the play *The Grasshopper and the Ant*. This activity is designed to help students understand the genre of drama and its elements.

TIP Have students follow along with the book walk using their own copy of the book.

READ

The Grasshopper and the Ant

Students will listen to and read along with *The Grasshopper and the Ant*, which is a play based on a fable by Aesop. They may choose to read the play on their own. Encourage students to reread their favorite parts.

TIP Explain to students that Aesop created a fable called "The Ant and the Grasshopper." The story and the play are similar, but the play adds details that are not in the story. The morals are also slightly different.

LEARN AND TRY IT

LEARN   Plot and Moral in Drama

Students will learn about the plot and moral.

TRY IT   Explain Plot and Moral in a Drama

Students will answer questions about the plot, moral, and characteristics of drama.

LEARN   Adjective or Adverb?

Students will learn a strategy for determining whether to use an adjective or an adverb in a sentence.

NOTE   We can often determine what is grammatical based on what sounds correct in a sentence. That method may not be reliable for determining whether to use an adjective or an adverb. Focusing on function—*What is this word doing in the sentence?*—is a more reliable strategy.

TRY IT   Choose Between Adjectives and Adverbs

Students will practice choosing whether to use an adjective or an adverb in a sentence.

LEARN   Spelling List 16

Students will learn and sort words with two r-controlled spelling patterns with the vowel *i* and words that begin with a consonant-r (Cr) blend.

- In an online activity, students will learn about the spelling patterns and the sounds they represent. They will learn how to sort words according to those sounds and patterns. They will also complete a word sort.

- In *English Language Arts 2 Activity Book 1*, students will complete Spelling List 16.

NOTE   Students will need scissors to cut out the spelling words on the activity page. Have students store their cutouts in a safe place, such as an envelope.

This is the complete list of words students will work with to learn the spelling patterns.

ire *fire*	ir *bird*	Cr blends
hire	dirt	drip
tire	first	friend
wire	girl	grill
	shirt	trick

WRAP-UP

Questions About Fables (F)

Students will answer questions to show that they understand the reading, writing, and spelling skills they learned in this lesson.

Handwriting

Students should gather their handwriting materials and begin where they left off. Remind students to form letters carefully and correctly.

TIP Set a timer to help students stay focused during handwriting practice.

Go Read!

Students will read for pleasure. They should choose a book or a magazine that interests them, or they may choose a selection from the digital library, linked in the online lesson.

- Have students read aloud a few paragraphs of their selection.

- Then have students read silently for the rest of the time.

SUPPORT Students should make no more than five errors in decoding when they read aloud a few paragraphs of their Go Read! selection. If students struggle or make more than five errors, they need to select a different (and easier) text for the Go Read! activity.

TIP Have students select something to read ahead of time to help them stay focused.

Fables (G)

Lesson Overview

ACTIVITY	ACTIVITY TITLE	TIME	ONLINE/OFFLINE
GET READY	Introduction: Fables (G)	**1** minute	🛜
READ	"The Lion and the Fox"	**10** minutes	🛜 and 📄
LEARN AND **TRY IT**	Follow the Clues in the Plot and Moral	**15** minutes	🖥
	Connect the Clues in the Plot and Moral	**10** minutes	🖥
ALL ABOUT ME	Brain Break	**1** minute	🛜 or 📄
LEARN AND **TRY IT**	Descriptive Paragraphs	**10** minutes	🛜
	Freewrite for Your Descriptive Paragraph	**20** minutes	📄
ALL ABOUT ME	Brain Break	**1** minute	🛜 or 📄
TRY IT	Practice: Spelling List 16	**20** minutes	🛜 and 📄
WRAP-UP	Questions About Fables (G)	**2** minutes	🛜
	More Language Arts Practice	**10** minutes	🛜
	Handwriting	**10** minutes	📄
	Go Read!	**10** minutes	🛜 or 📄

Content Background

Students will continue a series of lessons about fables. In this lesson, they will read the fable "The Lion and the Fox." They will learn about the plot and the moral of the fable. Students will also learn about writing a descriptive paragraph.

Writing Skills **Sensory language** describes the five senses—touch, sight, sound, taste, and smell. In a **descriptive paragraph**, writers use sensory language to convey their main idea.

Students will begin writing their own descriptive paragraph. They will complete this assignment over the course of several lessons by following a modified version of the writing process. (Students will not revise, proofread, or publish their descriptive paragraph in this course.)

1 Prewriting	2 Drafting	3 Revising	4 Proofreading	5 Publishing

In this lesson, students will begin prewriting by choosing a topic and freewriting about it.

Advance Preparation

Gather a folder that students can use to keep all activity pages related to their descriptive paragraph.

Gather students' cutouts from the Spelling List 16 activity page from Fables (F). They will use the cutouts during Try It: Practice: Spelling List 16.

During the Go Read! activity, students will have the option of using the digital library. Allow extra time for students to make their reading selection, or have students make a selection before beginning the lesson.

"The Lion and the Fox" Synopsis

A weak, old lion pretends to be sick so he doesn't have to go out and hunt. The other animals go into his den to see how sick he is. The lion catches the animals and eats them. A fox goes by the lion's den and stays outside. He calls to the lion to ask him how he's feeling. The lion begs the fox to come inside. The fox doesn't go in because he sees footprints that go into the den but don't come out. He's figured out the clues! Moral: Learn from the mistakes of others.

Lesson Goals

- Listen to a read-aloud of "The Lion and the Fox."
- Learn about the plot and the moral of the story.
- Learn about descriptive writing.
- Choose a topic for your descriptive paragraph.
- Identify and write spelling patterns that stand for sounds within words.
- Develop letter formation fluency.
- Read independently to develop fluency.

Supplied

- *Fables and Folktales*
  - "The Lion and the Fox"
- *English Language Arts 2 Activity Book 1*
  - Model Descriptive Paragraph
  - Freewrite for Your Descriptive Paragraph
  - Practice: Spelling List 16
- handwriting workbook

Also Needed

- folder for organizing descriptive paragraph assignment pages
- Spelling List 16 activity page cutouts from Fables (F)
- crayons or markers (optional)
- reading material for Go Read!

KEYWORDS

description – words that show how something looks, sounds, feels, tastes, or smells
Example: The sky is a soft, powdery blue, and the golden sun feels warm on my face.

sensory language – language that appeals to the five senses

Introduction: Fables (G)

Students will get a glimpse of what they will learn about in the lesson.

"The Lion and the Fox"

Students will listen to and read along with "The Lion and the Fox" by Aesop. They may choose to read the story on their own. Encourage students to reread their favorite parts.

LEARN   Follow the Clues in the Plot and Moral

Students will learn about the plot and moral.

> **TIP**   Look at the illustration together to help students understand that the footprints go into the den but not back out in the other direction. Students may not be aware that footprints have a front and back to their pattern.

TRY IT   Connect the Clues in the Plot and Moral

Students will answer questions about the plot and moral.

LEARN   Descriptive Paragraphs

Students will learn about descriptive writing by exploring a model descriptive paragraph.

TRY IT   Freewrite for Your Descriptive Paragraph

Students will complete Freewrite for Your Descriptive Paragraph in *English Language Arts 2 Activity Book 1*.

> **TIP**   Read the Model Descriptive Paragraph together to ensure that students understand the assignment before they choose a topic and freewrite.

> **NOTE**   Have students put the Model Descriptive Paragraph and their completed Freewrite for Your Descriptive Paragraph activity page into a folder for safe keeping.

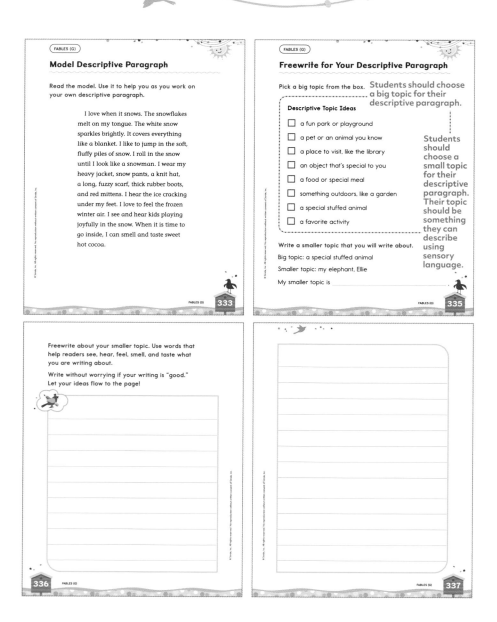

TRY IT   Practice: Spelling List 16

Students will practice the spelling patterns for Spelling List 16.

- In *English Language Arts 2 Activity Book 1*, students will complete Practice: Spelling List 16.

- Online, students will answer questions that require them to reflect on the spelling patterns.

NOTE   Students will need their cutouts from the Spelling List 16 activity page to complete Practice: Spelling List 16.

NOTE   Students may wish to use crayons or markers to draw their pictures or comic strip.

Practice: Spelling List 16

Get your spelling cutouts. Set up the headings, and sort the spelling words again.

Look at your sort, and write down each spelling word under the correct heading on the chart.

ire fire	ir bird	Cr blends
hire	dirt	drip
tire	first	friend
wire	girl	grill
	shirt	trick

Do one of the following activities to practice your spelling words:

Draw and label.

Choose four of your spelling words. Draw a picture for each word. Then write the word under the picture.

Create a comic strip.

Create four panels of a comic strip. Draw pictures and write text with four or more of your spelling words.

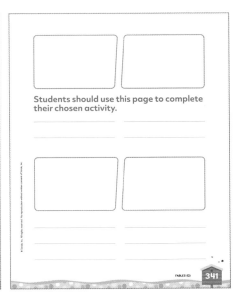

Students should use this page to complete their chosen activity.

WRAP-UP

Questions About Fables (G)

Students will answer questions to show that they understand the reading and spelling skills they learned in this lesson.

More Language Arts Practice

Students will practice skills according to their individual needs.

Handwriting

Students should gather their handwriting materials and begin where they left off. Remind students to form letters carefully and correctly.

TIP Set a timer to help students stay focused during handwriting practice.

Go Read!

Students will read for pleasure. They should choose a book or a magazine that interests them, or they may choose a selection from the digital library, linked in the online lesson.

- Have students read aloud a few paragraphs of their selection.

- Then have students read silently for the rest of the time.

SUPPORT Students should make no more than five errors in decoding when they read aloud a few paragraphs of their Go Read! selection. If students struggle or make more than five errors, they need to select a different (and easier) text for the Go Read! activity.

TIP Have students select something to read ahead of time to help them stay focused.

Fables (H)

Lesson Overview

ACTIVITY	ACTIVITY TITLE	TIME	ONLINE/OFFLINE
GET READY	Introduction: Fables (H)	**1** minute	🖥️
	Using Context	**10** minutes	🖥️
	Words to Know: Fables (H)	**5** minutes	🖥️
READ	"The Hound and the Hare"	**10** minutes	🖥️ and 📄
LEARN AND **TRY IT**	Plot, Moral, and Character's Perspective	**15** minutes	🖥️
	Examine Plot and Moral	**10** minutes	🖥️
ALL ABOUT ME	Brain Break	**1** minute	🖥️ or 📄
TRY IT	Plan Your Descriptive Paragraph	**25** minutes	📄
ALL ABOUT ME	Brain Break	**1** minute	🖥️ or 📄
TRY IT	Apply: Spelling List 16	**20** minutes	🖥️ and 📄
WRAP-UP	Questions About Fables (H)	**2** minutes	🖥️
	Handwriting	**10** minutes	📄
	Go Read!	**10** minutes	🖥️ or 📄

Content Background

Students will continue a series of lessons about fables. In this lesson, they will read the fable "The Hound and the Hare." They will learn about the plot, moral, and character's perspective. Students will also plan their descriptive paragraph.

Vocabulary   Students will review this word from the story: *startle*. This is the definition for how the word is used in "The Hound and the Hare":

• **startle** (verb) – to surprise or jump suddenly

Reading   Sometimes authors state a character's **perspective**; they tell readers exactly what a character believes or feels. Other times, authors reveal a character's perspective through the character's words, actions, and reactions to others.

In "The Hound and the Hare," the Hound's perspective is unclear and must be inferred by readers. This choice on the part of the author makes sense given the fable's moral: Beware of those whose intentions are not clear.

Writing Skills   Students will continue working on their **descriptive paragraph**. They will complete this assignment over the course of several lessons by following a modified version of the writing process. (Students will not revise, proofread, or publish their descriptive paragraph in this course.)

Writing Process

1 Prewriting	2 Drafting	3 Revising	4 Proofreading	5 Publishing

In this lesson, students will use a graphic organizer to plan their main idea, details, and the language they will use to describe those details.

Advance Preparation

Gather the folder that students are using to keep all activity pages related to their descriptive paragraph.

- Model Descriptive Paragraph from Fables (G)

- Students' completed Freewrite for Your Descriptive Paragraph activity page from Fables (G)

Gather students' cutouts from the Spelling List 16 activity page from Fables (F). They will use the cutouts during Try It: Apply: Spelling List 16.

If students have removed My Speed Sort Times from the activity book, have them gather this activity page. They will use this activity page in Try It: Apply: Spelling List 16.

During the Go Read! activity, students will have the option of using the digital library. Allow extra time for students to make their reading selection, or have students make a selection before beginning the lesson.

"The Hound and the Hare" Synopsis

A Hound chases a Hare, first biting him, then rolling him in the grass. The Hare is very confused. If the Hound bites him, then she's his enemy. If she plays with him, then she's his friend. But, which is it? The Hare stops running and asks the Hound to be truthful—is she a friend or a foe? The story is told from the Hare's perspective, so there's no way to know what the Hound thinks. We never find out if she intends to be the Hare's friend or enemy. Moral: She is no friend who plays double.

MATERIALS

Supplied
- *Fables and Folktales*
  - "The Hound and the Hare"
- *English Language Arts 2 Activity Book 1*
  - Plan Your Descriptive Paragraph
  - Apply: Spelling List 16
  - My Speed Sort Times
- handwriting workbook

Also Needed
- folder in which students are storing descriptive paragraph assignment pages
- Spelling List 16 activity page cutouts from Fables (F)
- reading material for Go Read!

KEYWORDS

context – the parts of a sentence or passage surrounding a word

context clue – a word or phrase in a text that helps you figure out the meaning of an unknown word

perspective – what a character thinks or believes

Lesson Goals

- Learn about using context to determine word meanings.
- Learn new vocabulary.
- Listen to a read-aloud of "The Hound and the Hare."
- Learn about plot, moral, and a character's perspective.
- Plan your descriptive paragraph.
- Identify reasons for when and how to use certain spelling patterns.
- Develop letter formation fluency.
- Read independently to develop fluency.

GET READY

Introduction: Fables (H)

Students will get a glimpse of what they will learn about in the lesson.

Using Context

Students will learn how to use context to determine the meaning of words.

Words to Know: Fables (H)

Students will review and answer questions about one new vocabulary word.

READ

"The Hound and Hare"

Students will listen to and read along with "The Hound and the Hare" by Aesop. They may choose to read the story on their own. Encourage students to reread their favorite parts.

LEARN AND TRY IT

LEARN   Plot, Moral, and Character's Perspective

Students will examine the plot, moral, and seeing things from one character's perspective.

TRY IT   Examine Plot and Moral

Students will answer questions about the plot and moral.

TRY IT   Plan Your Descriptive Paragraph

Students will complete Plan Your Descriptive Paragraph in *English Language Arts 2 Activity Book 1*. They will need to refer to both the Model Descriptive Paragraph and their completed Freewrite for Your Descriptive Paragraph activity page.

NOTE   Have students add their completed Plan Your Descriptive Paragraph activity page to the folder they are using to store their descriptive paragraph assignment pages.

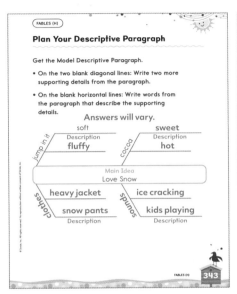
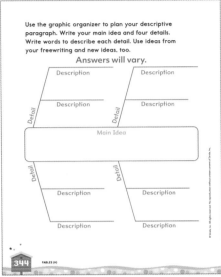

TRY IT   Apply: Spelling List 16

Students will apply what they have learned about the spelling patterns for Spelling List 16.

- In an online activity, students will complete a word sort and answer reflection questions.

- In *English Language Arts 2 Activity Book 1*, students will complete Apply: Spelling List 16.

NOTE   Students will need their cutouts from the Spelling List 16 activity page to complete the word sort.

TIP   Have students record their speed sort times on the My Speed Sort Times activity page, which is located at the back of the activity book. It can be motivating for students to see their progress as their ability to complete speed sorts should improve over time.

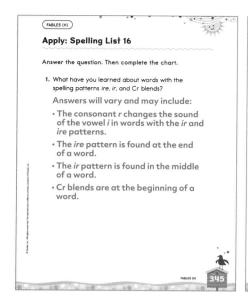
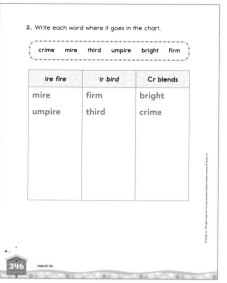

Apply: Spelling List 16

Answer the question. Then complete the chart.

1. What have you learned about words with the spelling patterns *ire*, *ir*, and Cr blends?

Answers will vary and may include:

- The consonant *r* changes the sound of the vowel *i* in words with the *ir* and *ire* patterns.
- The *ire* pattern is found at the end of a word.
- The *ir* pattern is found in the middle of a word.
- Cr blends are at the beginning of a word.

2. Write each word where it goes in the chart.

crime   mire   third   umpire   bright   firm

ire *fire*	ir *bird*	Cr blends
mire	firm	bright
umpire	third	crime

WRAP-UP

Questions About Fables (H)

Students will answer questions to show that they understand the reading and spelling skills they learned in this lesson.

Handwriting

Students should gather their handwriting materials and begin where they left off. Remind students to form letters carefully and correctly.

TIP   Set a timer to help students stay focused during handwriting practice.

Go Read!

Students will read for pleasure. They should choose a book or a magazine that interests them, or they may choose a selection from the digital library, linked in the online lesson.

- Have students read aloud a few paragraphs of their selection.

- Then have students read silently for the rest of the time.

SUPPORT   Students should make no more than five errors in decoding when they read aloud a few paragraphs of their Go Read! selection. If students struggle or make more than five errors, they need to select a different (and easier) text for the Go Read! activity.

TIP   Have students select something to read ahead of time to help them stay focused.

Fables (I)

Lesson Overview

ACTIVITY	ACTIVITY TITLE	TIME	ONLINE/OFFLINE
GET READY	Introduction: Fables (I)	**1** minute	🖥️
	C-le Syllables	**10** minutes	🖥️
READ	Choose a Fable (A)	**20** minutes	🖥️ or 📄
TRY IT	Fable Questions	**15** minutes	📄
ALL ABOUT ME	Brain Break	**1** minute	🖥️ or 📄
TRY IT	Start Writing Your Descriptive Paragraph	**42** minutes	📄
ALL ABOUT ME	Brain Break	**1** minute	🖥️ or 📄
TRY IT	More Practice: Spelling List 16	**20** minutes	🖥️ and 📄
WRAP-UP	More Language Arts Practice	**10** minutes	🖥️

Content Background

Students will continue a series of lessons about fables. In this lesson, they will read a fable of their choice. They will also start writing their descriptive paragraph.

Writing Skills   Students will continue working on their **descriptive paragraph**. They will complete this assignment over the course of several lessons by following a modified version of the writing process. (Students will not revise, proofread, or publish their descriptive paragraph in this course.)

Writing Process

1 Prewriting	2 Drafting	3 Revising	4 Proofreading	5 Publishing

In this lesson, students will start writing their paragraph.

Advance Preparation

Gather the folder that students are using to keep all activity pages related to their descriptive paragraph.

MATERIALS

Supplied
- *The Fabled Life of Aesop* by Ian Lendler
- *English Language Arts 2 Activity Book 1*
  - Fable Questions
  - Write Your Descriptive Paragraph
  - More Practice: Spelling List 16
  - My Speed Sort Times
- Writing Paper (printout)

Also Needed
- folder in which students are storing descriptive paragraph assignment pages
- Spelling List 16 activity page cutouts from Fables (F)

- Model Descriptive Paragraph from Fables (G)

- Students' completed Freewrite for Your Descriptive Paragraph activity page from Fables (G)

- Students' completed Plan Your Descriptive Paragraph activity page from Fables (H)

Gather students' cutouts from the Spelling List 16 activity page from Fables (F). They will use the cutouts during Try It: More Practice: Spelling List 16.

If students have removed My Speed Sort Times from the activity book, have them gather this activity page. They will use this activity page in Try It: More Practice: Spelling List 16.

Lesson Goals

- Learn about C-le syllables.

- Read a fable of your choice.

- Start writing your descriptive paragraph.

- Identify and write spelling patterns that stand for sounds within words.

GET READY

Introduction: Fables (I)
Students will get a glimpse of what they will learn about in the lesson.

C-le Syllables
Students will learn about consonant-le syllables.

READ

Choose a Fable (A)
Students will choose one of the following fables to read from *The Fabled Life of Aesop* by Ian Lendler:

- "The North Wind and the Sun"

- "The Donkey and the Lapdog"

- "The Fox and the Crow"

- "The Town Mouse and the Country Mouse"

- "The Ant and the Grasshopper"

- "The Lion and the Statue"

Fable Questions

Students will complete Fable Questions in *English Language Arts 2 Activity Book 1*.

Start Writing Your Descriptive Paragraph

Students will complete about half of their paragraph using Write Your Descriptive Paragraph in *English Language Arts 2 Activity Book 1*. They will have time to complete this activity page in Fables (J). Make sure students have their completed Plan Your Descriptive Paragraph activity page to refer to as they work.

NOTE Have students put their in-progress Write Your Descriptive Paragraph activity page in the folder they are using to store their descriptive paragraph assignment pages.

NOTE Additional sheets of Writing Paper are available online.

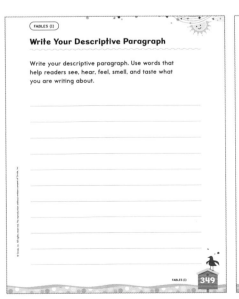

More Practice: Spelling List 16

Students will continue to practice the spelling patterns for Spelling List 16 to increase automatic recognition of the patterns.

- In an online activity, students will practice the spelling words and patterns.
- In *English Language Arts 2 Activity Book 1*, students will complete More Practice: Spelling List 16.

NOTE Students will need their cutouts from the Spelling List 16 activity page to complete the word sort.

TIP Have students record their speed sort times on the My Speed Sort Times activity page, which is located at the back of the activity book. It can be motivating for students to see their progress as their ability to complete speed sorts should improve over time.

WRAP-UP

More Language Arts Practice

Students will practice skills according to their individual needs.

Fables (J)

Lesson Overview

ACTIVITY	ACTIVITY TITLE	TIME	ONLINE/OFFLINE
GET READY	Introduction: Fables (J)	**1** minute	🖥️
	More C-le Syllables	**10** minutes	🖥️
READ	Choose a Fable (B)	**20** minutes	🖥️ or 📄
TRY IT	More Fable Questions	**15** minutes	📄
ALL ABOUT ME	Brain Break	**1** minute	🖥️ or 📄
TRY IT	Finish Writing Your Descriptive Paragraph **LEARNING COACH CHECK-IN**	**37** minutes	📄
ALL ABOUT ME	Brain Break	**1** minute	🖥️ or 📄
QUIZ	Spelling List 16	**25** minutes	🖥️
WRAP-UP	Read and Record	**10** minutes	🖥️

Content Background

Students will conclude a series of lessons about fables. In this lesson, they will read a fable of their choice. They will also finish writing their descriptive paragraph.

Writing Skills   Students will finish writing their **descriptive paragraph**. (Students will not revise, proofread, or publish their descriptive paragraph in this course.)

Writing Process

1 Prewriting	2 **Drafting**	3 Revising	4 Proofreading	5 Publishing

In this lesson, students will finish writing their paragraph

Advance Preparation

Gather the folder that students are using to keep all activity pages related to their descriptive paragraph.

MATERIALS

Supplied
- *The Fabled Life of Aesop* by Ian Lendler
- *English Language Arts 2 Activity Book 1*
  - More Fable Questions
- Writing Paper (printout)

Also Needed
- folder in which students are storing descriptive paragraph assignment pages

- Model Descriptive Paragraph from Fables (G)

- Students' completed Freewrite for Your Descriptive Paragraph activity page from Fables (G)

- Students' completed Plan Your Descriptive Paragraph activity page from Fables (H)

- Students' in-progress Write Your Descriptive Paragraph activity page from Fables (I)

Lesson Goals

- Learn more about consonant-le syllables.

- Read a fable of your choice.

- Finish writing your descriptive paragraph.

- Take a spelling quiz.

- Read aloud to practice fluency.

GET READY

Introduction: Fables (J)
Students will get a glimpse of what they will learn about in the lesson.

More C-le Syllables
Students will continue to learn about consonant-le syllables.

READ

Choose a Fable (B)
Students will choose one of the following fables to read from *The Fabled Life of Aesop* by Ian Lendler:

- "The North Wind and the Sun"

- "The Donkey and the Lapdog"

- "The Fox and the Crow"

- "The Town Mouse and the Country Mouse"

- "The Ant and the Grasshopper"

- "The Lion and the Statue"

More Fable Questions

Students will complete More Fable Questions in *English Language Arts 2 Activity Book 1*.

Finish Writing Your Descriptive Paragraph

Students will complete Write Your Descriptive Paragraph in *English Language Arts 2 Activity Book 1*. In addition to their in-progress paragraph, make sure students have their completed Plan Your Descriptive Paragraph activity page to refer to as they work.

LEARNING COACH CHECK-IN   Provide students feedback on their paragraph, focusing on their writing growth.

NOTE   Additional sheets of Writing Paper are available online.

NOTE   Students will not turn in this assignment for grading.

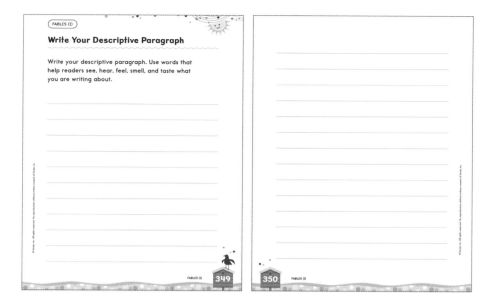

Write Your Descriptive Paragraph

Write your descriptive paragraph. Use words that help readers see, hear, feel, smell, and taste what you are writing about.

QUIZ

Spelling List 16

Students will complete the Spelling List 16 quiz.

WRAP-UP

Read and Record

Good readers read quickly, smoothly, and with expression. This is called *fluency*. Students will record themselves reading aloud. They will listen to their recording and think about how quick, smooth, and expressive they sound.

TIP Encourage students to rerecord as needed.

Fables Wrap-Up (A)

Lesson Overview

ACTIVITY	ACTIVITY TITLE	TIME	ONLINE/OFFLINE
GET READY	Introduction: Fables Wrap-Up (A)	**1** minute	🖥️
	Syllable Review	**20** minutes	🖥️
REVIEW	Fables	**25** minutes	🖥️
ALL ABOUT ME	Brain Break	**1** minute	🖥️ or 📄
WRAP-UP	Theme Time: Fables **LEARNING COACH CHECK-IN**	**47** minutes	📄
ALL ABOUT ME	Brain Break	**1** minute	🖥️ or 📄
WRAP-UP	Your Choice Time	**25** minutes	🖥️ or 📄

Advance Preparation

During the Your Choice Time activity, students will be given the option to read something of their choice. If students are using the digital library, allow extra time for them to make their reading selection, or have them make a selection before beginning the lesson.

Lesson Goals

- Review all syllable types.
- Review writing, vocabulary, and reading skills from the unit.
- Make connections among the texts in the unit.

MATERIALS

Supplied
- *English Language Arts 2 Activity Book 1*
  - Theme Time: Fables

Also Needed
- reading material for Your Choice Time (optional)

GET READY

Introduction: Fables Wrap-Up (A)

Students will get a glimpse of what they will do in the lesson.

Syllable Review

Students will review all six syllable types: open, closed, r-controlled, vowel teams, C-le, and VCe.

REVIEW

Fables

Students will answer questions to review the vocabulary, writing, and reading skills they learned in the unit.

WRAP-UP

Theme Time: Fables

Students will complete Theme Time: Fables in *English Language Arts 2 Activity Book 1*.

NOTE   This activity page includes an optional ungraded project. Students may need additional materials to complete the project.

LEARNING COACH CHECK-IN   Discuss students' responses to the questions. If they completed the optional project, have them present it to you.

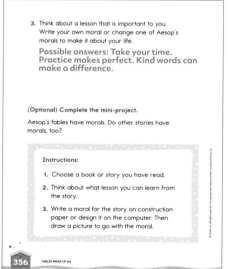

Your Choice Time

Students will choose among the following activities:

- Independent reading

- Independent writing

- Completing the optional project from the Theme Time: Fables activity page

Fables Wrap-Up (B)

Lesson Overview

ACTIVITY	ACTIVITY TITLE	TIME	ONLINE/OFFLINE
GET READY	Introduction: Fables Wrap-Up (B)	**1** minute	🖥️
QUIZ	Fables	**33** minutes	🖥️
ALL ABOUT ME	Brain Break	**1** minute	🖥️ or 📄
REFLECTION	Go Write! and Set a Goal **LEARNING COACH CHECK-IN**	**30** minutes	📄
WRAP-UP	Celebrate: Fables	**20** minutes	📄
	Discussion: Speak with Detail **LEARNING COACH CHECK-IN**	**15** minutes	🖥️
	More Language Arts Practice	**10** minutes	🖥️
	Your Choice Time	**10** minutes	🖥️ or 📄

Advance Preparation

If students have removed the My Reading Log and My Badge Book activity pages from the activity book, have them gather these pages. They will use these activity pages in the Celebrate: Fables activity.

During the Your Choice Time activity, students will be given the option to read something of their choice. If students are using the digital library, allow extra time for them to make their reading selection, or have them make a selection before beginning the lesson.

Lesson Goals

- Take a quiz on the writing, vocabulary, and reading skills from the unit.
- Freewrite to develop fluency and reflect on learning.
- Set a goal for future learning.
- Celebrate accomplishments from the unit.
- Participate in a discussion.

MATERIALS

Supplied
- *English Language Arts 2 Activity Book 1*
  - Go Write! and Set a Goal
  - My Reading Log
  - My Badge Book

Also Needed
- crayons or markers
- reading material for Your Choice Time (optional)

Introduction: Fables Wrap-Up (B)

Students will get a glimpse of what they will do in the lesson.

QUIZ

Fables

Students will complete the Fables quiz.

REFLECTION

Go Write! and Set a Goal

Students will complete Go Write! and Set a Goal in *English Language Arts 2 Activity Book 1.*

NOTE The Go Write! activity is intended to build writing fluency. Students should write for 10 minutes.

LEARNING COACH CHECK-IN Discuss students' goal, including any steps they can take as well as support you can provide in helping them meet it.

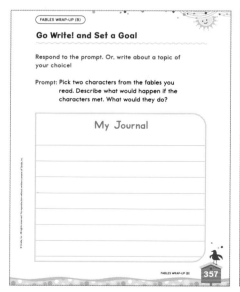

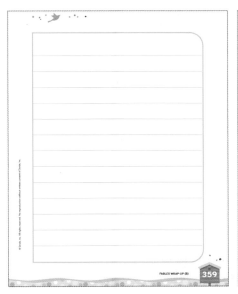

A goal is something that you want to do.

You are getting ready to start a new unit. Choose one goal for yourself as a reader or writer. Or, write your own goal.

My GOAL!

☐ Read each book twice.

☐ Read for 10 minutes a day.

☐ Use adjectives and adverbs correctly in my writing.

☐ _____

Write one thing you can do to help reach your goal.

I will _____

WRAP-UP

Celebrate: Fables

Students will celebrate accomplishments from the unit.

- They will record what they read in this unit in their reading log.

- They will color the badge for this unit in their badge book. They may also color a badge to celebrate reading accomplishments.

NOTE Students will need crayons or markers to color in their badges.

NOTE My Reading Log and My Badge Book are located at the back of the activity book.

Discussion: Speak with Detail

Students will respond to a discussion prompt.

LEARNING COACH CHECK-IN Students should respond to the prompt shown on-screen with an adult. In some cases, teachers may facilitate a group discussion.

More Language Arts Practice

Students will practice skills according to their individual needs.

Your Choice Time

Students will choose among the following activities:

- Independent reading

- Independent writing

- Completing the optional project from the Theme Time: Fables activity page